Champions
in Conflict

Champions in Conflict

The Bath Rugby Revolution

Dick Tugwell

Robson Books

To Sarah and Reg,
builders of dreams.

First published in Great Britain in 1998 by Robson Books Ltd,
Bolsover House, 5–6 Clipstone Street, London W1P 8LE

British Library Cataloguing in Publication Data
A catalogue record for this title is available from the British
Library

ISBN 1 86105 213 8

Typeset by Derek Doyle & Associates, Mold, Flintshire, North
Wales.
Printed in Great Britain by St Edmundsbury Press Ltd, Bury
St Edmunds, Suffolk

PART ONE

The Prologue

For a man who only minutes earlier had ensured his place in the rugby union record books with a match-winning performance of epic proportions, Jon Callard looked a picture of desolation – utterly spent by the fulfilment of his own destiny. Or perhaps it was the realisation of an elusive, long-cherished dream, the triumphant end of an obsessive two-year campaign to conquer new horizons, that had left him visibly overcome by the magnitude of the achievement.

Sitting hunched, head in hands, still covered by the stains of combat, at a plain table in the gymnasium attached to the Stade Lescure in Bordeaux, Callard's eyes revealed none of the euphoria that was breaking out all around the stadium.

When his silent reverie was eventually interrupted by the assembled press, he fielded questions in the same calm, forthright manner that he had just displayed on the field and modestly brushed aside the value of his own contribution to what had unarguably been the greatest of Bath's 17 cup and league triumphs over the previous 14 years.

I was standing to one side of the packed gathering, the only non-working journalist on hand, but when the inquest was over and Callard turned towards the exit, he provided me with a moment I will never forget. As I extended my hand in congratulation, he shook it firmly, looked me straight in the eye and said quite simply, 'That was for you,' before passing on through the door and again being surrounded by an eager throng of press, radio and television reporters anxious to record his every word. No one else heard those four brief words and their significance would have been lost on anyone other than him and me, but they will remain with me for the rest of my days.

Why did he proffer that unsolicited dedication to an out-of-work sports journalist who had paid his own way to Bordeaux for the privilege of watching Bath confront reigning champions Brive in a European Cup final showdown that would determine the future of Britain's greatest Rugby Union club? The answer to that question will emerge as this singular story unfolds, but for Callard, and everyone else associated with Bath Rugby Club, that day – Saturday, 31 January 1998 – will forever be enshrined as Bath's day of sporting deliverance.

When it dawned that historic day unfolded like some tortuous script fashioned by the gods, with Bath having to wait until the very last seconds to know their fate, in the most dramatic climax to any sporting conflict that I have ever witnessed. But when Scottish match referee Jim Fleming eventually blew a decisive final blast on his whistle Bath had won by the skin of their teeth, 19-18, to become the first British club to capture the Heineken European Cup and the survival of top class professional rugby in England's only world heritage city seemed assured.

Somewhere between five and six thousand Bath fans had found their way to Bordeaux to support their heroes on this, the greatest day in the club's 133-year history, and not a single man, woman or wide-eyed youngster would depart with anything other than a sense of wonder and indelible pride at having been present to witness the experience.

Someone always has to win on such occasions and no finalist in any major competition is ever without a slim chance. But this sensational triumph, by a team bereft of form and dogged by raging controversy, against apparently overwhelming odds, was one for the annals of any anthology of great sporting upsets.

Bath had precious little going for the them that January afternoon. They had arrived in Bordeaux having been dumped out of the Tetley's Bitter Cup seven days earlier by Allied Dunbar Premiership One rivals Richmond, who had outplayed them in extra time to win 29-17 on their own Recreation Ground turf. And the club was still reeling under a welter of media publicity and speculation caused by the intense furore that had erupted after the notorious ear-biting incident in their previous Tetley's clash at home to London Scottish fourteen days earlier, when they had been extremely fortunate to beat the Premiership Two side 24-23.

Brive had already convincingly mastered Bath in the second of their qualifying group games and had also gone close to lowering their colours in their initial encounter at the Rec when Bath had edged home by two points despite trailing 2-3 on the try count. The European champions had stunned a redoubtable Leicester side with a convincing victory in the final at Cardiff Arms Park 12 months previously, had edged out powerful French rivals Toulouse to reach a second successive final, and were hot favourites to repeat that success.

While Bath had to travel hundreds of miles to a strange city and a hostile environment, Brive had merely to take a leisurely two-hour coach ride to the Atlantic coast where their support would outnumber Bath's by six to one, and few among a fanatical French following were in any doubt of the outcome.

Confidence in English ranks was hardly at an all-time high either. The national press had written off Bath's chances in their previews and even their most ardent followers were fearful of a humiliating setback, considering the disasters that had marred their preparations for the most crucial contest in the club's history. If there was any shred of comfort to be found, it came from Bath's domination of the English club scene over the previous fifteen seasons, in which they had swept all before them in their pursuit of trophies.

Since 1984, when Bath first captured the John Player Cup,

the club had not lost a single final in ten Twickenham appearances. Six championship wins and four cup and league double triumphs had established them as the most successful team in any major sport in Britain, bar none. And not even soccer giants Liverpool and Manchester United could match that sustained record of achievement.

Another factor that should have been recalled by those who doubted their cause was that throughout that period of domestic dominance, the legend had become established that Bath were always at their most redoubtable and dangerous with their backs to the wall, when all appeared lost and defeat seemed inevitable. So often had Bath dragged themselves back from the brink of disaster to win vital matches, that the myth of their big game invincibility had transcended folklore. Opposing teams might catch them on an off day and dictate proceedings for most of the game. But, if Bath were still in contention, they invariably summoned inspiration to confound opponents at the death, with an opportunist try, an unlikely dropped goal or an unerring penalty to snatch victory from the jaws of defeat.

That envied reputation for never-say-die heroics had not noticeably manifested itself in the first century or so of Bath's existence, although for most of that time the club had enjoyed first class status and contributed some gifted player to international colours. I once incurred the wrath of one member of the Bath Old Players Association when I wrote that prior to the 1980s the club's impact had rarely been much more than mediocre, but it was not too inaccurate an assessment. The fixture list had long been impressive, including top sides like Leicester, Wasps and Harlequins and a strong Welsh club element. But, on the whole, the playing record had been unremarkable. And, in terms of standing, Bath's West Country rivals, Bristol and Gloucester, were held in higher regard nationally.

That situation remained unchanged for nearly a decade after the game's governing body, the Rugby Football Union, finally responded to a rising demand for more competitive rugby by sanctioning the introduction in 1971/72 of the RFU Knockout Cup, later to become the John Player Special Cup and won inaugurally by Gloucester, with Bristol losing to Coventry in the following season's final.

Bath's record in the competition in the seventies was nondescript to say the least, but then, in 1979, a northerner named Jack Rowell was appointed head coach at the Rec, and slowly the first seeds of Bath's meteoric rise began to emerge. Rowell, an Oxford honours graduate and successful business-man, had captained an emerging Gosforth side in his playing days, coached them to successive cup triumphs in 1976 and 1977 and was already acknowledged as a shrewd and innov-ative rugby brain.

At Bath he soon formed a flourishing coaching liaison with two other astute rugby fanatics, Tom Hudson, sports supremo at Bath University, and David Robson, a local accountant with a midas touch for recruiting potential future stars, and in no time Bath were riding a rollercoaster of success that was to astonish the rugby world.

That dramatic upward spiral was forged in the rugby stronghold of South Wales where Bath, long regarded as easy victims on their frequent forays into the valleys, suddenly began to raise eyebrows by matching and then beating many of the major Welsh clubs.

Such temerity in the heartland of Welsh rugby was no mean feat in those days when the principality was still inspired by the glorious exploits of Gareth Edwards, Phil Bennett, JPR Williams and Mervyn Davies, and it was evidence that Bath were quietly building a squad of players who demanded respect wherever they took the field.

Mike Beese, a skilful centre capped by England, led Bath on many of those successful outings across the Severn in the late 1970s, while former Bristol fly-half John Horton and flying winger David Trick added further quality to a talented set of backs. But it was a Cornishman, Roger Spurrell, who lit the touchpaper that ignited Bath's sudden rise to national promi-nence. A charismatic, flaxen-haired openside flanker, Spurrell took over the captaincy for the 1982/83 season and his fiery example set the standard for the triumphs that were soon to follow as Bath began to assemble a pack of forwards who would add power to an already accomplished back line.

Alongside him, Paul Simpson's impressive displays at blindside flanker would soon see him elevated to England ranks. But the final piece in Bath's back row jigsaw was put in place by the arrival at the Rec of a hulking, 18-year-old youngster from a local club side, Oldfield Old Boys, whose Bath rugby pedigree could hardly be faulted.

John Hall's great-grandfather, Harry Vowles, a talented scrum-half, had captained the club to first-class prominence in the successful years before and after the First World War, while his father Peter had been a Bath stalwart in the late 1950s and early 1960s. So it was hardly surprising that the powerful former Beechen Cliff schoolboy should follow family tradition and make his own mark on the rugby field. Hall made his first team debut against a formidable Pontypool side that could boast not only a fabled front row but an all-international back row in Jeff Squire, Terry Cobner and Eddie Butler, who gave the raw youngster a torrid time. But he soon learned how to cope and thrive.

Bath began the 1982/83 season by recording six home wins on the trot and by the end of that campaign, when they crushed a strong Cardiff side 28-9, Hall was a permanent fixture at number eight in a team that was beginning to compete with the very best. However, respect is one thing and achievement another and in terms of trophies Bath's record was hardly impressive. The RFU Knockout Cup had been in existence for over a decade, but the club had never figured in the later stages of the competition. Envied rivals Gloucester had already won it twice and shared the trophy with Moseley in 1981/82, while neighbours Bristol, in their second final appearance, had overcome Leicester 28-22 in front of a record 34,000 crowd the following year.

Nevertheless, the climax of the 1983/84 season, when John Player first sponsored the competition, was destined to bring

Bath's trophy frustration to a triumphant end and herald the beginning of an unprecedented chapter in the club's existence. This time Bath managed to avoid disaster in the early rounds and in a nerve-racking final toppled holders Bristol 10-9, stand-in kicker John Palmer, already an England international and still on the coaching staff at the Rec, missing five attempts at goal.

Bristol fly-half Stuart Barnes missed a late chance to win the game and tasted cup final defeat for the first and only time in his eventful career. After a controversial move to the Rec, he and Bath were to savour the sweet flavour of Twickenham victory on a regular basis, as that initial success became an accustomed end of season ritual.

Horton, established as England's stand-off, wore the No ten shirt as London Welsh were eclipsed 24-15 in the 1985 final. And Bath went on to complete four successive final triumphs with 25-17 and 19-12 victories over Wasps in 1986 and 1987.

By that time Bath's strength had been significantly boosted by the arrival of a posse of gifted and ambitious young players who were quick to establish themselves at club and international level. Richard Hill, a stocky, combative scrum-half who would briefly captain England, made the number nine shirt his own, enjoying productive partnerships, first with Horton and then the mercurial Barnes, while centre Simon Halliday also earned England honours.

Nigel Redman, a late selection for the 1984 final when aged only nineteen, gained his first England cap at lock against Australia six months later, and Bath were soon boasting a complete international front row, as hooker Graham Dawe followed props Gareth Chilcott and Scotland's David Sole into the Rec's photographic hall of fame which was rapidly expanding around the clubhouse bar.

Change was also evidenced in Bath's back row, where Hall remained a dominant force, but Simpson gave way to David Egerton and Spurrell was eventually forced out by the emergence of another Rec legend – Andy Robinson, from Taunton. He made his Bath debut in 1986, his first England appearance against Australia barely two years later and he was called up for the British Lions tour of Australia and Fiji in 1989.

Simultaneously, new faces were emerging in the backs, where a tall, graceful full-back, Jonathan Webb, soon made his mark at club and international level, while Tony Swift, a stocky, darting winger and deadly finisher, arrived from Swansea to launch a career that would earn him England recognition and a record number of tries for Bath.

Already firmly established in the Bath centre was a home-grown player whose good looks and silky running and handling skills were to set him apart from his contemporaries on the world stage for the next decade and beyond. Jeremy Guscott had made his first-team debut at nineteen in 1985, but was already a Bath veteran of twelve years' standing, having played for the club's mini-rugby section at the tender age of seven and progressed through every stage of junior development. A brilliant hat-trick of tries on his 1989 England debut in Romania would lead to more than 50 caps. A record number of British Lions test appearances on three tours in 1989, 1993 and 1997, when he dropped a series-clinching goal in the second test against world champions South Africa, have since sealed his place among rugby's world superstars.

With four John Player Cup victories under their belt, Bath were ideally placed to continue to set the pace when, under mounting pressure from its member clubs, the RFU finally gave a tentative nod of approval to league rugby in the 1986/87 season. Initially it involved only a select band of clubs competing on a winning percentage basis in their normal friendly fixtures under the sponsorship mantle of the John Smith's Merit Table (which Bath duly won); but it proved to be the thin edge of the wedge as far as the clubs were concerned. The competition provoked scant interest among supporters, especially diehard traditionalists, but that small concession to a competitive system provided the lever that was to undermine the RFU's power over rugby in England.

Increasing pressure to expand competition soon led to the formation of the nationwide Courage Clubs' Championship in season 1988/89, opening up a new and exciting era in what was still, ostensibly at least, a strictly amateur code. The previous season of 1987/88 had seen Bath endure a frustrating hiccup in their all-conquering progression. After four years of unbroken success, the club had to endure a rare barren campaign in terms of trophies, amid widespread controversy over what was seen as an over-physical attitude by some of its leading players.

Richard Hill had lost the England captaincy in a storm of controversy that followed a brutal clash against Wales in Cardiff in the spring of 1987, a game which also threatened the future international prospects of Bath's Gareth Chilcott and Graham Dawe, who were both promptly discarded. Dawe was particularly affected as he was forced to play second fiddle to Wasps rival Brian Moore for virtually the rest of his career, in which he amassed a record number of appearances on the England bench.

By the autumn of 1988 Bath had recovered from these setbacks, sweeping all before them in an unprecedented run of 27 unbeaten games, winning 26 and drawing one, in their most successful start to a season ever. And it was then, on Saturday, 28 January 1989, when Bath were due to host Oxford in a third round Pilkington Cup tie (Pilkington having succeeded John Player as sponsors) that I first visited the Rec to seek an insight into a club that was rapidly becoming a sporting phenomenon.

As sports editor of the *Oxford Times*, I could have reported Oxford United's FA Cup tie against Manchester United at Old Trafford that afternoon, but for once the lure of a contest between rugby minnows Oxford and Bath, undisputed kings of the union code, drew me away from soccer. I was not disappointed.

Despite the handicap of a Rec quagmire and some heroic resistance from Oxford who fought manfully for the full 80 minutes to stem a mounting tide of points, the quality of

Bath's rugby was simply breathtaking. Winger Tony Swift and full back Audley Lumsden each scored four tries out of Bath's total of 16 as they swept to an 82-9 victory – just two points short of their highest score ever, an 84-0 cup annihilation of Streatham/Croydon the previous year.

The ruthless efficiency of their play that day made a lasting impression on me and not surprisingly provided the subject matter for my subsequent weekly column 'Second Thoughts', in which I expounded a scenario that perhaps has relevance even now, nearly a decade hence.

Of Bath's performance that afternoon, my report included the following excerpts from *The Oxford Times*:

'Over the past few seasons, while their better-known rivals have apparently been content to slumber, Bath have attracted a steady stream of outstanding players to boost their strength until suddenly they have become almost unbeatable, as Oxford vividly discovered on Saturday. . .

'If you like, they have emerged as the "Liverpool" of still-amateur rugby union and few would dispute that they are now the most talented and best organised club in Britain. . .

'Heavily sponsored by the South West Electricity Board and currently considering a massive redevelopment scheme on an unparalleled scale, Bath are clearly aiming to entrench themselves as the kings of club rugby.

'And in so doing they are accelerating the process which will change the game, as we know it, beyond all recognition in the not so distant future.

'Of that I have no doubt. Already the Rugby Football Union is being coaxed and prodded into increasing professionalism from all quarters and if the example of Bath is followed, as it surely must be, the revolution cannot be suppressed much longer.

'It seems to me that this inexorable pressure cannot and will not be contained, and Bath – consciously or not – are rapidly becoming the catalyst of rugby's future.

'Oxford, who among all minor clubs probably epitomise the old traditions, earned medals for gallantry on the day, but were ruthlessly swept aside by the finest display of rugby it has been my pleasure to behold.

'Bath were simply out of this world, in approach and execution of all the skills that are still cherished in the game. If that was a vision of the future then I was converted in the space of 80 minutes at the Recreation ground that afternoon.'

Professional rugby union was not even a subject for discussion in those far-off days, although it had long been accepted that the game was not strictly amateur in the purest definition of the word. Payment, of one kind or another, whether in the form of inflated expenses, a surreptitious brown envelope in the boot, the provision of expensive items of consumer goods, or offers of lucrative and largely undemanding employment within the local community, had been rife in the union game for at least two decades, if not longer. It went on, notoriously, in the rugby hotbed of South Wales, but unless taken to excess or blatantly exposed, when an occasional example was made, it was largely ignored by the game's governing bodies, who seemed more concerned with how things looked rather than how they were in reality.

All that began to change in the late 1980s when rising demands by clubs and national teams exerted increasing pressure on players to intensify their commitment to training and playing. But opinions were still deeply divided on whether players should be more suitably compensated for their endeavours. And the RFU, under the zealous administration of its powerful secretary, Dudley Wood, remained adamant that, while competitive rugby might be tolerated, the English game at least would never abandon the principles of amateurism.

As a result, my premonition that rugby union was close to the brink of a professional breakthrough began to look premature. And after that initial introduction to the Rec, I carried on editing the sports coverage of the *Oxford Times* and reporting the waning fortunes of an Oxford United side stripped of its idols of recent years and struggling to survive in Division 1 of the Football League.

It was a period in which Bath went from strength to strength and, as I had predicted in that January column, the club completed a first cup and league double that spring, a feat repeated on three more occasions over the next six seasons as their star scaled new heights in rugby union's amateur firmament.

The trickle of talented recruits that had first begun to flow in the early 1980s had now become a stream. Jon Callard, a young teacher from Leicester, educated at Bassaleg School, Newport, like Stuart Barnes, joined Bath from Newport, only to live too long in the shadow of Jonathan Webb for his own comfort; while over the next 12 months a crop of up-and-coming players arrived to swell a flourishing academy of rugby talent.

A future Bath and England captain, Phil de Glanville, Yorkshire-born hooker Gareth Adams, a Bath University student, and a trio of Nigerian youngsters headed the new intake. Victor Ubogu, whom I had first noticed propping for Oxford in the varsity match, back row forward Steve Ojomoh and winger Adedayo Adebayo all joined that influx as Bath sought to build on the foundations of unprecedented success.

Meanwhile, Brian Ashton, a former scrum-half with Sale, had taken a teaching post at Kings Bruton School, near Taunton, and joined the Rec coaching staff in 1989, quickly forming a formidable partnership with Jack Rowell, before taking over as head coach when Rowell eventually succeeded Dick Best as England coach five years later.

Predictably, the Pilkington Cup stayed in the Rec trophy cabinet at the climax of the 1989/90 season, and while the league title eluded them that year, it was reclaimed in 1991. Bath's name was engraved on it for the next three seasons, in which the club twice repeated their cup and league double triumph of 1989.

By the time Rowell moved on in 1994, Bath fans were already enjoying the fruits of a further recruiting campaign, while reluctantly saying farewell to several stalwarts of the 1980s. Gareth Chilcott, whose bulldog frame had provided the bulwark of the front row for a dozen years, trudged off the Rec for the last time to an ovation befitting a legend. And quixotic fly-half Stuart Barnes was soon to follow, along with Richard Hill, both of them ending careers that should have earned them far more England caps than they accrued.

As they bowed out, two other members of the Rec hall of fame were about to embark on a swansong season. Tony Swift, whose lethal finishing had destroyed defences for a decade in which he amassed a club record tally of tries, announced his retirement after scoring on his farewell appearance in Bath's ninth cup final win at Twickenham in the spring of 1995, when Wasps were eclipsed 36-16 in front of 60,000 spectators.

That afternoon also brought a sad end to the illustrious career of one of the founding members of Bath's reign of supremacy and a player who perhaps had more influence on the club's phenomenal rise to prominence than any of his contemporaries. John Hall had achieved just about everything in his 13-year career with Bath. And but for a succession of cruel injuries he would almost certainly have gained recognition as a British Lion and many more than his 21 appearances in an England shirt. Elected captain that season, Hall was desperate to lead Bath out at Twickenham, but he damaged his shoulder against Sale shortly before the big day and was forced to sit in the stands as Phil de Glanville took over and Wasps were put to the sword. Hall went up to accept the trophy, but it was scant consolation for not playing. It was not, however, the end of John Hall's long involvement with Bath because, by the end of a momentous summer when rugby union was suddenly thrown into disarray, he was back in harness, in a non-playing role, to guide the club's progress in a new and exciting chapter in its history.

That summer of 1995 also brought a turning point in my career. After eleven years as sports editor of the *Oxford Times*, I had become increasingly restless, so when the company announced a limited offer of voluntary redundancy I accepted it in the hope of finding a more rewarding challenge elsewhere.

I had been unemployed barely two months when, on 26 August 1995, a decision was announced that would ignite a bitter civil war: the International Rugby Board issued a declaration stating that the amateur principles on which the game had been founded should be repealed and it should henceforth become an 'open' game. That dramatic decision was subsequently ratified by the IRB at their meeting in Tokyo on 28 September and suddenly a whole new world had opened up for Britain's leading clubs, not to mention their players, whose hitherto muted campaign for proper financial recognition of for their commitment to the game had at long last been addressed.

To suggest that this sudden and unexpected development hit the RFU like a bombshell would be something of an understatement, coming as it did after over a century of their implacable opposition to professionalism in any shape or form. Unfortunately for a hierarchy of traditionalists who frequented the committee rooms at Twickenham, the other national governing bodies, and legions of similarly minded club officials who until then had controlled the game in Britain, the cat was out of the bag. They might not have welcomed the IRB declaration, and a great many were vehement in opposing it, but they could not be seen to openly defy a democratic decision reached by the supreme authority in the world game.

In consequence, the RFU declared a moratorium until the end of that 1995/96 season on changes within the game in England and formed the Rugby Union Commission to conduct a full review of its regulations, rules and structures. But there was no going back. When the Commission reported, it concluded that English rugby was club-based and should remain so. It proposed a restructuring of the Courage League, an end to the Divisional Championship and the introduction of cross-border and European competition, which was considered vital in order to attract additional revenues from sponsorship and television rights.

Meanwhile, the major clubs, aware of the need for a collective approach to the new era, formed their own organisation, English First Division Rugby Clubs (EFDRC); later a further body, English Professional Rugby Union Clubs (EPRUC), was introduced, extending the professional franchise even further.

Amid all these frantic discussions and preparations, the factor that everyone involved in rugby union was absolutely certain about, right from the outset, was that running a professional club would need financial input beyond the means of existing committees. Clubs like Bath, Gloucester, Harlequins and Wasps were not poor or badly run, but they were not in any position to launch themselves as professional entities, capable of financing the staffing and salary structure that was already envisaged within the game.

Only one club, and one not counted among the first division elite, could be said to be ready for that kind of transformation: Newcastle, who months earlier had escaped relegation from Courage League Division 2 by the skin of their teeth. Sir John Hall, the multi-millionaire chairman of Newcastle United FC, acting with typical speed and foresight, had acquired control of the old Gosforth club, renamed it and taken it into his portfolio of business interests, so there was no shortage of financial clout as far as they were concerned. Sir John had acted promptly in setting up his rugby union offshoot, recruiting veteran England stalwart Rob Andrew as his director of rugby and giving him what amounted to a blank cheque book to transform a struggling team into a potentially top flight outfit.

Andrew responded to the challenge with equal alacrity, taking coach Steve Bates and number eight Dean Ryan with him from Wasps and soon developing a side that would narrowly retain second division status that season and gain promotion in 1997.

Elsewhere, another millionaire entrepreneur, Ashley Levett, took control at Richmond, who quickly began waving their apparently unlimited cheque book around in a quest for new players to put them back among the elite clubs. Their eye fell on quite a few of Bath's glittering array of international performers.

Bath, still run by a well-intentioned but unwieldy 27-man amateur committee, were not exactly quick to appreciate the ramifications of rugby union's revolution, although they had made certain strategic changes in the run-up to the 1995/96 season. John Hall had emerged triumphant from an internal power struggle with Richard Hill to take over the management of the side, first as chairman of selectors and later as the club's first director of rugby.

That battle had been settled in the traditional Bath way by a player vote. Hill, who had done some coaching at the club, soon took up an offer from rivals Gloucester to become director of coaching at Kingsholm, where he was assisted part-time by his former Bath colleague Gareth Chilcott. An indication of Bath's initial failure to react to rugby's dawning revolution could be ascertained by the fact that, the club insisted that Hall's role should be unpaid, and it was quite a while before his input was recognised in financial terms.

However, that oversight made little apparent difference to the team as the 1995/96 season, the last to be contested under the old amateur regime, got under way. Bath made a superb start, running up a sequence of 12 straight victories and playing some dazzling rugby before a depleted side lost 19-17 at home to Loughborough Students.

That run included eight Courage League wins in a row, many by emphatic margins, as Bath romped to the top of the table, before finally slipping to a first league defeat on 6 January 1996, when they lost 15-14 at home to traditional foes Leicester, whom they had already beaten 14-9 in September at Welford Road.

A week later Bath suffered another setback, losing 21-12 in a friendly encounter at Northampton. January was to prove a frustrating month as the weather took a turn for the worse. And it was around then that I received a telephone call that would lead to an eventful new chapter in my working career.

Neville Smith, a friend and former companion on my travels to Oxford, rang to tell me about a vacancy for a rugby writer on the *Bath Chronicle* and suggested I apply for the job. He had recently been appointed as the paper's sports editor and, intrigued by the challenge of covering Bath rugby, I answered the advertisement, attended an interview and was offered the job.

My new employment commenced on Monday, 26 February 1996. And so, after seven months away from the daily grind of provincial journalism, I was back in harness and back hitting the early morning road with Neville Smith – with one significant difference. This time he was the newly fledged sports editor, while I was a down-table sports writer/sub. It was a role reversal that meant little to me. I was content not to have the responsibilty for a change. All I really wanted was to renew my acquaintance with the enthralling brand of rugby I had encountered on that memorable first visit to the Rec in 1989. And more than that, I was looking forward to the chance to write about the exploits of a special band of men who had established themselves as the dominant force in British rugby union.

Even then, before I began what was to be a helter-skelter assignment within a game that was just about to embark on a kaleidoscopic period of disruption, change and development, I had few illusions about just how difficult the task might be. I had a premonition that my time in Bath would be exhilarating, eventful, exhausting and, as likely as not, short-lived. But I was totally unprepared for the drama that was about to unfold. I was there just 22 months, a period that encompassed every imaginable twist of fortune as far as Bath Rugby Club was concerned.

Triumph, disaster, boundless optimism, dark despair and the ultimate achievement of an ambition that became something akin to the legendary pursuit of the Holy Grail lay in store for the rugby gladiators of Bath over the next two years. I was drawn into that fateful plot like a moth to a flame, but I shall never forget or regret my part in it.

It was one of those chapters in life that seems pre-ordained and at times it felt like hell on earth, but it was tremendous fun. If I had a choice of retracing my steps I would willingly go through that extraordinary experience all over again just for the satisfaction, delight and insight it gave me.

PART TWO

Spring Fever and a Double Celebration

CHAPTER ONE

The International Set

Curiously, considering the hectic maelstrom of activity that would soon ensue, my first month of commuting to the *Bath Chronicle*'s head offices in Westgate Street was conspicuous only as a period of frustrating inactivity on the playing front. But perhaps that was just as well, because it gave me a useful opportunity to gently ease myself into the Bath rugby scene, although it was nonetheless a profoundly annoying time for all concerned.

The first story I wrote for the *Chronicle*, on my second day in residence, was a preview of the Pilkington Cup semi-final draw, which from Bath's point of view had produced the ideal prospect: a home tie against local rivals Gloucester on Saturday, 23 March. It ended a bizarre sequence of nine successive away draws at that stage of the competition for Bath, all of which they had won on their way to cup final glory at Twickenham.

I managed to get telephone quotes from skipper Phil de Glanville and head coach Brian Ashton that day; but, for one reason or another, it was some time before I actually got to meet any of Bath's leading personalities.

Not least among these was John Hall, recently confirmed in the new post of director of rugby at the club, and obviously committed to his responsibilities to such an extent that he had scant time to talk to the latest rugby writer in town.

I found no difficulty in contacting his secretary, Susie Holmes, a charming, sympathetic and extremely loyal lady, who was always a delight to talk to. But, invariably in that first fortnight, she was unable to put me through to her boss or arrange a convenient time for me to introduce myself to Bath's legendary former captain. Eventually, when I did meet him face to face for the first time, Hall was affable enough, but somewhat guarded in his responses and my initial impression was that he was not someone who had much time or respect for the press, or felt comfortable in the presence of reporters. For a man of his imposing physical presence, long experience at the top level and high standing within the game, he seemed unsure and suspicious when responding to even the most straightforward of questions, as though he felt that each one was a potential trap which could lead to problems he would rather do without.

I could understand that attitude because 25 years in journalism had taught me that the relationship of trust between top sportsmen and members of my profession had become precarious, especially in recent times when national newspapers had often been criticised for their relentless pursuit of revelatory stories about anyone remotely deemed to be in the public spotlight, not least in the realm of sport.

In contrast to 'Mr Grumpy', a nickname John Hall had picked up from his playing days (and which he was said to detest), I was to find that the majority of people I came into contact with in Bath were forthcoming and helpful, from the chairman Richard Mawditt down to the most minor of club officials. As the man charged with the hazardous task of supervising Bath's metamorphosis from amateur to professional status, Mawditt had a lot on his plate at a precarious stage in the club's development. And not surprisingly he became the focus of attack by a vociferous minority among the membership, who opposed the changes that were about to occur. But from my point of view, as a hopefully unbiased observer, he was always pleasant and polite and a natural communicator, who invariably returned a phone call if he was not immediately available and took pains to explain the club's position on whatever issue that arose. Likewise, on the rare occasions I needed to talk to them, the president Brendan Perry, a former Bath centre, and father of future Bath and England full-back Matt Perry; the secretary Major John Quin; the assistant secretary Peter Hall, also a former player and father of John; and the treasurer Colin Gale were equally accommodating and businesslike in their dealings.

As far as team matters were concerned, however, my efforts to obtain up-to-date news and information were initially laborious and unrewarding, making life difficult on a newspaper whose sports coverage depended so heavily on Bath rugby, which was the staple news diet for the majority of Bath's sporting fraternity. However, unlike their soccer counterparts, Bath City FC, Bath Rugby Club appeared to have no pressing need to drum up paying customers. After twelve years of constant success, the club was used to full house attendances and on most home match days the demand for tickets easily exceeded availability, without any real need for promotional or marketing activity. That demand had risen to the point where that the club felt justified in advising people purchasing seats in the stands to be in their place well before kick-off, or run the risk of the tickets being resold to other supporters. So it was hardly surprising that the club's management were not inclined to spend too much time catering to the requirements of the local press or feel over concerned about their public relations image.

The team was riding high at the top of the Courage League and looked set to enter the professional era with every expectation of yet more glory days to come. No one then had any realistic perception of the developments that were soon to be set in motion by the most contentious decision in the game's history, or even a premonition that Bath's entire future in rugby union's top flight might come under threat. Inevitably, after such a long period of supremacy, an element of complacency, and even arrogance, had crept into the club's attitude to the game.

Sporting history is littered with examples of how such frailties have led to the periodic or permanent decline of great clubs through the ages. Most, like Manchester United, Liverpool and Arsenal in soccer, survive the barren years, rebuild and flourish once more through renewed managerial vision, vigour and sound investment policy. But many once-famous clubs have not been so fortunate, discovering too late that the elusive blueprint for success, once discarded, can be impossible to rediscover.

Certainly under the influence of Rowell, Robson and Hudson in the 1980s, and then Rowell and Ashton in the early 1990s, Bath had rarely allowed complacency and arrogance to take root on the playing side of the club's affairs – although occasionally, more often than not against unconsidered opponents, the team had suffered the odd unexpected setback. One of the overriding factors in Bath's emergence as rugby union's dominant force had been a constant awareness that no club can afford to relax its standards or neglect to take on board new ideas and changing trends if success is to be sustained. Yet, even at the highest level, this is easy to do without comprehending until too late that the club has imperceptibly lost impetus and direction.

That awareness of a continual need for honest self-appraisal, reassessment and positive updating had kept Bath way out ahead of their established rivals for more than a decade. But, as I gradually became more familiar with my new surroundings, I began to wonder whether those core beliefs had, however unwittingly, been diluted, especially off the field of play, by such a prolonged reign at the top.

If there was one single word that I came to hear more than any other from players and management in countless interviews with them over the next two years, it was 'focus'. But I think that word had begun to lose much of its original impact, simply through endless repetition when Bath were at their invincible best. However, there was no doubt that in terms of readiness for the approaching switch to professionalism the club was infinitely better prepared on the field than it was behind the scenes.

If there was one official who was invariably willing to talk to me in that instructive first month at Westgate Street, it was Ken Johnstone, the club's veteran press officer, who seemed to have plenty of time to chew the fat. The problem was that Ken, now an amazingly spry and still enthusiastic octogenarian, rarely rang up with any tangible news about Bath's activities. He came on the phone almost daily, sometimes two or three times each morning, and always in the frantic last hour or so before our 10am edition deadline.

I didn't really mind on those rare days when we were ahead of schedule, because his chatter and wicked asides often provided an amusing break in an otherwise routine day. But when we were busy Ken's ceaseless patter could be irksome, to say the least. It became something of a standing joke and what made it even more amusing was that Ken's interest seemed to lie more in finding out what was going on at the hub of Bath's command centre, rather than informing us of any developments – which hardly seemed to match up to the accepted idea of a press officer's role.

On reflection, and having got to know him much better since then, it's clear that we were doing Ken a disservice. It wasn't his fault that the people in authority at Bath chose not to brief him about major developments and failed to use his services in the appropriate manner. Had he been consulted promptly over a plethora of situations that arose it might have saved the club no little embarrassment when stories leaked out and caught them on the hop, which happened on numerous occasions in my first year at Bath.

When I did come to know Ken and share his company, notably on Bath's initial venture into Europe for a Heineken Cup qualifying group game against Treviso, I found him to be a gentleman, a genuine character and far more shrewd than I had ever realised. He enjoyed playing the buffoon, proudly doffing his lucky beige fedora wherever Bath were in action and he was quite happy to be considered one of rugby's celebrated 'old farts' (to quote Will Carling), but there was a lot more to Ken than met the eye. For a long time I was unaware of his track record in media and public relations circles and I was surprised to discover that this Geordie-born pensioner had been ITV's first head of sport, with the dubious distinction of being the man who had introduced professional wrestling to the nation's Saturday afternoon audience.

In the circumstances in which he was forced to operate, Ken Johnstone undertook the club's media chores and match-day press arrangements in an invariably cheerful and welcoming manner. And when he eventually retired after Bath's home game against Sale in 1998, I for one was sorry to see him go, although I am glad to say he is still involved on match-days.

Those first few weeks of my introduction to new surroundings and an unfamiliar role in Bath may have been instructive, but they were also a frustrating time for everyone connected with Bath Rugby Club. For a start, rugby had been virtually brought to a halt thanks to the combination of inclement weather, last minute cancellations and the commencement of the highlight of the international season, the annual Five Nations Championship. Those factors meant that Bath's loyal supporters had not seen any worthwhile action at the Rec for over two months, since Leicester had narrowly put paid to the club's unbeaten Courage League run on 6 January. Since then Bath had lost at Northampton 21-12, beaten Moseley 20-11 and gone down 27-10 at Swansea in friendly clashes, before only just overcoming Wakefield 16-12 in a postponed Pilkington Cup fourth round clash, thanks to a dramatic late try by fly-half Richard Butland.

The weekend before I joined the *Chronicle*, Bath had clinched a semi-final place with a lacklustre 19-12 away win over Bristol, who had not beaten them for some ten years. So, although they were well on target for a coveted fourth league and cup double, no one at the Rec was feeling too contented with a severely disrupted period since the New Year. Head coach Brian Ashton had few qualms about criticising the farcical nature of the fixture situation from the club's viewpoint, describing it as ridiculous and expressing his sympathy with supporters over the lack of competitive games at the Rec. In one sense it was not too damaging in terms of match fitness, because most of Bath's senior players were involved in Five Nations combat, but that was scant consolation for Ashton, who was naturally anxious to achieve some semblance of continuity in training and preparation for the crucial climax to the club's winter campaign.

After Newbridge called off a friendly game due to a shortage of players, Bath had no game on the second weekend in March, owing to England's preparations for their final Five Nations encounter against Ireland on 16 March, when victory would guarantee them the Triple Crown and an outside chance of snatching the championship title if France lost to Wales on the same afternoon.

As it turned out, that Twickenham clash was to be my first opportunity to see any Bath players perform in the flesh and it ended in a blaze of glory for the latest recruit to the Rec's international fold, a 23-year-old Yorkshireman who had been with Bath for just over a season and had still to claim a regular place at first team level. Jon Sleightholme, a stocky, powerful, direct right-winger, had already made an impact with Grimsby, Hull Ionians and then Wakefield. After studying sports science and physical education at Chester College, he arrived in Bath as a postgraduate student in the school of education at Bath University, where he joined a number of sports scholars who eventually made their way to the Rec.

Jack Rowell, still living on the outskirts of Bath, quickly got wind of the promising young newcomer whose searing pace had raised eyebrows at his old club, and early in 1995 Sleightholme was selected on the wing for England A, appearing in successive victories over Ireland, France and Italy and scoring a try in each of the last two games. A place on the England A tour to South Africa and Australia soon followed, but it was still a major surprise when Rowell called up the 5ft 10in, 14-stone Sleightholme for his full England debut in the Five Nations Championship opener against France in Paris.

After guiding England to a grand slam the previous year, Rowell had indicated his wish to see the side play a more expansive game, but he was destined to be disappointed by their initial display as France triumphed 15-12, although Sleightholme, despite having scant opportunity to run with the ball, made a pleasing impression. In his next outing, against Wales at Twickenham, the winger confirmed that promising impact with another solid display, as England, forced to revert to forward power to subdue the stubborn Welsh, scrambled home 21-15. And he did nothing wrong when winning his third cap against Scotland at Murrayfield early in March, in a dour game that saw the redoubtable Leicester number eight Dean Richards turn in a typically powerful display to grind the Scots into subjection.

Now with a Triple Crown beckoning, and the championship still not out of England's reach, Rowell was hoping his backs would at last get the chance to show their paces against an Irish side that could be guaranteed to show plenty of fire and aggression, but were expected to buckle under the pressure of England's superior firepower.

It was a milestone encounter, not least because England's charismatic skipper Will Carling had already announced that it would be his 58th and last game as captain, after filling the role with unrivalled success for almost a decade. For almost all that time Carling had partnered Jeremy Guscott at centre in an England team that had rarely thrown caution to the wind. But they tried hard to in the first half on this occasion and nearly paid a high price for it, as some indifferent handling was punished by the lighter, more mobile Irish forwards, who continually outpaced their lumbering English counterparts to the the loose ball.

By the time Carling was carried off the field with 35 minutes gone, having fallen awkwardly and damaged an ankle, Ireland were six points ahead. But the second half was a different story as England wisely reverted to type, their pack eventually wearing Ireland down to clinch a comfortable victory. The highlight of that second-half revival was a jet-propelled burst of acceleration from Sleightholme that brought him his first international try and marked him down as a real prospect for the future. And when the news filtered through from Cardiff Arms Park that Wales had foiled France, leaving England as unexpected champions, an unlikely celebration was soon under way, to the relief of none more than Jack Rowell.

Apart from Carling's retirement as captain (he was to play one more Five Nations series before retiring from the international scene), that victory over Ireland marked the end of an era for other reasons. It was the last Five Nations Championship clash played under the amateur code, and, coincidentally, it saw one England captain replaced, as substitute, by his successor, although no one was aware of that possibility when Bath's Phil de Glanville, who had spent the past two seasons on the bench, came on to play a significant part in England's success.

De Glanville had often despaired of escaping the shadow of Carling and Guscott, but, to the surprise of many rugby pundits, he would go on to enjoy a golden year in the limelight as his country's first professional captain, although it was a Rowell decision that caused no little controversy the following autumn.

For two other members of Bath's international elite on display that afternoon it was a day which marked a significant downturn in their career prospects. Ben Clarke, a British Lion and an England regular since making a dazzling debut in a splendid victory over South Africa in 1992, was soon to find himself consigned to the international wilderness when he accepted a lucrative offer to leave Bath and join second division Richmond a few weeks later. And for Ireland winger Simon Geoghegan, who had already established himself as a world-class performer before joining Bath in 1994, it was to mark the beginning of a nightmare period in his life, involving a constant battle to overcome a rare toe injury that still threatens to end a glittering career.

Geoghegan, a London solicitor, had made an explosive impact on the international scene almost from the moment he was first capped at the age of 23 in 1991, and quickly went from strength to strength, impressing everyone with his pace, tigerish tackling and deadly try-scoring ability. He won 24 caps in rapid succession before leaving London Irish to join Bath three years later, when it seemed that the rugby world was at his feet. Sadly his move to the Rec coincided with the onset of an injury jinx that severely limited his appearances at club level for the next four years.

Unfortunately, I saw him play only a handful of games for Bath while I was reporting their progress, but when he did play, often in some discomfort, he usually managed to score a typically opportunist try and fleetingly demonstrate the immense talent that Bath were to sorely miss when the game went professional. Over the next two years, Geoghegan was to endure no fewer than nine operations on the troublesome toe joints that defied surgeons in England and the United States, but his regular attempts at a comeback were invariably cut short by cruel disappointment. I found him full of hope each time, but his struggle has so far been in vain. Had it gained the reward he deserved, Bath might just have avoided some of the bitter setbacks that were to befall the club later that year.

Meanwhile, with a momentous climax to the Five Nations Championship out of the way, John Hall and Brian Ashton were finally able to gather their international stars together at the Rec, to prepare for what was to be an equally dramatic conclusion to the domestic campaign. And suddenly, after a month of relative peace and quiet, life began to move into the fast lane with increasing velocity as far as I was concerned.

While other clubs had been busily formulating strategies for the professional revolution that now seemed irreversible,

Bath had initially dragged their feet in response to the challenge, but in the fortnight prior to that international finale, the wheels had begun to turn with increasing momentum. Club chairman Richard Mawditt and his 27-strong committee hardly needed reminding that the key factor in ensuring Bath's future among rugby union's elite would be money and plenty of it, but where it was to come from was a burning question that had yet to be resolved, and time was of the essence. Without substantial financial investment over the next few months it was clear that the club's prime asset, an envied playing squad, containing seventeen internationals and many other blossoming talents on the fringe of national recognition, could fall apart.

The potentially disastrous prospect of a mass exodus of leading players tempted by lucrative offers from rival clubs, who had already begun making overtures to top stars worldwide, let alone on the domestic front, was already a major concern for John Hall, in his first season as director of rugby. And he admitted as much, while predicting that the next few months would be the hardest of his life.

Bath had already taken one ground-breaking initiative that would not only shake the rugby world but bring in much-needed ready cash, by announcing their intention to take on Rugby League giants Wigan in a two-legged clash at the end of the season. Negotiations between the two clubs to stage a unique confrontation between the two undisputed champions of rugby's divided and intensely alienated codes had gone well. Wigan, beset by their own financial problems, had proved only too willing to share the anticipated proceeds of a contest which could not have been contemplated only months earlier, considering the acrimonious friction that had existed between the rival codes for the best part of a century.

Not everyone was as enthusiastic as the boards of the two clubs. Many of their fans were lukewarm about the proposed rapprochement between the warring codes and one particular Bath legend steadfastly refused to have anything to do with it. Jeremy Guscott had long been a prime target for Britain's leading rugby league clubs, but had turned down all offers to switch codes in the past, some of them extremely lucrative. And, as he was under no contractual obligation to Bath to take part in what he regarded as a gimmick, he emphatically rejected all pleas to become involved.

Nevertheless the proposal was eventually sanctioned by the RFU. And it was agreed that Manchester City's Maine Road ground would stage the rugby league encounter on Wednesday, 8 May, four days after the Pilkington Cup final, with the second leg to be played under union rules on Twickenham's hallowed turf on Saturday, 25 May.

Both matches were highly entertaining and thoroughly enjoyed by both sets of partisan supporters, although Wigan, who had been a professional outfit for many years and boasted several players with union experience, eventually emerged comfortably ahead on points difference over the two legs. The cross-code saga provided an interesting diversion for Bath's players, as well as netting the club upwards of £250,000 as their share of the gate receipts, which proved more than welcome.

Such a figure, however, was chicken feed compared with what would be required to launch and maintain a professional set-up at the Rec for the following season. So with that dilemma in mind, Bath's management committee had been hard at work on a draft proposal that would effectively transform the club into a public limited company and dissolve an institution which had been governed by its membership for over 130 years. The proposal was refined into a resolution to be put before the membership at an extraordinary general meeting on Monday, 11 March at the Pavilion, adjacent to the ground, when Bath's future would be determined. Prior to that meeting it was by no means certain that the membership would approve the measures that had been recommended by the committee. Unsurprisingly, the proposal gained unanimous backing from the players, who obviously stood to benefit from such a change. And a number of them, led by skipper Phil de Glanville, who moved the resolution along with

Richard Mawditt, were present to support their case and try to persuade members to give the move their blessing.

For several months, however, there had been rumblings of dissent from a small, but vocal, group of members who were vehemently opposed to professional rugby union in principle and none too happy at the prospect of seeing control of their club's affairs passing out of the hands of the membership. It had been hard to gauge the extent of likely support for that rebellious group, but a number of letters had been published in the *Chronicle* criticising the club's intentions, and doubtless there were a lot of fingers crossed at the Pavilion when the fateful moment of decision arrived.

In all some 820 members, about one fifth of the total membership, packed into the auditorium to participate in a crucial event in the club's history. But when it came to a vote, it was all but unanimous, with 806 members approving the motion, only six opposing it and eight abstaining.

That decision, to create a new professional club, Bath Football Club plc, was a major stepping stone in the process that would sweep away the old 'shamateur' regime that had ruled the game for so long. And, although those who opposed it alleged that the meeting had been stage-managed to produce the desired outcome and that members had been railroaded into voting against their better instincts, the die was cast.

Next morning chairman Richard Mawditt forecast that it would require in the region of £3 million a year to run the club, and with players' contracts accounting for between £1 million and £1,500,000 of that, he indicated that further investment was being sought and the club would look to attract individual backers. Phil de Glanville also welcomed the important step forward and was hopeful that the club would be able to attract underwriters by the end of the month, while John Hall claimed that the club was now in a wonderful position and targeted 30 March as the date set for contract agreements to be settled.

As it turned out, those deliberations and negotiations

would take a lot longer than that, and would involve Hall and the club in far more intricate and prolonged bargaining than they anticipated. But for the moment it was a time for celebratory contemplation of a new and exciting epoch, and also time to get back to the routine grind of trophy pursuit.

In the fortnight following that emphatic EGM vote, I came to know John Hall a little better, as he set out his stall with regard to the issues he faced over players' contracts and his vision of Bath's future impact on the world club scene. And it soon became apparent that, as far as he was concerned, Bath was committed to policies that would not only keep the club at the forefront of the domestic rugby union scene but enable it to scale new heights of conquest in Europe and eventually match the standards currently being set in the Southern Hemisphere as well.

The 'Super 12' series, a recently introduced championship involving leading district and state teams from South Africa, Australia and New Zealand, had already made a huge impression on rugby-minded television viewers around the world. And it had excited great interest among coaches of Northern Hemisphere clubs, who were impressed by the high skill levels on show, not to mention the superb fitness of the combatants.

One of the crucial factors in Bath's rise to prominence had been a continual striving to set, maintain and constantly improve standards of playing performance year on year, which had become almost an obsession within the club. So, having gained approval to embrace professionalism, Hall was quick (perhaps, on reflection, too quick) to outline his vision of the club's potential impact on rugby worldwide. Only hours after an EGM he described as the most positive move in the club's history Hall confidently proclaimed that Bath would be able to offer his playing squad contract packages that would at least match, if not better, any available elsewhere. He predicted that around thirty players would be offered varying contracts, depending on individual circumstances. And although he was aware that rival clubs had made lucrative offers to many Bath players, he was sure the squad would remain virtually intact.

Quizzed about the likelihood of the squad being strengthened by the import of top stars from Britain and abroad, Hall refused to rule out the possibility, but he confirmed that the club's main priority was to keep the current squad together. And in an assessment he was to repeat frequently over the coming months, he propounded the view that Bath already possessed the best squad in Europe.

It was a bold statement that, on reflection, he was perhaps unwise to make in such unequivocal terms, not only because it put increased pressure on a team that would soon come under far greater pressure than it had ever known, but also because unwittingly he was making a rod for his own back. It was an assertion that would return to haunt John Hall, when suddenly and dramatically, the pressure of the professional spotlight was turned on his own broad shoulders over the next 12 months.

However, that painful experience was some way ahead and the immediate concern for Bath was to concentrate on confirming their status as the best club in England, starting with a local derby Pilkington Cup semi-final against Gloucester. That clash, which Bath were expected to win comfortably, was also to see my belated introduction to a sell-out match day at the Rec and provide my first real opportunity to meet some of Bath's rugby legends, although I had already spoken to a number of the players on the telephone in the course of my duties.

As a prelude to the game, I reported Bath's efforts to placate a significant and militant section of their Teacher's Stand debenture holders, who were up in arms over plans to charge them an extra £12 to watch the game and were eventually offered a refund. And I spoke to Richard Hill about his team's chances of beating his former club. Hill had been appointed coaching director at Kingsholm early in the season and after a disappointing pre-Christmas period which saw Gloucester floundering near the foot of the table, he had inspired a dramatic improvement in form and an encouraging run of victories that moved them away from the relegation zone.

It was the first time I had spoken to him, and he was still combining his coaching duties at Gloucester with a managerial job in Bristol, but right from the outset I found him co-operative, helpful and articulate, clearly someone with business experience and communication skills. He obviously wasn't afraid to take new and fairly unconventional ideas on board, and the theme of the story I wrote three days before the game highlighted his recruitment of a leading London-based sports psychologist who had been working with the Gloucester players with a view to improving their mental preparation for matches. Hill had also appointed a full-time fitness adviser for the squad, a policy that Bath were to follow a year later when they brought in the former Auckland Blues and All Blacks fitness coach Jim Blair from New Zealand.

Despite these innovations and his side's recent revival Hill was candidly realistic about their chances of beating Bath at the Rec, pointing out that very few sides had managed to win there in the past decade. Gloucester still possessed a formidable pack, but their backs were not renowned for flair or penetration and, on paper, could not be expected to match the international quality of the likes of Guscott, Catt, de Glanville and Sleightholme, among Bath's elite set of threequarters.

However, Bath were fully aware of Gloucester's battling qualities and had not shown consistent winning form in friendly action in recent weeks, their latest setback coming four days before the semi-final when they lost 27-16 to the Army at the Rec. Their season had been badly disrupted over the three months since Christmas, and now with Richard Butland sidelined by a rib injury they were forced to revamp their back line by switching Mike Catt from full-back to fly-half and recalling Jon Callard in his place. It was to prove a pivotal game for this talented trio and an unfortunate setback for the unlucky Butland, who had fought hard to establish his place in the team, but would find himself languishing in Catt's shadow for the next two seasons.

That situation became a frustrating stumbling block for Butland, who may have lacked Catt's mercurial brilliance in broken play, but was a fine player in his own right, an astute tactician and kicker and the model of a solid, capable, conventional fly-half. Callard had lost his Bath place partly because Jack Rowell had elected to play Catt in the full-back role for England that season and Bath had accommodated Rowell's desire that he should become used to playing there at club level. But losing his place was nothing new to Callard, who, like many players at the Rec, could never be certain of selection for his club even though he might be first choice at international level. In his early years at Bath Callard had been largely confined to playing for the United, the club's second team, owing to the presence of England full-back Jonathan Webb. And when Webb retired, he briefly, and successfully, took over the latter's England shirt, notably kicking a crucial match-winning penalty in the last minute of a nerve-racking 15-14 victory over Scotland at Murrayfield in the 1994 Five Nations Championship.

Jack Rowell, who was once reputed to have vowed that Callard would never take a kick for Bath again after a rare below par performance, promptly discarded him the following season and the combative, sometimes abrasive, full-back seemed fated to be made the scapegoat whenever things went wrong, however well he had played. Whenever the side needed a solid, steadying influnce, however, Callard could usually be relied on to produce it, and when the chips were down that Saturday he would again prove his worth with a typically committed display, especially with the boot.

Fortunately, although the pitch was fairly cloying, as it frequently is at the Rec owing to its proximity to the river, the overhead conditions were ideal, a sunny afternoon that suited Bath's running style, while Gloucester's powerful pack would probably have preferred it wet, favouring their less expansive game plan.

After a quiet start Bath made nearly all the first half running, but failed to penetrate a blanket Gloucester defence and were forced to rely on four penalties from Callard for a 12-3 interval lead, visiting fly-half Martyn Kimber responding with a dropped goal. Gloucester were still in contention, but seconds after the interval Bath took a quick penalty in their own half and left-winger Adedayo Adebayo scored a virtuoso try, powering half the length of the field to crash over wide out, Callard's conversion giving him a return of 14 points and sealing yet another Twickenham appearance.

Bath had to withstand a determined Gloucester revival in the closing stages, scrum-half Scott Benton fleetingly raising their hopes with an opportunist try converted by Mark Mapletoft. But there were no real hard-luck stories in a 19-10 win, Bath's extra class seeing them through to their tenth final. Richard Hill took some consolation from a resolute second half display by his side; but John Hall was less than satisfied with Bath's failure to extend a comfortable lead, and he warned that some hard work would be required if his side were to overcome Leicester, who had eased through against Division 2 outfit London Irish in the other semi-final.

With their Pilkington Cup final place assured, the holders now faced a daunting end-of-season run of six league games inside a month that would determine whether they had the talent and stamina to capture the Division 1 title and set up the possibility of a fourth cup and league double celebration at Twickenham in May.

At that stage of the season it was already a three-horse race. Leicester, who had been Bath's main rivals in their quest for honours since the early 1980s, were just a couple of points behind the leaders. And Harlequins, who Bath still had to host at the Rec, were still in touch in third place. But the rest were trailing, in a division that had been dominated by these three clubs over the years.

Bath's next game, at Bristol, did not appear to pose too many problems, given the long run of defeats they had suffered at the hand of their near neighbours. And the following Saturday I set out for the Memorial Ground, Bristol, already contemplating a mouth-watering trip to Twickenham.

Meanwhile, Bath's playing squad were concentrating on the job in hand, with some of the players currently on the fringe of the first team intent on forcing their way into the side for the final against Leicester by dint of taking advantage of any chances of inclusion that came their way over the ensuing month.

Adebayo, scorer of that memorable try against Gloucester, and Jon Sleightolme were out of contention, having flown out with the England squad for the annual Hong Kong Sevens tournament, which meant a return for Simon Geoghegan and Audley Lumsden on the wings. Lumsden, a pacy black winger and brilliant Sevens performer, who had been a regular try-scorer since joining Bath as an England colt ten years earlier, had seen his career tragically interrupted three times since then, first when suffering a broken neck in a friendly game at Plymouth and then by twice breaking a leg. But he was to battle back into the first team reckoning and ultimately win another cup-winners medal with Bath before eventually teaming up with Richard Hill at Gloucester when the game went professional the following season.

In the pack John Mallett, a powerful England A prop was selected in preference to Victor Ubogu, who was involved in a mysterious absence at that time, which was initially attributed to his being away on business. It eventually emerged that Victor, who had lost his place in the England front row, was out in Hong Kong, not playing in the Sevens, but apparently active enough to sprain his ankle at a wedding celebration, a repercussion that kept him out of the Bath team for much of the rest of the campaign, although he was later to return in style. I had to write a couple of stories about his mysterious absence at the time, which the club were none too keen to elaborate on, and it took me a long time to forge any reasonable contact with him after that episode. But I am glad to say that in the end, as he began to mellow, I came to know him quite well and appreciate his highly individual personality.

As expected, Bristol proved no match for a Bath side that showed encouraging signs of returning to peak form that afternoon. Simon Geoghegan grabbed two sparkling tries in a decisive 43-5 victory that sadly left him struggling with a recurrence of his injury problems, this time attributable to a calf strain. That was enough to put him out of the home clash against Harlequins the following week, which saw the return of Adebayo and Sleightholme, while Bath even had the nerve to rest influential number eight Ben Clarke and Scottish international tighthead prop Dave Hilton for a game which would either heat up the championship tussle or effectively leave Harlequins out of it.

In the event with another Scotland star, Eric Peters replacing Clarke in the back row, Bath shattered any illusions that Harlequins might have harboured about pipping them for the title with an awesome second-half display of power and pace to gain a handsome 41-15 victory, after trailing 12-3 early on and 15-9 at the interval. It was a vintage Bath exhibition, which would be reproduced equally vividly against Harlequins on another momentous Saturday the following season at the Rec. More importantly, at that stage it kept them perched two points clear at the top of the table and virtually ended the challenge of one of their two rivals, although Harlequins were still to play a significant part in the eventual destination of the title.

On the back of two convincing league victories and having already beaten Gloucester less than three weeks earlier, the team's confidence should have been sky high as they set out on the short trip up the M5 four days later. But a Kingsholm full house on a wet Tuesday night in April, with the notorious 'Shed' in full cry, is about as inhospitable an atmosphere as you can get in rugby.

Bath's confidence may have been high, but their morale was hardly boosted by the fact that they were again forced to make changes to the team, with Jon Callard unavailable and Jeremy Guscott also otherwise engaged. Guscott, who over the years had combined playing rugby with a burgeoning career that ranged from modelling fashion to radio and television work, was contracted to take part in an episode of the

ITV programme 'Body Heat', being filmed on location in South Africa. And in his absence a fit-again Richard Butland returned at fly-half with Mike Catt switching to centre and Audley Lumsden replacing Callard at full-back.

With Ubogu still under a cloud following his impromptu trip to the Far East, it was a depleted Bath side that took the field that night, and Gloucester made them pay with a fiery display that shook the leaders out of their stride from the outset. Lumsden, still uncertain after a long lay-off, suffered a nightmare at full-back, slipping up on the wet turf to gift home winger Paul Holford a fourth-minute try converted by Tim Smith, who then added a simple penalty after Lumsden had taken a quick tap penalty from the wrong place in front of his own posts. To add to Bath's misery, Butland, taking over Callard's kicking duties, missed three out of four first-half penalty attempts, and although Nigel Redman reigned supreme at the lineout, Gloucester's ferocious loose play and tackling gave the visitors little chance to establish any rhythm.

Trailing 10-3 at the interval, Bath conceded another Smith penalty before Catt's break put Phil de Glanville in under the posts for Butland to convert. But the rally came too late, and Smith's third penalty earned Gloucester a deserved 16-10 win that sent the entire crowd wild. It was a poor performance from Bath and the bad news soon became far worse when it was revealed over the next few days that Ben Clarke, who had limped off with a shin injury late in the game, was likely to miss the last three league games and might not recover in time for the Pilkington Cup final clash with Leicester on 4 May.

In the event, it proved to be Clarke's last game in a blue, black and white shirt, which was a sad way to end his highly successful five-year career at the Rec. In that time he had been a towering influence for Bath, England and the Lions, but speculation was already mounting that he was a key target for several big clubs, and eventually the lure of a huge offer from ambitious Richmond proved too tempting to resist, although the move was to affect his pursuit of further international recognition.

As for Bath, that defeat provided a stark warning that the celebration champagne could not yet be put on ice. In the aftermath of that setback at Kingsholm they would have to regroup, recharge their flagging batteries and learn some hard lessons if their dream of a fourth double triumph was to be realised.

CHAPTER TWO

History in the Making

That unpalatable defeat by Gloucester offered Leicester renewed hope of catching their deadly rivals on the title run-in and meant that both teams had now lost twice, although Bath still retained a superior points difference. It also left John Hall and Brian Ashton with the difficult task of restoring the dented morale of their squad for the final three games of the season, away to Saracens and Orrell and a home finale against Sale.

Bath's management team had enough problems on their plate in the week leading up to the Saracens game, with injuries to Clarke and Ubogu being compounded by the absence of Guscott and rising speculation about which players might soon be leaving. Hall offered an optimistic scenario on the latter front, claiming he was hopeful Clarke would stay with Bath, although he was delaying a decision until the end of the season.

He confirmed reports that Nigel Redman, who had enjoyed an outstanding season at lock, was weighing up an offer of a five-year contract to take over as player-coach at Division 2 side Moseley. But Hall predicted he would stay, and was equally confident that Guscott would remain loyal to a club he had first represented at mini-rugby level. One piece of good news for Hall that week came from 32-year-old Andy Robinson, the club's long-serving openside flanker, who announced he would be giving up his job of teaching rugby at Colston Collegiate School in Bristol and pledged the rest of his career to Bath as a full-time professional.

Already there were ominous political stirrings on the national scene with EPRUC, representing the top two divisions in club rugby, confirming their intention to boycott all RFU league and cup competitions the following season unless agreement could be reached over a number of key issues, including cash allocations to the clubs. On the eve of the trip to Saracens, Hall confirmed Bath's backing for EPRUC and opposition to the stance adopted by the RFU's newly elected chairman Cliff Brittle, whose views were to provoke inflamed debate over the next two years.

One of those key issues was the need for a radically reconstructed fixture programme that should, in the clubs' view, recognise the increasing importance of competitive club rugby and enable clubs to generate a regular volume of gate income to support their aspirations of achieving full-time professional status. But Brittle, with the backing of the rump of the RFU's less exalted club membership, insisted that the needs and ambitions of the leading clubs should be subordinate to the interests of international and Five Nations Championship competitions and that overall control of all such matters should remain with the governing body.

At that stage the clubs were still expressing a united willingness to compromise and co-operate with the RFU over the running of the professional game, and Hall's comments reflected that conciliatory mood. But the dispute would soon lead to an impasse that would eventually evolve into a prolonged and bitter power struggle, which has yet to be resolved and still threatens to hurl rugby union into worldwide chaos and disruption, such has been the acrimony engendered between rival factions in the game.

My sympathies, then as now, lay with the aspirations of the clubs. They may have been harbouring delusions of grandeur, but at least they seemed positive and progressive in their vision of the future compared to the hidebound attitude of a powerful reactionary element at RFU headquarters, who appeared to want to deny them any influence over their own destiny. I took that view because I felt a drastic change in attitude and conception was urgently required if rugby union was to grow and prosper in the new open order of things. And my first sight of Saracens' Bramley Road ground the following Saturday was enough to convince me that such change was long overdue.

Devoted rugby traditionalists had no doubt delighted in its cosy informality for several generations. But, as a stadium playing host to a high standard of sporting entertainment, Bramley Road was a throwback to the Ark. One tiny permanent stand, adjoining a couple of overcrowded marquees, provided the only semblance of spectator facilities for the fans who flocked there that day to see a contest that was to have a major bearing on the destination of the Courage League championship, the most prestigious competition in the English rugby union calendar.

It was a prospect that may have captured the romance of the English sporting scene before and after the Second World War, but as a supposedly top class competitive venue, Bramley Road almost defied credulity. Imagine Arsenal playing Liverpool in a vital Premiership clash on Clapham Common, instead of Highbury or Anfield, and you have the equivalent image of my first venture to Saracens. But there was nothing sub-standard about the entertainment on view, or the nail-biting intensity of the action as it drew to a fraught and exciting climax that April afternoon.

On form, Bath should have encountered few problems in disposing of a Saracens side still awaiting the fanfare arrival of world famous performers like Philippe Sella, Michael Lynagh and François Pienaar, not to mention England scrum-half Kyran Bracken. But with Guscott, Clarke and Ubogu missing from their line-up and the jarring setback at Gloucester still fresh in their minds, Bath were keenly aware that another below par display could wreck their double dream. They opened up in style, dominating the opening quarter to establish a 13-point lead. Two coolly despatched penalties by Callard, restored at full-back, soon settled Bath's nerves and when Phil de Glanville raced clear to send Adedayo Adebayo over for an unchallenged try converted by Callard, their worries seemed to be over.

Unfortunately, as Bath's early supremacy began to fade, the home forwards took their cue to launch a determined recovery, marred only by wayward kicking which was eventually to prove costly. Saracens steadily upped the tempo to dictate the early second-half pace and storm into a 15-13 lead with just 11 minutes left, before a stroke of brilliance by Mike Catt, back instead of Butland at fly-half, sparked Bath to life again. Gathering his own chip ahead, Catt shot clear on a scything run through the middle, but, as the Saracens cover closed him down, support seemed wanting, until suddenly the unlikely form of hooker Graham Dawe loomed up alongside to grasp the pass, step neatly inside two defenders and drop triumphantly over the line.

It was a try the veteran Dawe will surely savour with relish when he finally calls time on a lengthy and eventful career. And it could hardly have come at a more opportune moment for a Bath side whose backs had been firmly against the wall. Callard missed the conversion and Bath were forced to defend with all their renowned tenacity in the closing minutes. John Hall's nerves became so frayed that he took refuge behind the stand in mute prayer, before Callard popped over an injury-time penalty to seal a desperate and somewhat fortunate 21-15 victory.

The sense of relief and euphoria that followed the final whistle was etched on the faces of Bath's players as I sought their reaction afterwards. And it was then I discovered the true depth of their special brand of camaraderie and also, to my own satisfaction, that I was making a measurable impact in my new role. As I walked up to chat to John Mallett and 'Ollie' (as the gentle giant Nigel Redman is universally known in Bath rugby circles), I enquired about the possibility of speaking to Graham Dawe – to be met with faces that instantly broke into conspiratorial smirks. 'Dawesy', it transpired, was none too pleased with me, having been informed that I had marked him down with 4 out of 10 in my player-ratings summary following the defeat by Gloucester.

I was already aware that Dawe, Bath's legendary man of iron, is not a character you want to get on the wrong side of, on or off the field, so this revelation filled me with foreboding as I watched him emerge from the changing rooms.

Of course, I had not given him a 4 rating (in fact, no Bath player ever received a 4 from me in my time reporting their exploits). But, farming on the borders of Devon and Cornwall, as he still does, Dawe was unlikely to take the *Bath Chronicle* through the week and thus had been an ideal target for a leg-pull.

The problem was convincing Dawe that he had been the butt of a typical piece of Bath squad banter. And when he finally sauntered into the marquee bar, I had to endure a few straight looks and some frank interrogation from the great man, before I finally persuaded him that he had not been awarded such a dismal rating and that his artful team-mates had been taking the proverbial. In fact I'm not sure even now that he fully believed my protestations of innocence. But that minor incident broke the ice, as far as he and I were concerned. And to my relief it was to prove a thaw in relations that eventually spread to the rest of the squad as we came to know each other better over the coming months.

Further evidence that, if not yet entirely trusted, I was at least beginning to enjoy some measure of confidence among the players was evidenced soon afterwards, when I spoke to Ben Clarke (who had watched the game with his leg in plaster) and tried to get him to talk not just about his fitness but also about his future contract plans. He responded readily enough concerning the injury, but when I asked him whether he would be staying with Bath or moving to another club, a big grin spread slowly over his face and suddenly we were laughing in unison, both of us knowing that he would not be saying a single word about that rather delicate and confidential subject.

Some journalists, I suppose, might have pressed the point further and eventually been given a less light-hearted brush off, but I have always preferred to trust my instincts with regard to how far to delve into sensitive areas. And they have usually stood me in good stead in the long run, especially where the relationship between sportsman and reporter is of an ongoing nature, when respect and trust have to be earned and valued. National newspapers expect a more forceful approach from their writers and can also afford to pay liberally for exclusive information. But these writers don't have to come back the next day, so they can usually escape any flak from players who feel they have been caught unawares in an interview.

That afternoon confirmed some useful lessons as far as close contact reporting of top-class sport was concerned and also a great deal about the men who had made Bath a household name in rugby over the past dozen years. They were not all easy to deal with. And some older players were invariably extremely guarded and sometimes downright uncommunicative whenever the press were around, perhaps with good reason on past experience.

But, if you could convince them you were genuine, professional in your approach and sincere in attitude, they were as good as gold to work with and they would often put themselves out to accommodate your requirements, provided they were treated with normal courtesy and respect. I was to find that, although I might not be universally popular with Bath's management over the next two fraught seasons of professional endeavour, as far as the players were concerned, the relationship was, by and large, both trusting and rewarding.

As for Graham Dawe, I never did get to have what could be described as an in-depth interview with him, although I bought him a drink and we had a reasonable chat after Bath's penultimate league game against Orrell the following week.

Not that I didn't enjoy talking to him, because that was certainly not the case. But he was usually so cagey about what he said that he rarely uttered anything worth noting. And he was a past master at the art of answering a question in a couple of unquotable words or turning it round so that you were forced to give an opinion, which he would then blandly dismiss. It got to the stage where I would be happy to speak to 'Dawesy' just for the challenge of getting him to talk freely, which he never did. But, although our conversations were often exasperatingly unproductive, as far as our columns were concerned, they were always fun and usually ended with me, and sometimes both of us, chuckling almost hysterically at the outcome of yet another mission impossible.

Another thing I gleaned from that enjoyable interlude at Saracens was that, although I was fairly unenthusiastic about the value of those match facts and player ratings which it was my duty to compile on match days, Bath's players were interested in them.

I found them a nuisance, because they distracted my attention from the game, which meant I sometimes missed part of the action, especially in the frantic exchanges at the ruck and maul, but as far as our rugby coverage was concerned they were deemed to be important, although I often wondered how many readers actually studied them. The other drawback to the duty of rating players was that it was potentially damaging to my efforts to forge a productive working relationship with the squad, which in the circumstances was never an easy task.

That encounter with Graham Dawe made me realise that Bath's players were only too aware of my evaluation of their individual contributions, even if, quite naturally, they did not always agree with or approve of my assessment. And, although I tried hard to be fair and unbiased in those ratings, I had no wish to set myself up as some arbitrary judge and jury as far as their performance was concerned, especially when, as soon would be the case, professional livelihoods were at stake.

I had played the game at a decent club and district level for a number of years, mainly as a fly-half and full-back, and that at least gave me a better working knowledge of its intricacies than some of my colleagues in the press box. But I would never claim to be a true rugby connoisseur or even by any stretch of the imagination an expert judge of a player, so from then on I tended to err on the generous side in my ratings. An average display in my estimation rated a six, a good performance merited a seven, excellent warranted an eight, outstanding a nine, and a ten – a mark I was to award only twice in my time at the Rec, indicated that the player in question had produced an out-of-this-world performance. Mike Catt was the first Bath player to receive a ten from me, for a breathtaking display in a crucial Heineken European Cup qualifying group game in Treviso later that year, when he scored four superb tries and kicked flawlessly. And Jon Sleightholme got the other perfect score for a brilliant hat-trick of tries in a Courage League clash against Northampton at the Rec that same season.

Apart from that the only other rating I awarded was a five, which generally covered a range from below average to poor. It was a mark I used sparingly because, most of the time, Bath were winning and, when they didn't win, it was rarely due to a lack of effort or commitment from the team.

Only once can I recall having real cause to regret a rating, when I sat at the same table as the club's talented but inexperienced young scrum-half Charlie Harrison at Bath's annual dinner in the Guild Hall, after awarding him a five. He let me know it rankled, but was polite about it, which was typical of the general attitude shown by the players. They came in for some stick at times, but took it in their stride like men, which showed what a proud and resilient bunch they were as a squad – full of character, determination and courage, whatever the odds, or their own personal fortunes at any given time.

Victory over Saracens left Bath and Leicester still neck and neck at the top of the table with two games left. And as Bath prepared for a penultimate league clash at mid-table Orrell, it looked certain that the title race would go right down to the wire, which was exactly how it turned out, although no one could have forecast how dramatically that seasonal curtain would fall.

With Jeremy Guscott due back from filming in South Africa in time to play, John Hall's selection worries appeared to be easing. But any relief he may have anticipated soon disappeared when it was revealed that Guscott had picked up a hamstring injury on his travels and would require a fitness test before the team travelled north on the Friday.

As it transpired, he failed the test and Bath left without him. When the squad arrived that evening at Central Park in time to watch Wigan's 22-6 Super League win over Bradford Bulls, Guscott's name was loudly jeered by home fans, who did not think much of his refusal to play in the forthoming inter-code challenge matches. Not that Jerry would have been concerned, given his ability to ignore such sniping. And it failed to impress his team-mates the following afternoon as, in front of a reasonable sprinkling of regular rugby league followers, they put Orrell firmly in their place, 44-11.

The occasion had a unique flavour, Orrell having gained permission to switch the game to Central Park in the hope of boosting the attendance, the first time two union teams had set foot on league soil in several generations. But the unprecedented move failed to disconcert Bath, who gave fans of the 13-man game, and several watching Wigan players, a liberal taste of their championship vintage. Martin Haag and Sleightholme both scored twice, and Callard contributed a 14-point haul, in a comfortable win.

That result left Bath needing to beat Sale at home the following Saturday to clinch the first leg of the double, but there were a few more setbacks in store before that bridge was crossed. The first bombshell exploded two days after the Orrell excursion, when Bath revealed that the RFU had decreed that the attendance for their rugby union showpiece clash against Wigan at Twickenham would be restricted to a half-capacity 37,500. The reason given was that major repairs to the Twickenham section of the Waterloo to Reading railway line were scheduled that weekend, and the Transport Police and Railtrack were concerned that the network would not be able to cope with the traffic likely to be generated by a capacity 75,000 attendance.

After a hastily arranged meeting between these bodies and the RFU – of which Bath had been given barely two hours' notice, making it impossible for club officials to attend – a decision to impose the limit was taken. Not unnaturally it left officials of the two clubs fuming, not least Bath's match co-ordinator Danny Sacco and director of rugby John Hall, who claimed it could cost the clubs £500,000 each in lost revenue.

Two days later Hall was forced to concede that Ben Clarke, who had only just had the plaster removed from his damaged ankle, would not be fit to face Sale, and was also unlikely to make the Pilkington Cup final against Leicester. Jeremy Guscott was pronounced fit, although his return to action would prove fleeting as he aggravated his thigh injury against Sale and eventually missed the Pilkington Cup final. His centre partner, Phil de Glanville, was also ruled out of the title showdown.

Two other significant items of news cropped up that week. The first came with the revelation that Leicester were being linked with Australia's former national coach Bob Dwyer, who was later to lead the Tigers to a European Cup final and Pilkington Cup success before suddenly parting company with the club less than two years later. The second item was a report that the former Wales flanker Richard Webster was set to join Orrell from rugby league club Salford on a one-year contract.

Not surprisingly, with the last amateur season nearly at an end, clubs were already frantically turning their attentions to their managerial and playing requirements for the onset of professionalism the following season. But Webster's was one move that, fortunately for Bath, was never completed. Webster, capped 13 times by Wales before embracing the league code in 1993, would be one of a number of new faces to make their presence felt at the Rec that autumn, a change of heart that neither he nor Bath would have cause to regret in the turbulent era that was about to ensue.

However, the only thing that really mattered that week was beating Sale and clinching another league title, and although Bath were some way short of full strength when they took the field that Saturday, the destination of the crown appeared to be in little doubt as they made their Lancastrian visitors look second rate in a one-sided first half which saw Bath sweep into a convincing lead.

Leicester, meanwhile, were at home to Harlequins, but few present among the capacity crowd at the Rec gave much thought to the outcome at Welford Road, as their heroes ran Sale ragged early on – until a sudden second-half transformation threw a spanner in the works. Sale had often caused Bath problems in the past, but showed little sign of doing so on this occasion until their experienced player-coach Paul Turner came on at fly-half to turn the contest on its head. Some of the blame lay with Bath, who clearly thought they had done enough and nearly paid a heavy price for complacency as the visitors suddenly moved up a couple of gears. As the champions took their foot off the pedal, Turner inspired his side to a superb rally in a pulsating finale, which saw them run Bath ragged in the final half-hour. And, with news filtering through of an equally tight contest developing at Welford Road, nerves were on a knife edge all around the ground as the minutes ticked away.

At the final whistle Bath were left clinging grimly to a 38-38 draw. But then the Rec erupted as the news spread that Harlequins had triumphed 21-19, veteran Leicester full-back John Liley missing an injury-time penalty that would have snatched the title.

John Hall and head coach Brian Ashton were understandably relieved and overjoyed at the outcome, after the nail-biting tension of those closing moments. And afterwards, with the championship safely under lock and key, both men were optimistic about the club's future as a professional entity. Hall targeted victory over Leicester in the Pilkington Cup final seven days later, which would clinch an unprecedented fourth double, as the springboard for Bath's continued domination of the English scene, and he repeated his view that most of his players would stay and give Bath the strongest squad in Division 1 the following season. And Ashton, who days earlier had announced he would be giving up his teaching job at Kings Bruton School to become the club's first professonal coach, was fulsome in his praise, claiming the side was on a par with the best Bath had ever fielded.

However, although they had played some scintillating rugby throughout the season and gained some outstanding victories, especially before Christmas, the climax of the title race had stretched the squad's stamina and mental strength to the limit, and over those gruelling closing weeks their weariness on both counts was beginning to take its toll. Now, after retaining the league crown by the skin of their teeth, Bath had to raise their dwindling reserves of energy and resolve for one last challenge, against a Leicester side desperate to salvage something from the wreckage of their own season after the bitter blow of losing to Harlequins and handing the title to their rivals.

It was a contest that had been a sell-out just days after the semi-finals had been played and was destined to attract a world record 75,000 crowd for a final at Twickenham. But sadly it would be recalled more for its controversial ending than for the quality of entertainment on view.

Historically, encounters between the two clubs had rarely been classics and few people expected such fare on that momentous first Saturday in May, a day which would bring down the curtain on over a century of tradition, under the rigid governance of the old amateur ethos. There was no doubt that both teams were jaded after a long and strenuous campaign. I was feeling the strain as well, after two eventful but increasingly hectic months at Westgate Street. Events had gathered pace to such an extent that I was working all hours to keep up with the constant demand for rugby news, that fortnight before the 1996 Pilkington Cup final proving one of the busiest of my working life.

As well as charting Bath's progress towards the Courage League title and undertaking my share in the daily routine of helping to produce our sports pages, I found myself providing most of the written material for the *Chronicle*'s 16-page Pilkington Cup supplement which went out on the Tuesday before the big game at Twickenham. Armed with a tape recorder, I hammered out a series of features and interviews previewing the forthcoming final and by the time I had completed the final piece – an interview with Bath skipper Phil de Glanville, written up in a frenzy, with just minutes to spare before the copy deadline – I was all but exhausted as well.

I thoroughly enjoyed an enlightening interview with Julie Bardner, the most senior of Bath's all-female team of physiotherapists, who had helped prepare the side for most of their Twickenham cup final triumphs and proved a mine of useful background material. Somehow, I dragged a few more words than usual out of a phlegmatic Graham Dawe and talked at length to John Hall who spoke with obvious pride about his own career and the development of the Bath family ethos, to which he had made a crucial contribution in his long and successful association with the club.

I wrote a sentimental flashback article on the *Chronicle*'s specialist rugby photographer Bob Ascott, who had played scrum-half for the club in the early 1970s and had scored an amazing try on his first team debut against Wasps. Bob covered the final from the touchline that Saturday, and still provides a constant flow of tremendous action photographs for the paper, thanks to his instinct for knowing exactly where and when the best picture is likely to emerge on the field.

Last, but not least, among my interviews for that cup final supplement was an initial encounter with the man credited with founding Bath's trophy-winning dynasty, Jack Rowell.

And to my surprise, when I came face to face with the England coach, it was to be greeted by a compliment that made me realise that my journalistic efforts were being appreciated among rugby-loving readers of the *Bath Chronicle*, of whom Jack, who still lives on the fringe of the city, was clearly one. As he welcomed me, he said that in his opinion the quality of the rugby coverage in the paper's sports columns had gone up several notches since my arrival. And after that morale-boost any nervousness I had felt on being confronted by such a world famous figure in the game rapidly dissolved. We got on well, although he was ultra careful to be as even-handed and circumspect as possible in response to my questions regarding the respective merits of the two sides and I couldn't pin him down to a firm prediction of the outcome. He believed, rightly as it turned out, that the issue hinged on Bath's ability to counter Leicester's forward power and gain sufficient ball to feed their talented backs. But, although I gained the distinct impression he hoped they would succeed, he was far too canny to say so outright.

My initial impression of Rowell, and it was one that would be amply confirmed on further acquaintance, was that he was a man who liked to keep his own counsel and his cards as close to his chest as possible. In contrast to that fairly relaxed interview, he rarely appeared comfortable in the press and public relations limelight thrust upon him by his role in the England hierarchy. And I have often wondered whether Bath's frequently precarious and sensitive relationship with the media could be traced back to his huge and formative influence at the Rec. That close-knit family feeling, which John Hall and almost everyone involved with the club were so proud of and fiercely determined to retain, was one lasting Rowell legacy that had stood the test of time and proved crucial to Bath's extended run of almost unbroken success over the years. But with rugby on the brink of a startling metamorphosis, there were indications that, in a drastically changing world, it was perhaps time for the club to embrace a more open approach in the conduct of its affairs, to give more thought to the projection of a modern image and a more positive attitude towards communication at all levels of its operation.

For a man of his undoubted business acumen and prowess as a coach and motivator, Rowell was to remain very much an enigma, not only to me, but also to many players who came under his influence and were variously affected by it.

Meanwhile, in the days leading up to that cup final, I began to realise that I had, in the space of nine short weeks, become almost as big a Bath fan as anyone else.

It was not just the flair and quality of Bath's performances on the field that had won me over, but the whole ambience of the rugby scene at the Rec, which inspired me with the feeling of sharing an involvement in something truly special in sport. Although the pressure of maintaining high standards of achievement was constantly in evidence, there was a real bond of camaraderie, not just within the squad but also between the players and supporters, which I could only admire and respect. It was a unity that was always evident immediately after home games at the Rec, when a large section of the crowd would linger over a beer in the clubhouse or out·on the pitch. And Bath's players and officials seemed content to mingle with them, signing autographs, posing for photographs with excited youngsters, and talking freely to supporters who had paid good money for the privilege of seeing them perform.

It struck me vividly then that such an informal bonhomie and relaxed atmosphere was one of the ingredients that had made Bath almost invincible for so many years. It was a real family environment – not without its divided loyalties, conflicting interests and jealous factions, but joined together by a common allegiance to the pursuit of rugby excellence.

And from my point of view, I had found the players a delight to deal with. They were rational, self-critical to a fault, whether they had won or lost and, above all, intensely loyal to the club that had fostered their ambitions. Even when players were out of form or favour, or sidelined by injury, that loyalty shone through in their invariably diplomatic and honest reactions, and their patience in dealing with press questions that must have seemed yawningly mundane and repetitive at times was beyond reproach.

With precious few exceptions, they were a terrific bunch of people to work with and their courtesy and willingness to co-operate made life much easier for me throughout our association.

It was a huge pity, then, that the Pilkington Cup final, the showpiece finale of the rugby union season, was to be remembered that year not for quality of performance by the two finest teams in Britain but for reasons that detracted from what should have been a great and memorable occasion. It was a frustrating, disjointed and niggling contest from start to finish, with Leicester unarguably the chief culprits, in denying a capacity Twickenham crowd, and ultimately themselves, the glorious spectacle the occasion deserved.

As many pundits, including Jack Rowell, had anticipated the Tigers' formidable pack soon made their presence felt, and with towering England lock Martin Johnson dominating the lineout and Neil Back foraging voraciously in the loose, Bath were denied clean, quick possession for long periods of the game. However, Callard's penalty gave Bath an early lead, before Leicester produced a telling forward surge that allowed fly-half Niall Malone to knife through a ragged defensive line and give John Liley the chance to put his side 7-3 ahead with a neat conversion.

Callard cut the deficit with his second penalty as Bath, without the lethal opportunism of the injured Guscott, tried to feed off scraps of untidy possession, and thanks to a Mike Catt dropped goal they somehow managed to regain a 9-7 lead at the interval. But in the second half the Leicester juggernaut, led by the daunting bulk of number eight Dean Richards, looked set to grind their opponents into the turf. That they failed to do so was Leicester's own fault, because they created enough chances to have settled the issue long before the end, while Liley also let Bath off the hook with a couple of errant penalty attempts. But, when lock Matt Poole stole the ball from a lineout to snatch the Tigers' second try with five minutes left, Bath's double dream looked dead and buried even though Liley missed a conversion that would have left them chasing an unlikely two scores.

With his side trailing 15-9 as the contest reached a climax, John Hall – not for the first time in recent weeks – could not bear to watch, retreating to the empty solace of the changing rooms. But he, of all people, should have remembered Bath's reputation for amazing fightbacks, and so, to their cost, should Leicester.

Anxious to preserve their slender advantage the Tigers ceded territory and in a sudden explosion of frustrated passion Bath's beaten pack dredged up their last of ounces of energy to mount a sustained assault on the Leicester line. The offensive was thwarted only by suicidal defensive resistance, punished by a succession of five penalties in 90 seconds, before referee Steve Lander, tired of Leicester's illegal tactics, ran to the posts, his raised arm signalling a penalty try.

In the mayhem that ensued, an incensed Back clearly appeared to push Lander to the turf, an offence which later would see him receive a six-month ban. And from the brink of defeat Bath suddenly found themselves one easy kick away from a coveted double. The ice-cool Callard was never going to miss that golden opportunity and over the ball went from in front of the posts, Lander's final blast on the whistle sending the Bath team and their disbelieving supporters wild with jubilation at their undreamt-of reprieve, while Leicester fans were left understandably aggrieved and inconsolable.

I was among a majority of observers who were to applaud Steve Lander's brave and controversial decision that afternoon, along with some 18,000 partisan Bath followers whose joy was unrestrained. But, justified or not, that penalty try award was to have repercussions which would leave a sour taste in the mouths of those who would have preferred a more decisive and fitting outcome.

Neither club was entirely blameless in the recriminations that followed Lander's final whistle. Leicester's Back and Richards were castigated for a lack of sportsmanship in defeat, Back refusing to go up to receive his loser's medal, although he did eventually apologise to Lander for the push, which he claimed was a case of mistaken identity as he mistook the referee for a Bath player.

But Bath were less than magnanimous in their response to a victory that many deemed extremely fortunate on the run of play, although to their credit they produced most of what little flowing rugby had been played, and their defensive work had been nothing short of heroic. However, John Hall voiced his strong condemnation of Leicester's negative tactical game plan at the subsequent press conference. This achieved little except perhaps to tarnish a noble effort by his double-winning team.

It was the kind of regrettable reaction that would surface again in the future, but for the moment it was soon forgotten amid the joyous celebrations that followed. Bath had proved themselves, if not quite undisputably, the kings of English rugby once more. And John Hall, at the climax of his first season at the helm, had every reason to relish a glorious double achievement and the gleaming prospect of continued domination in the professional era that was about to commence.

Before that, however, and while other clubs around the country were busily packing for hard-earned holidays in the sun, Bath's battle-weary troops were steeling themselves for three more weeks of training-ground toil and what looked likely to be a gruelling two-leg showdown against Wigan, unchallenged kings of the rugby league code for almost as long as Bath had reigned supreme at rugby union. No one, not even John Hall, expected Bath to have any chance in the first leg under league rules at Manchester City's Maine Road ground, especially as the tie came just four days after their draining Pilkington Cup final exertions against Leicester.

As they travelled north on the day before their historic first encounter, Bath's heavily depleted squad were still digesting the news that Ben Clarke had agreed to join second division Richmond in a three-year deal reported to be worth around £500,000, along with England Under-21 prop Darren Crompton, who had become disenchanted with his lack of first-team opportunities at the Rec. Hall revealed that he had known Clarke would be leaving several months before and while regretting that decision, he expressed confidence that no other senior players would be following Clarke's example and seeking pastures new. His confidence was somewhat misplaced: winger Audley Lumsden would play his last game for Bath against Wigan at Maine Road that week, before eventually joining Richard Hill at Gloucester. And experienced lock Andy Reed, having fought his way back to fitness from a serious back injury, would follow his Scottish international second row partner Damian Cronin to Wasps.

The good news for Bath was that Mike Catt seemed certain to reject a massively tempting offer from Richmond. And Hall was hopeful that Victor Ubogu and Simon Geogheghan would also elect to remain with the club. They did eventually stay put and Catt's decision would prove a crucial turning point in John Hall's protracted negotiations with his squad, most of whom were loath to leave the Rec, where they had made their names, and where they were only too aware of having a realistic chance of further honours.

For Crompton, who was unlikely to figure in Hall's first-team plans, a move which would at least give him a chance of first-team status was probably wise, as it would also be for several other promising young players whose prospects at the Rec looked bleak in the face of the intense competition for places that had been the norm for years. Talented youngsters like scrum-half Marcus Olsen, eventually to make his mark with Saracens, flanker Adam Vander, England Under-21 hooker Neil McCarthy and centre Fraser Waters would all follow Crompton in seeking greater opportunities elsewhere, as Bath began to lay plans to add to the club's glittering array of international stars in the coming months.

Wigan, after generations of experience in the unrelenting grind of professional combat, knew everything there was to know on that score, and, as the two teams took the field that night in front of 20,418 expectant fans at Maine Road, it soon became clear they were intent not just on demonstrating their overwhelming superiority, but on rubbing Bath's upstart noses in the dirt.

What transpired was an eye-opening feast of unbelievably fluid rugby, with a gallant Bath outfit, way below full strength and barely familiar with the rules, let alone any real vestige of tactical awareness, being mercilessly swamped in a totally one-sided first half as Wigan ran in a hatful of tries to lead 52-0 at the break. Bath were unable to cope with the mesmeric skills of Shaun Edwards, Gary Connolly, Henry Paul and Jason Robinson, the power of Va'aiga Tuigamala and the pace of Wigan's smaller, but more mobile forwards, let alone the blistering speed of winger Martin Offiah who strolled over for six scintillating tries. But despite being under constant siege for almost the entire 80 minutes, Bath's courage never faltered. They took the severest of poundings without complaint or rancour and exerted fleeting pressure on Wigan in the second half, culminating in a consolation try by Jon Callard, in the unaccustomed role of scrum-half, which he converted himself.

When a merciful final whistle brought the slaughter to an end Wigan had stretched the lead to 82-6, but even they could only salute Bath's dogged resistance after a game which had a profound effect on all who witnessed it.

And there were many influential rugby union people present, not least Bath's own management team, for whom it would prove a positive eye-opener as far as recruitment plans were concerned.

I was so struck by the pace and precision of Wigan's attacking play that I actually felt they had a real chance of inflicting Bath's first defeat of any kind on Twickenham turf when the second leg, this time under union rules, got under way on Saturday, 25 May, but my fears that Bath might suffer the ultimate humiliation proved groundless.

Wigan had done their homework and looked dangerous with ball in hand, especially in broken play, but they rarely managed to achieve sufficient possession to allow their lethal backs enough time or space to display their superb running and handling skills. Bath paid them the compliment of keeping their own game tightly disciplined and for the most part forward-dominated in the first half, and had forged into a decisive 39-0 lead by the fiftieth minute, when they gradually began to look weary and eased their foot off the accelerator, allowing Wigan to make a dramatic impression in the final quarter.

Running the ball at pace, sometimes from behind their own line, Wigan suddenly took control to run in three brilliantly conceived and executed tries. Craig Murdock twice finished off blinding moves and Tuigamala burst clear for another try as the supremely fit northern champions brought a near 50,000 crowd to its feet in rapt admiration.

Scrum-half Ian Sanders added Bath's seventh try to leave them comfortable 44-19 victors and seal a more than adequate revenge for that Maine Road mauling. But there was no doubt that Wigan had more than enhanced their own standing in the rugby world in an enthralling display that fully vindicated the decision to stage it. Naturally the revenue would be useful too, but over the course of two historic games, Bath and Wigan had more than given value for money, and, in so doing, they had also learned useful lessons from each other, while raising the enticing prospect of further interplay between two codes of the same game that had been bitterly divorced for longer than anyone could remember.

For John Hall, Brian Ashton, and a bevy of rugby union club officials and scouts in the stands at Twickenham that afternoon, the sight of Wigan's professional expertise, albeit in a form of the game that was entirely foreign to most of their team, must have been a profound and salutary experience. These men were superbly trained and finely tuned athletes, fearless in all the physical aspects of the game, amazingly adept at spinning out of the tackle when cornered, and to a man, forwards included, they were supremely aware in terms of all-round vision, with mesmeric running, handling and passing skills.

Rugby League, with its established professional disciplines, was clearly a gold-mine of potentially massive and as yet untapped proportions for the coaches and rugby directors who would be at the forefront of the rugby union's charge towards paid employment. And many of them already had plenty of money burning holes in their pockets. Hall and Ashton were not quite in that bracket yet, but they soon would be as Bath's doomed committee resigned themselves to the inevitable and completed plans for their own abdication from all power and responsibility. As they set about plotting their own carefully charted course for the following autumn they must have been quietly delighted by their shared vision of even greater glories in store for a club that could barely remember the meaning of failure.

After all, what could possibly go wrong? They already had the best playing squad in the country, if not the whole of Europe, with the prospect of another batch of world-class recruits in the pipeline. They were once again established as double champions, still ahead of the chasing pack and the envy of all their rivals, as they had been for a dozen years and more. Hardly a dark cloud was visible on the horizon, and surely nothing, short of an unprecedented disaster, could halt Bath's relentless pursuit of excellence and trophy domination once those crucial financial resources were securely in place. But a setback of huge magnitude was about to envelop the club, and when it did, no amount of money could avert the sudden calamitous crisis that descended on the Rec in the dark, dying days of that fateful year, when the traditional countenance of rugby union changed forever beyond all recognition or redemption.

PART THREE

A Leap Too Far

CHAPTER ONE

Feeling the Heat

I can recollect a distinct feeling of being present at a water-shed in sporting history as I surveyed the scene in Twickenham's crowded tea room only minutes after Bath and Wigan had brought the 1995/96 rugby union season to such a momentous close. It was incredible, and incongruous to observe so many players, personalities and administrators from two long-estranged rugby codes in such an animated display of harmony and goodwill.

Both sets of players seemed uplifted by the experience. RFU secretary Tony Hallett and RFL chief executive Maurice Lindsay staged a press conference that enhanced the over-whelming feeling of euphoria, and I can remember that notable northern actor and author Colin Welland, an enthusi-astic supporter of rugby league since childhood, being quite overcome by the occasion. But if you scanned that sea of beaming faces hard enough it was possible to detect that not everyone present was quite as enthused by the reconciliation between the codes. I remember seeing RFU management committee chairman Cliff Brittle flitting here and there among the jostling throng with a face betraying very little of pleasure, and there were others present who also seemed less than overwhelmed.

It was easy, in the euphoria of the moment, to believe that the two rugby codes might have arrived at the brink of an unprecedented reunion. In the real world, however, it requires something more substantial than 30 players taking the field together to erase generations of prejudice. But for a week or two, before and after that heartwarming confrontation, the possibility of amalgamation was on the tip of many a tongue, not least that of John Hall, who had openly called for such a merger on the eve of the game. Hall's enthusiasm, however, was not too widely shared elsewhere and significantly many of his senior players were more cautious in their appraisal of the situation as the debate continued in the weeks after the game. Andy Robinson, voted man of the match in that second Wigan clash, welcomed closer contact between the codes, but considered they should retain separate identities. And both Jon Callard and Nigel Redman expressed reservations over the reunification issue.

In a sense it was easy to see why they were reluctant to comtemplate a merger, considering the likely threat to the career ambitions of union players and also the anarchic state that the union code was already rapidly descending into, with the RFU and its member clubs engaged in open conflict over control of the game. Reunification was hardly a realistic possibility when clubs in the top two divisions of the Courage Championship were already weighing up the possibility of breaking away from the RFU in pursuit of their own ambitions. This danger was eventually averted by the first in a series of uneasy compromises that would frequently threaten to make things worse over the next two years.

With the first professional campaign coming ever closer, clubs were busy finalising plans for the new era, which left scant time for dealing with the issue of unification and it soon became a non-starter. John Hall and his counterparts elsewhere were not to dismiss the league scene entirely from their minds when it came to bolstering their squads in the weeks to come. But for now time was of the essence for Hall, in an all too short and disrupted summer that was to become a challenge of nerve, character and stamina for all those concerned with transforming Bath into a professional entity.

It was a torrid period that Hall would later reflect had often left him close to despair. And the fact that Bath's season had extended nearly a month longer than any of the club's rivals had only added to his problems. In any other year, he and his players would have enjoyed the reward of an extended close-season holiday before returning refreshed for the autumn. But this summer was to be different from any that had gone before and it soon became essential that business took priority over rest and recuperation.

For a start Hall had to tie up negotiations with a number of players who had not yet committed themselves to the club. And that was no easy task, considering that he was bargaining from the unenviable position of not knowing if and when Bath would attract a major backer to put up the finance required to deliver those contracts. All this took much longer than anticipated, and there was still the problem of attracting and recruiting additions to the squad who were already being targeted by Hall, Brian Ashton and a band of assistant coaches and scouts who had been scouring the globe for available talent.

Altogether, June and July were to prove traumatic for everyone concerned with setting up a professional regime at the Rec. And, of necessity, it was no time for them to be airing their intentions in public, which naturally made my job as a rugby writer, in a city obsessed by the game, that much more difficult. It was one of those periods when, in the absence of credible information or anyone to talk to, with people on holiday or just about to depart, the only alternative was to resort to speculation. A lot of that, much of it inaccurate, went on that summer. With John Hall adamantly, and understandably, refusing to reveal or discuss his squad plans, other than to repeat his claim that it would be the best in the country, much of the speculation centred on the identity of Bath's prospective new owner. All sorts of rumours were being touted within days of the season ending, while club chairman

Richard Mawditt was already hinting that the answer was on the brink of being revealed. But, as with everything else in that frustrating early summer lull, the truth took far longer to emerge than expected.

In the meantime, while everyone waited for momentous events to unfold, I turned my attention to other sports, reporting the exploits of local cricket clubs Bath, Lansdown and Keynsham in the Western League, which proved to be a rewarding and enjoyable distraction from my rugby responsibilities. As well as those cricket interludes I also managed to make fleeting acquaintance with the local golf scene, once following Jeremy Guscott, Jon Callard and former Scotland captain Gavin Hastings on a headlong circuit of Lansdowne Golf Club, where Guscott was a 12-handicap member. The event was *The Sun* Longest Day Golf Challenge in aid of charity, with Guscott and Hastings undertaking a whistle-stop plane and car chase around Britain playing four courses in Wales, England, Ireland and Scotland in the space of 18 hours.

It was fun to watch, but offered little opportunity to talk to the participants, who were too busy rushing from tee to green to offer much more than idle chat, particularly from Jerry, who was not in a communicative mood. Sportsmen, of course, have as much right as anyone else to their own space and privacy. I have never been one to harass players. In my experience, if you treat them with respect they usually accept that you have a job to do and respond willingly. Jerry eventually did, although it took a while, and his co-operation could never be taken for granted. He could be uncompromisingly blunt in refusing to comment at times, while on other occasions he would be more than forthcoming. But I always admired his capacity to distinguish between those moments and, when he was inclined to talk, his comments were usually to the point and sensible.

Guscott, from my first-hand observation, was and still is the finest centre in the world on his day. His ability to leave quality opponents floundering with one silky bodyswerve, or electric change of pace, has been unmatched over the last decade in world rugby. And he is only too aware of that fact, even if England's management, obsessed with tactical limitations elsewhere, chose to ignore his unique talents far too often.

When Bath's internal troubles erupted later that year Guscott was as loyal to the club as anyone could have expected him to be. And later, when a new management team took over, he was one of the first to demonstrate his allegiance by signing an extension to his contract that virtually tied him to Bath until the end of his career. No doubt he was well compensated for doing so. But he would be a much wealthier man had he not turned down a host of lucrative offers earlier in his career in order to stay with Bath. Even now he could probably earn more elsewhere.

Like him or not, Guscott is his own man. And he was shrewd enough to put his finger on the root of the club's problems in that first professional season when he observed that Bath had talked too openly about what they aimed to achieve and by doing so had put added pressure on the squad to fulfil those ambitions. He was referring by implication to those oft-repeated statements of intent by John Hall, who had been his staunch friend and team-mate through many successful campaigns, and in Guscott's estimation was the finest rugby player he had ever known.

But it was not just a surfeit of bold talk that undermined those lofty ambitions before a ball was kicked in anger. There were other critical shortcomings that would surface, notably flawed policy, organisational and logistical teething problems, poor communication and personnel management, and tactical and selection inconsistency. And all these would contribute to the disasters that were to follow.

To be fair to John Hall, not all of those mistakes could be laid at his door alone. There was a general air of self-satisfaction bordering on arrogance prevailing at the Rec, and later on at the club's plush new offices in Queen Square, as that busy summer wore on and the nuts and bolts of Bath's vision of professional pre-eminence were put in place. On the eve of his departure as chairman, Richard Mawditt, in an extensive article in the club's newsletter, *The Recorder*, published at the end of June, waxed lyrical about the club's past achievements and proud standing in the rugby world. And, somewhat immodestly, the magazine itself proclaimed Bath's record as ' a story of unbroken success' achieved by 'probably the world's greatest rugby club'. It was by no means a ridiculously overblown claim because Bath had undeniably ruled the domestic rugby union scene for years. But the club had not yet entered European competition, let alone conquered the continent, and it had certainly not earned the right to depict itself as the greatest club in the world, although the impression given was that these conquests were merely a matter of time. And, more importantly, of money. John Hall was already discovering that time was a precious commodity. And, in hindsight, he might reflect that money, unless wisely spent, is no guarantee of success in sport, although no one would dispute that it helps.

There was no question that, as June gave way to July, the pressure intensified on Hall and Bath to reveal their master plan for continued trophy domination in the new professional era. On 1 July most of the club's existing squad reported back for pre-season training under fitness coach Ged Roddy at the Bath University sports complex. They had enjoyed only a month's lay-off from their double-winning labours, and there was still no confirmation of major financial investment in the club, nor a whisper about any new signings.

Speculation was rife on both counts, but settling such matters was obviously proving much more complicated than anyone had anticipated. And, as far as the press and the club's supporters were concerned, the uncertainty seemed interminable. But four days later, on 5 July, our local rivals the *Western Daily Press* broke the story that the multi-millionaire greetings card magnate Andrew Brownsword was set to become Bath's financial saviour – although, typically, the news came in the form of an unconfirmed leak.

Not for the first time, nor the last, the club was slow to react to events and was caught napping by the premature airing of a major announcement that should have come from official sources. But in a rugby hotbed like Bath very little stays secret for long. Asked to comment on the revelation, Richard Mawditt would say only that the club was looking forward to making an announcement concerning a long-term arrangement that would ensure its stability and guarantee players contracts for several years. John Hall flatly refused to comment other than to say that a press conference would take place a week later. But he was markedly less reserved about Bath's prospects for the new season, reiterating his claim that the club would have the best squad in England, capable of winning every trophy on offer. He also said he would be looking at players from around the world, from both rugby codes, and that Bath's playing style would reflect some of the lessons they had learned from the previous season, especially the Wigan clashes. He predicted improved performance levels and professional standards in all aspects of the game, promising that Bath would be fitter, faster and stronger than ever.

Not surprisingly, the revelation that Bath had secured a major financial backer of Brownsword's stature, whose assets were estimated in some quarters at around £300 million, fuelled frenzied speculation about the size of his investment in the club. Initially, the *Bath Chronicle* followed most of its rivals in guessing that the initial input would be worth around £5 million. But that was to prove way over the mark when a week later the club belatedly staged a press conference to unveil Brownsword as its new owner. The event was something of a damp squib. But it did have its moments of drama, revelation and a touch of almost comic relief. For a start, the conference was delayed for some time owing to the late arrival of the guest of honour. And then it was put back even further by a mysterious late hitch that saw Richard Mawditt hastily flitting between the conference room in the Teachers stand and the clubhouse at the opposite end of the ground in a state of no little agitation.

When Andrew Brownsword eventually made his entrance, he read a prepared statement outlining his reasons for taking a hand in Bath's affairs, his future hopes and ambitions for the club, and his firm faith in the new board of directors, responsible for securing its future as a professional business. And then, without further ado, he was gone, striding out of the room to his next appointment, leaving others to cope with an inevitable flurry of questions. These were fielded mainly by John Hall, predictably confirmed as Bath's director of rugby, a position which now gave him almost unlimited control over the playing side of Bath's affairs.

Alongside him in Bath's new power base were Ed Goodall, a Brownsword nominee as the club's chief executive, and Stephen Hands, a former Coca Cola executive, recently appointed as commercial and marketing manager by the outgoing committee. They were soon joined by David Jenkins, a former Bath player recruited as operations director, and Thomas Sheppard, a Bath-based lawyer installed as company secretary. The major surprise at the press conference was the appointment of one of Bath's legendary former players, Tony Swift, in the role of non-executive chairman. Since his retirement some 14 months earlier, after scoring a farewell try in Bath's Pilkington Cup final victory over Wasps, Tony Swift had dropped right out of the Rec scene, preferring to concentrate on his regular job as an accountant with the Bath accountancy firm of Robson, Taylor Ltd. But, as he was to explain later, Swift had viewed the sudden prospect of professional rugby union at the Rec with great excitement and, when the opportunity arose to become involved, he had grasped it with alacrity.

That chance had come about through his friendship with former team-mate John Hall, who had supported his appointment to the Brownsword organisation for what was seen to be a figurehead role. Such nepotism was not unknown in Bath rugby circles where one of their own ilk was usually preferred to an outsider. In their eyes, as John Hall and Brian Ashton were only too fond of pointing out, Bath were the rugby union equivalent of the Liverpool of the eighties, and if such methods of internal advancement were good enough for Anfield they were good enough for the Rec.

As it happened, Tony Swift's return to the fold (initially on the basis of chairing meetings and a time contribution he estimated at half a day per week) would turn out to be one of the few saving graces in Bath's fateful first campaign as a professional club. But it would be a traumatic return for the popular Swift, who would quickly become enmeshed in the stress of intense disappointment, dire controversy, internal wrangling and above all, heartrending decisions that would stretch and ultimately sever the close friendship that had brought him back to the Rec and back into the game he loved.

Of his fellow board members in the new administrative headquarters at 4 Queen Square, I had no contact with Ed Goodall and Thomas Sheppard, who clearly had important roles within the club, but remained firmly in the background as far as my duties were concerned. From the start of his involvement, Goodall, a publicity-shy accountant, insisted that, like his even more reticent employer, he would not be available for interviews and he never budged from that position, which was frustrating from my point of view as a journalist, but at least the ground rules were clearly stated.

I can't say much about his influence on Bath's corporate development, except to suggest that it seemed incongruous for the chief executive of a high profile sporting concern like Bath, a club which by definition remains totally reliant on the support of the paying public, to insist on complete anonymity. When problems arose over a multitude of issues, as they soon would, there was no one in overriding authority to address the concerns of members, supporters, or journalists. And, because of this apparent lack of open communication, relations with the rugby-going public undoubtedly suffered.

As far as Andrew Brownsword was concerned, the barriers blocking communication and accountability were even more pronounced. He had bought a seventy-five per cent controlling interest in the club (a members' trust held the other twenty-five per cent), he had installed a board of directors to run it, and that was that, as far as his, and indeed the public, conception of his role was concerned. On that single and extremely brief foray into the public spotlight, the belated press conference announcing his takeover of control, a hopeful photographer had offered him a rugby ball to pose with for the cameras, which he regarded with suspicion and disdain, as if disclaiming any association with the game. Brownsword was clearly an intensely reticent and private personality. Initially that revelation, and his apparent lack of interest in the game, caused some foreboding, although many top sports clubs would probably welcome such a non-interfering owner with open arms. But as events began to unfold and dark clouds of controversy and disunity gathered over the Rec, Brownsword would be forced to assume a decisive role in the club's affairs. And he soon came to learn more about rugby, apparently developing quite a passion for the game.

With Stephen Hands and David Jenkins, shyness and reticence were never a problem. Both came from successful executive careers in sales and marketing for major companies, and they possessed all the market-place acumen and patter that goes with the territory, although they differed in approach and attitude. I was invited to talk to Stephen Hands soon after he arrived at Bath and quickly got the message that he intended taking a vigorous stance in promoting the club's image and revamping its marketing policies.

He was never rude or overbearing, but he wasted little time in asserting his view that close contact with Bath Rugby Club was an essential ingredient in terms of sales for the local newspaper and therefore the *Bath Chronicle* should do all it could to accommodate the club, particularly with respect to providing free advertising. That kind of statement was guaranteed to raise hackles, and not just with me. Back in the editorial department at Westgate Street the editor, David Gledhill, gave it short shrift. We acknowledged that Bath rugby was a vital feature of the paper's sports coverage, but felt strongly that the paper was equally important to the club, in that our blanket coverage of Bath's activities provided daily free advertising in itself. The reality was that both companies needed each other. And once that fact was established Stephen Hands and I communicated well enough on the few occasions our paths crossed.

David Jenkins, one of a family of three brothers who had played for Bath in the late 1960s and early 1970s proved to be even more voluble, rarely pausing for breath when you talked to him. But I always got on well with him and was amazed by his seemingly boundless enthusiasm and energy. A talented all-round sportsman in his playing days, his rugby career was sadly cut short by a horrific knee injury that today could almost certainly have been treated successfully. He was invariably positive and effervescent, and his hyperactive nature was ideally suited to the daunting task of bringing order and organisation to the management of the Rec and its facilities, which had been beset by problems before his arrival.

All things considered Bath's management team certainly didn't lack experience or know-how, but it consisted of strong-minded, opinionated people who, understandably perhaps, were not always on the same wavelength. On the one hand there was a strong element of former Bath players, whose experience and knowledge of the game was unquestioned, but whose business skills were limited and untested in the demanding commercial side of professional sport. On the other side of the table sat some acute business brains, who knew nothing about rugby and had scant experience of administering a sporting concern, in which the prime commodity was people, whether it was players, members or ordinary, itinerant fans.

Unfortunately a characteristic of both factions was a deep-seated reluctance to engage in open, straightforward communication about their intentions and plans with all those interested parties whose support was vital to the club's cause. And, in the case of the media, the accepted, if occasionally unreliable and uncontrolled channel of communication between the club and its public, that reluctance was almost pathological in its intensity in some quarters.

Add all that to the universal uncertainty, discord and financial over-indulgence that was already afflicting the game at that time, when every hesitant step was a matter of trial and error, and it was bound to present a difficult and potentially volatile situation. But the dire problems that were to befall Bath's new administration could hardly have been foreseen or anticipated in advance, as the board sat down with optimism to map out their campaign plans for a new and exciting future.

Meanwhile, in the middle of a long, hot and often irksome summer of uncertainty, I suddenly encountered problems of my own, which were to come as a warning signal that the responsibilities and demands of my new role were beginning to take their toll. A few days after the unveiling of Bath's newly professionalised administration, I was in the *Chronicle*'s paste-up area helping to supervise the completion of that morning's sports pages when I glanced upwards at the high brightly-lit ceiling and suddenly, for the first time in my life, I felt my head swim and my knees begin to buckle under me. Without understanding what was happening, I lurched sideways to rest my arms on the stone, the metal bench where stories are collated and distributed to their allotted pages. But I struggled to support myself and was sliding slowly to the floor until I managed to utter a cry for help, which alerted David Gledhill who was nearest to me. In an instant he grabbed me and lowered me gently to the ground. By then I was in a semi-faint and had lost all capacity to do anything other than lie back and attempt to regain my senses. After first-aid attention I still felt groggy, so eventually I was helped out of the building and driven home.

On arrival I was seen by my doctor who arranged a series of tests. It was a couple of days before I began to feel more like my usual self, but I was back at work the following week and apparently none the worse for my sudden mishap.

Only the day before, the dam had broken on Bath's rigid silence concerning player-recruitment plans, with the news that the former Wales and British Lions flanker Richard Webster was expected to join the club on a three-year contract, due to be signed on the very day I suffered that worrying scare. It was the first concrete evidence of John Hall's plans to build a squad that would be the envy of rival clubs in England and abroad. But there would still be a considerable delay before his full line-up would be revealed, during which, for the first time, our working relationship suffered its first major hiccup.

In the same back page lead in which I revealed that Webster would be joining Bath, Hall intimated that his first priority had been to secure the continued services of the club's existing squad, but he had already talked to a number of possible new players who had shown varying degrees of interest. He refused to discuss speculation that Bath were interested in Wigan backs Henry Paul and Va'aiga Tuigamala (later to sign a lucrative contract with Newcastle) or comment on individual players he might be interested in until he had completed his overall preparations. But he claimed there would definitely be some new players in the squad.

Once again he trotted out the familar line about Bath already possessing the strongest and most attractive squad in the country. And he also dropped a hint that there would be modifications to the team's playing style to take into account new laws governing the lineout and scrummage and developments in the way the game was being played in the Southern Hemisphere, particularly in the highly popular Super 12 series contested by district sides from New Zealand, Australia and South Africa. But the major talking point was whether Hall would invest some of Bath's newly acquired riches on bringing world-class rugby league performers into the union game at the Rec. He had already expressed his unqualified admiration for the fitness and ball skills of Wigan's elite stars. And, with the northern champions beset by financial problems, it was rumoured that for the right money they would be prepared to allow some of their players to ply their trade in professional rugby union, if only on a short-term loan basis.

The crux of the dispute between Hall and me arose from a telephone conversation in which I asked him about his purported interest in recruiting players from Wigan and asked him whether he had spoken to them about the possibility of a deal.

He said he had spoken to them and, by that, I took him to mean the players involved, which I duly conveyed in my report. The paper came out, there was no further reaction for the rest of the day, and I went home looking forward to an evening round of golf without an inkling that anything was amiss. However, when I returned from the golf course my wife informed me that a very irate Hall had phoned wanting to speak to me urgently and had even suggested that she should try and get hold of me at the golf club, which she had attempted to do, without success, because I was already well out of range of the clubhouse.

I could not imagine what all the fuss was about, but I didn't have to wait long to find out, because, when I eventually contacted Hall, he told me, in no uncertain terms, that he was extremely unhappy about the report of his interest in Wigan's players and that our relationship was under a considerable cloud as a result. I was taken aback at this outburst because I felt strongly that I had only reported what he had quite distinctly said, but over the next couple of days I gradually began to realise what had occurred.

At that time Westminster Press, who owned the *Chronicle*, ran its own news agency, UK News, to which all its newspapers were expected to contribute copy that might be of interest elsewhere. We usually faxed through stories that came into this category to the UK News headquarters in Leicester, where they were made available nationally.

Naturally, Hall's interest in Wigan players would be headline news for newspapers in that neck of the woods and, when my story was picked up by the local press there the revelation had obviously caused some consternation within the Wigan club, whose feelings about the matter had obviously been conveyed back to Hall.

In essence, as far as Hall and I were concerned, it was a tiny misunderstanding that can easily occur in a hasty telephone conversation and which had been blown up out of all proportion. But it did cause a rift between us for a while, in which time I found I was cold-shouldered whenever I tried to contact him.

One repercussion from that incident gave me some insight into Hall's complex mentality. I was to discover, from an impeccable source, that he had spoken to the players concerned and not to the Wigan club. The next time I met him, a couple of weeks later, his disposition had dramatically changed. I was walking across Queen Square towards Victoria Park to collect the *Chronicle*'s pool car for an assignment when I encountered Hall on his way to the club offices. He greeted me affably, as if nothing had happened, and then asked if I could do him a favour. He had been asked to write an article on rugby which had to be completed that day, and he offered me a a sizeable sum to write it for him as he didn't have time to do it himself. Unfortunately, there were only two of us on the sports desk that day and it would not have been fair or reasonable to have accepted the offer, so I had to turn him down. But the realisation that Hall was quite happy to bury the hatchet and be friendly when it suited his own purposes did not entirely escape me.

Apart from that contretemps over the Wigan episode, however, Hall and I got on well enough in that stressful time. He could be hard to contact at times and not exactly helpful or communicative when you did pin him down. But I was aware of how much he had on his plate and tried hard to be as sympathetic as I could.

He was obsessed with his dream of confirming Bath as the premier force in European, if not world rugby. And, in his mind, satisfying the needs of the local press represented a time-consuming distraction from the monumental task he had set himself. Likewise, I had my own job to do and I was equally determined to do it well, so it was inevitable that we occasionally crossed swords. But for the most part we communicated productively, until mounting pressure on Hall and Bath intensified to such a degree, that the bubbling pot eventually boiled over, enveloping everyone involved, not least the two men who, only months earlier, had guided the club to that glorious but soon forgotten cup and league double.

Meanwhile, the hour had nearly arrived when Hall would finally unveil the squad he had assembled to defend those trophies and, if all his hopes were fulfilled, annex two more – the ill-fated Anglo-Welsh Cup, a tournament that never got off the ground, and the biggest prize of all, the Heineken European Cup.

Bath had already captured everything on offer time and again on the domestic scene. And now, after years of waiting, the club was about to embark on its own European crusade in pursuit of a prize that in their eyes was rugby union's Holy Grail.

A whole new world was evolving at the Rec. And Bath, as undisputed champions of England, were soon to become the focus of more attention than ever. For a club that craved conquest, but not necessarily the often intrusive media interest it engendered, the prospect was inviting, if fraught with uncertainty. Not that the club had any real qualms or fears about exposing itself to the media gaze during that short, but stressful summer of transition from the constraints of amateur regulation to the promised land of professional freedom that lay just over the horizon.

At least the retiring club committee of unrepentant 'old farts' had harboured few doubts about Bath's continued domination after their own reluctant, but inevitable abdication. So confident were they that they had left the new regime an exciting legacy that would ensure its exploits would be proclaimed throughout the land on nationwide television. In one of its final decisions before handing over the reins at the Rec, the old committee had concluded an agreement allowing the BBC 2 cameras virtually free access to Bath's inner sanctums for a 'fly on the wall', six-part documentary series depicting a year in the life of Britain's greatest rugby union club. At the time it was seen as a real feather in Bath's cap to be selected for such extensive exposure, and the committee could hardly be blamed for giving the idea the go-ahead.

As Ken Johnstone, nearing octogenarian status but retained as the club's press officer, proudly trumpeted in *The Recorder*, it was fitting that such a famous club as Bath, rather than Manchester United or Arsenal, should be presented to the public on television. Such coverage, he proudly predicted, would not bear comparison with the coverage Bath had received on more controversial issues in the past. This was to be a glorious tribute to an enthralling new chapter in Bath's success story.

Well, not quite. If only he and Bath could have foreseen what was about to unfold. If only they could have envisaged the pitfalls that lay ahead. If only there had been more time to adjust, more opportunity to plan and prepare. If only... But time was running out. The sun was already rising on a changing landscape at the Rec and it was time for actions to speak louder than words, although there would be plenty more of those over the coming months, as Bath primed themselves for their baptism into the world of professional rugby.

CHAPTER TWO

New Style for a New Dawn

By chance I was away for a few days when John Hall finally took the wraps off his newly assembled squad on Thursday, 15 August, when several new arrivals were paraded for the benefit of the media at the Rec's annual photo-call. Neville Smith attended in my absence and quickly homed in on the main focus of press attention, which was undoubtedly Henry Paul, Wigan's brilliant New Zealander, who it was revealed had joined Bath on a four-month contract worth an estimated £100,000 and extending from 8 September to 11 January when he would return to rugby league.

He would later be joined by his equally famous Central Park team-mate Jason Robinson recruited on similar terms, which would work out at around £5000 a game. Paul revealed that he had chosen Bath in preference to several other lucrative offers from union clubs because in his opinion they were the best. He said he was impressed by the quality of players the club already possessed and also by the way they played the game.

Apart from Paul, who was not even a permanent signing, there was a marked absence of outstanding international stars of the calibre already being recruited by such rivals as

Harlequins, Wasps, Saracens and Leicester, which probably surprised many rugby correspondents present. Explaining that deficiency of big names, and why he had kept his squad strengthening such a secret, Hall said that he had wanted to wait until he was able to announce the finished product, and in his view it was not about individual star signings. He felt that Bath's success had been built on collective effort and the intention was to retain the existing squad, nurture younger players and enhance the overall strength of the squad, which he felt he had done. Hall refused to confirm suggestions that Bath's annual wage bill amounted to around £1.5 million and, commenting on the loan fee for Henry Paul, he admitted it was substantial but only a sum relative to his ability.

Nevertheless, apart from Paul and Webster, whose arrival had already been revealed, it was evident that Bath's other new recruits were mostly players who had yet to make a significant impact at the top level: promising youngsters and a couple of unknown quantities who might or might not make the grade.

It is important to evaluate the quality and possible future impact of Hall's summer shopping spree because the size, complement and potential of that initial professional squad would have a considerable bearing on the outcome of that ill-fated season and of a no less eventful, but ultimately more successful, campaign to follow. Included in the unknown category among the new intake were South African full-back Ruan Nel, who had played for Transvaal Under-21, and another rugby league recruit in Christian Tyrer, a utility back signed from Widnes, and said to be an outstanding prospect. In the event, neither player ever achieved first team selection in a competitive game and both made precious little impact in the few appearances they made in United colours, so it has to be said they were not successful investments.

Among the forwards on show were three men who had already achieved international recognition of sorts, but who could not be described as having established themselves at the highest level, although two of these would play a major part in Bath's second professional campaign just over 12 months later.

The one who did not make his mark, and struggled to establish himself at first-team level, was the 6ft 7in, seventeen and a half stone Brian Cusack, a second-row forward who had represented Ireland A, but who played only a handful of senior games in his two seasons at the Rec before being released in 1998.

Nathan Thomas, a 20-year-old flanker recruited from Bridgend and already a Wales A international, had been brought in as openside cover for Andy Robinson and would not have to wait long for a first-team place. And the one man among that new brood who would make perhaps the greatest impact of all was already captain of his country, but still virtually unknown in British rugby circles. Dan Lyle, the 25-year-old son of a United States Army general, had turned down a lucrative contract with American football giants Minnesota Vikings to try his luck with Bath at the English version of the oval ball game, where his earning potential was far less. But, although he was captain of the US Eagles, the American national team, he was still a novice by English standards when he arrived that August.

At 6ft 5in and around 18 stone in weight, he was an imposing physical presence, and he had shown enough ability as a back row forward to catch the eye of Bath's scouting set-up. Whether he would knuckle down to the hard grind of training at the Rec, and meet the daunting demands of regular Courage League conflict was another matter.

As it turned out Lyle, an intelligent, articulate character, with few hang-ups about talking to the press, was to stand as Hall's best buy and become an all-round inspiration to a team whose morale would be tested to the limit that season. It was a pity that when Bath needed his superb athleticism and ball-handling ability most, in a disappointing first half of the season, Lyle had not yet broken through into the first team. But when he did, after the New Year, the effect was electrifying. Lyle had made a sensational debut impact at the Rec, scoring a hat-trick of tries from number eight in his first game for the United against Orrell in September. But in his next appearance he suffered a knee injury which kept him out for eight weeks, and by the time he had recovered and fought his way into first-team contention, Bath's season was already going haywire.

Once he established himself, Lyle was to play a major part in Bath's stirring late revival that briefly put the club back in contention for the Courage League title and led to his nomination by the club's supporters as their player of the season. Not bad for a rookie at such a famous academy of rugby learning.

These then were the principal new faces who would ply their trade at the Rec in the coming season, which was now barely a fortnight away. Later, there would be more costly arrivals jetting in from South America, and there were plenty of youngsters just itching to be given their chance; but they would have to wait a while.

As for John Hall and Brian Ashton, they were satisfied that they had done everything in their power to provide Bath with the strength in depth they envisaged would be needed in what was expected to be the toughest season Bath had ever faced. No one had any reason to dispute the fact that Hall had worked a minor miracle in retaining the loyalty of the vast majority of his double-winning squad in the face of a flood of tempting offers from Bath's envious rivals. And although he had been forced to pay handsomely to achieve it, that loyalty was nonetheless impressive.

Now he and Ashton, the acknowledged supremo of training ground tactics, were to face a race against time to introduce and perfect an exciting new playing style to fully exploit the wealth of talent they had assembled and carry Bath forward to higher levels of performance and achievement than ever before. The immediate problem was that two weeks hardly seemed long enough to implement the drastic revision in style they envisaged. They could look forward to an uninterrupted pre-season training week in Jersey to refine their strategies, but it was still a tall order, even for Bath's immensely talented and versatile squad.

Nevertheless, reports indicated that the trip had been a worthwhile excercise and, on their return, the training and honing of the new style continued apace – so much so that hardly anyone connected with the playing side appeared to be available whenever I picked up the phone. Until that time I had never seen Bath in training. But it seemed that the only way I could get to talk to the players was to turn up at the University sports ground, where Bath trained on Monday and Tuesday mornings (their Thursday evening session reverting to the club's own training pitch at Lambridge on the eastern edge of the city).

It proved an inspired move and a change of routine that would make all the difference as far as my relationship with the players was concerned. And, to be fair, I was never discouraged from attending or denied access to anyone I wanted to talk to. To ensure that my presence was accepted, I tried to make sure that my own approach to attending training sessions was just as professional as that of the players and in that respect I followed a set policy which stood me in good stead from then on.

When I arrived at the University or Lambridge, if the players were busy (which they usually were) I kept well out of the way, confined myself to observing what was going on, and made no attempt to talk to anyone, unless they were obviously not involved. I usually waited until training had finished and the players had changed and had lunch before asking them politely for a quick word. Five minutes later I would have my story on tape, to be transcribed in the office and written up for the next day's edition.

That process became a familiar weekly routine, which the squad gradually became accustomed to and obviously preferred to being continually bothered on the phone, often at inconvenient times, especially for someone as busy as Phil de Glanville.

Bath's double-winning skipper was invariably polite and

helpful whenever, in the early days, I was asked to ring him, often before breakfast, for a comment on whatever story was breaking that day. Those calls must have been a nuisance to Phil and his wife Yolanda, as I discovered to my embarrassment when one of my Bath Cricket Club acquaintances, Barry Maggs, a friend and neighbour of the couple, once pulled my leg, claiming that my early morning calls had often interrupted the most delicate of marital situations.

Those weekly training-ground visits had all sorts of benefits from my point of view. And for their part the players seemed to appreciate the fact that I was interested in what they were trying to do in training and not just content to turn up at matches, criticise their performance whenever things went badly and then chase them for quotes afterwards, when they might not feel much like talking. It was time-saving from their point of view and mine, and it helped me to not only file a regular supply of stories (I usually did two or three interviews at each visit), but also to become much better acquainted with almost everyone on the staff, from the humblest training assistant to the brightest star in Bath's international firmament. Above all it was fun and it gave me the chance to build up a bond of trust with players, who were not always fond of the attentions of rugby journalists. In return I tried not to betray that trust, or their confidence, and I don't think I let any of them down, although I had to be objective, when reporting matches, assessing performances, or occasionally commenting on controversial situations that arose from time to time.

As I watched them go about the repetitive task of practising their skills and developing new tactical ploys, I was hugely impressed by the dedication and perseverance they put into those sessions, and also by their enthusiasm for the bold new playing style they were being asked to embrace. It was clear from the outset that Bath had decided that the Super 12 pattern of almost non-stop attack involving both backs and forwards was not only the brand of rugby they wanted to play, but also the style that suited the squad best in the professional era.

And, under the constant prompting of Ashton and Hall, they were clearly determined to ensure it would be effective when the action began in earnest. Time after time I would watch them sweep away in flowing movements, and then a second and third wave of forwards would swiftly recycle the ball and set the action in motion again in bewildering passages of almost non-stop interplay.

There was little tackling other than touch contact in those sessions. And it seemed that defensive work was of secondary priority, although that was understandable, bearing in mind the need for avoiding unnecessary injuries just before the season started. But I did wonder why Bath's vastly experienced coaching team had chosen to experiment so daringly with this totally uninhibited expansive approach and questioned whether it would stand up to closer inspection when the resistance was for real.

From talking to Hall, Ashton, Tony Swift and the club's newly appointed assistant coach, Andy Robinson, there was little doubt that the decision to plump for all-out attacking rugby had been unanimous, although whether they were all as entirely convinced of its practicality as they sounded then was another matter. All four supported the view that in a new professional era, although results were still the top priority, it was vital that the game should provide entertainment for the paying customer in order for rugby to become commercially viable and successful.

The chief architect of this 'total rugby' philosophy was undoubtedly Ashton, whose tactical genius had transformed Bath from a ruthlessly efficient outfit into the most attractive side in the land over the previous seven years. The quietly spoken Lancastrian rarely sought the limelight, but, in my experience, he was always willing to answer press enquiries in his own forthright way, if asked; and as a devotee of the running game he clearly saw a great opportunity for Bath to lead rugby into a new dimension in terms of playing style. His vision was partly derived from appreciation of the amazing developments that had emanated from the Southern

Hemisphere and the Super 12 experience and also because he considered that a batch of newly revised laws, to be introduced that season, were ideally framed to accommodate a more adventurous style. The principal changes that encouraged his thinking were revisions to the law governing the scrummage, preventing back row forwards from detaching themselves until the ball was cleared, and also preventing the defending scrum-half from leaving the side of the scrum, both of which had been designed to create more space for running the ball. And there was also an amendment to the line-out laws, allowing jumpers to be supported, which would ensure that teams could expect to secure more ball at their own throw-in.

Ashton was convinced that these changes would favour a more expansive approach and that Bath possessed the requisite quality in their back line, soon to be bolstered by rugby league imports of world-class pedigree, to fully exploit the advantages they were now being afforded. And in his view – one shared by many other free-thinkers in the game – it was time rugby union shed its traditional image of ponderous combatants slogging it out in six inches of mud. At the same time, he stressed that it would still be important to achieve the right balance between entertaining and winning.

John Hall, who seemed much more at ease out on the training ground with his squad than sitting in the confines of his office in his executive role, was effusive about Bath's new style, describing the pre-season sessions as phenomenal and claiming that the squad was much better placed than it had been at the same stage the previous year. He cast doubt on the policy other clubs had adopted of investing heavily in high profile international players from abroad, outlining his own preference for a balanced approach of strengthening the squad in areas that needed improving and building a system that would develop young talent within the club.

Bath, he insisted, didn't want to plunge into the market every two minutes to pay ridiculous transfer fees for big-name players and, with the quality already in the squad, they didn't need to. How soon his mind would change, and how expensive would be the consequences! But for now he was content to be in charge of the best squad of players in the country.

Andy Robinson, with his foot firmly on the coaching ladder and also in charge of developing future Rec stars at Bath's University-based Rugby Academy, was certain the club was on the right track to extend its trophy-winning traditions and stake its claim to be the best team in Europe. There was no turning back, he claimed, when asked for his opinion of Bath's style change. Southern Hemisphere rugby was the only way forward, because it would take players out of the comfort zone and force them to play to their limits in every game.

He, too, would be forced to reassess this appraisal before long. And he would also have the chance to put his own ideas into practice much sooner than he could ever have antici-pated. But on the eve of a new campaign everyone was whistling a similar optimistic tune. Well, not quite everyone. Tony Swift, still familiarising himself with the responsibilities and demands of his new role as Bath's non-executive chair-man, was more restrained in his predictions about what the future might hold, but hoped that professionalism would herald a big step forward. He defined his role as advisory and supportive as a public figurehead, and said he was deter-mined not to get in the way of the executive board members. However, he was keen to do something about what he saw as a pressing need to improve the lot of members and spectators and looked forward to discovering their concerns and complaints.

When I asked him about Bath's long-term future at the Rec, the possibility of the club moving to a new purpose-built stadium, and the prospects of flotation on the stock market Swift was noncommittal, suggesting it was too early to evalu-ate these matters. But he was convinced about the single factor that was essential for the prosperity of the club's newly fledged corporate structure: success as a business was intrin-sically linked with Bath's continued success on the field of play. He thought that John Hall had done an unbelievable job in keeping the playing squad together in difficult circumstances and had been impressed by the motives and commitment of the Brownsword organisation in providing the financial backing that would enable Bath to remain successful in the professional era.

For a club that had scarcely contemplated the prospect of failure in the fourteen years preceding the onset of professionalism, the overall prognosis looked both positive and exciting as Bath prepared to open its new account at Orrell's Edgehall Road stadium on the last Saturday in August. And there was yet more good news in store. Four days before the game, in another coup for Hall, Bath confirmed that Jason Robinson – 'Billy Whizz' as he was known to his legion of Wigan fans – was on his way to the Rec, having signed a similar £5,000 a game four-month contract to that of his league colleague Henry Paul, which would intensify the competition for first-team places among Bath's cavalcade of world-class threequarters.

All things considered, the new season was a mouth-watering prospect to contemplate as I drove up the M6 that Saturday morning. However, I was fairly sure that Bath would soon be under greater pressure to retain their status as Britain's leading rugby union club than ever before, and so would the men responsible for guiding their fortunes.

As far back as April, I had penned a *Bath Chronicle* column gently suggesting to John Hall that his life was about to undergo a drastic and irreversible change, and warning him of the inherent uncertainties and pitfalls that invariably afflicted anyone employed at the helm of a top-class professional sports club. Rugby Union, in its amateur state, could hardly be compared with professional soccer, which had, by established tradition, become an employment minefield for managers and coaches. But once high finance became involved, it was inevitable that it would not be long before the pressures of paid combat also began to take their toll in rugby.

Not that Orrell were able to inflict much pressure on Hall or Bath when the two teams took the field in their first professional outing that afternoon. The unsung Lancashire outfit had often caused Bath problems in the past, but they had not benefited from the financial backing and subsequent squad strengthening that their wealthier southern rivals had enjoyed over the summer break. In consequence they were already candidates for relegation in the estimation of most rugby pundits, whose glum forecasts would be amply vindicated by the end of the season.

Bath were without Jon Sleightholme and Phil de Glanville, both sidelined with shoulder problems, while Richard Webster, who had made an instant impression in pre-season training, and Gareth Adams were preferred to Steve Ojomoh and Graham Dawe in the pack. But, although it took the champions nearly an hour to exert their authority, when they did so it was in emphatic fashion. Five superb tries in the final 20 minutes saw Bath romp to a record 56-13 victory, with Webster grabbing one on his debut and Simon Geogheghan another, before he limped out of the fray and resigned himself to the prospect of yet another operation on his troublesome toe joints.

In his place, Bath sent on a little-known new recruit in Mike Horne, who took the field in distinctive white boots and raced over for a debut try with his first touch of the ball just a minute later. And with Jon Callard successful with nine out of eleven kicks at goal there was never any danger of Bath falling at the first hurdle, leaving John Hall a satisfied man after an impressive campaign opener.

In hindsight, Bath could probably have done with a harder contest to launch their title defence. But that was to come a week later when they visited Welford Road for a vital return clash against old foes Leicester, who were clearly relishing an early opportunity to avenge that controversial Pilkington Cup final defeat back in May. If I had to select one game and one definitive moment of action that would reflect the variously fluctuating fortunes Bath were to endure for the rest of that traumatic season it would be Mike Catt's fateful decision to attempt a dropped goal in the dying minutes of what turned out to be an epic contest.

With Bath clinging to a 25-21 lead, having outscored Leicester 3-0 on the try count thanks to opportunist touchdowns from scrum-half Andy Nicol, Catt himself with a brilliant solo effort, and Jeremy Guscott, it seemed that all they had to do was retain possession deep in Leicester territory to clinch a deserved victory. Instead, Catt suddenly unleashed a wayward attempt at a dropped goal when he might instead have set up position for a decisive try. From the restart the Tigers stormed upfield to mount a final desperate bombardment of the Bath 22.

Five times in rapid succession Leicester were awarded penalties by Bristol referee Ed Morrison before – like Steve Lander in that momentous Twickenham finale – he raised his arm and ran to the posts to signal a penalty try, which John Liley, who had already landed seven out of eight penalties, duly converted to send a 16,000 Welford Road full house ecstatic with delight at the delicious irony of it all.

It was not so much the defeat that mattered, because Leicester had always been capable of beating Bath on their day, as they so nearly proved at Twickenham. And, by tradition, clashes between the clubs had invariably been closely fought. It was the fact that on this occasion, Bath had proved themselves superior and had lost through their own profligacy, which was a bitter pill to swallow for a side that had long prided itself on its ability to find winning inspiration when the chips were down.

Important lessons needed to be learned as well about the stark realities of competing in the new professional order of things and the tactical priorities that would become paramount to success on the pitch, some of which Hall put his finger on in his post-match summary of what had gone wrong. It was one thing to go out and throw the ball about with abandon, but possession still had to be won and Bath's forwards had not produced the goods in that department, especially in the lineout, where Martin Haag and Nigel Redman had once again been outshone by Leicester jumpers Martin Johnson and Matt Poole. Bath had competed productively in the loose, defended and tackled superbly at times, and shown superior attacking potential. But they had conceded far too many penalties, mercilessly punished by Liley's unerring boot, and had committed too many unforced handling errors, which had allowed Leicester to win the day.

What the setback revealed was that, under the new laws, possession was even more vital than ever. More crucially, it had to be retained and ruthlessly converted into points, because regaining possession would be much more difficult in future and to waste it needlessly was potentially disastrous. As Jeremy Guscott would later put it so succinctly: 'Forwards win matches, backs just decide by how many'. And, as Hall and Brian Ashton were about to discover, it was one thing to fill a squad with outstanding runners, but without a plentiful supply of quick, clean ball their potency would be drastically reduced.

Nevertheless, after only two games into the season and one unfortunate defeat, it was rather hard on Haag and Redman for Hall to assert that Bath would need to go out and find some lineout forwards because in his view the club just didn't have it in that department. Both players had given Bath sterling service over many years of consistent trophy success and would continue to do so for the rest of that season and the next. Nine months on, albeit by dint of a spate of injury problems to several rivals, Haag, a dogged, determined and forthright character and a superbly mobile forward, would deservedly earn two cherished England caps on the summer tour to Argentina.

And for the veteran Redman, who had played in Bath's first John Player Cup triumph in 1984 at the tender age of 19 and had made his England debut against Australia later the same year, the summer of 1997 would provide a fairytale climax to his chequered international career. Having miraculously recovered from a serious knee operation after being injured late in the season, he would be called up by Jack Rowell for England's Argentina tour, and then by Fran Cotton's British Lions as a tour replacement for Scotland lock Doddie Weir, who had suffered a horrendous leg injury. He distinguished himself on both tours, never letting England or the Lions down and ending up with the ultimate honour of captaining the Lions to a resounding victory over Orange Free State when six weeks short of his 33rd birthday.

Neither Haag nor Redman ever let Bath down in my time of reporting their endeavours at the Rec, and indeed Redman in particular would have strong claims to receive my vote as Bath's most consistent performer over that period. But both these likeable and honest characters would probably admit that there were times when Bath struggled to achieve consistent lineout possession against opponents whose extra height gave then a distinct natural advantage. They were rarely outplayed at the scrummage or in the loose, but, at 6ft 5in and 6ft 4in respectively, they were comparatively short for lineout jumpers, and occasionally their lack of height told, particularly (from my recollection) against Leicester.

Although Hall had identified a potential problem, he failed to solve it, despite a belated foray into the transfer market a few months later, shortly before he and Bath were to part company in distressing circumstances. Today, two years after that pivotal league defeat at Leicester, Bath have still to recruit a second row forward capable of permanently splitting up the old firm of Haag and Redman, who look like soldiering on together in perpetuity.

CHAPTER THREE

Countdown to Calamity

John Hall made one other singular remark following that Leicester setback which was to be a portent of things to come, when he predicted that Bath were going to destroy some sides that season although it had not been their day against the Tigers. The validity of that prediction came precisely four days later on Wednesday, 11 September, when Bath played host to Swansea in their first encounter in the Anglo-Welsh Cup, a competition which, owing to lack of interest from potential sponsors, was to fail before it got off the ground.

The game held specific and widespread interest because it marked the union debut of Bath's two rugby league loan signings from Wigan, Jason Robinson and Henry Paul, whose arrival had been delayed by their commitments in the Stone's Premiership.

That requirement had ended the previous Sunday when both men scored dazzling tries in an emphatic 44-14 win over Superleague champions and Rugby League Challenge Cup holders St Helens (Wigan's deadliest rivals), and now everyone was interested to see how this gifted pair would fare in the 15-man game. The answer was both emphatic and sensational in its impact on all who felt privileged to be present at the Rec on a night of pure rugby magic. But, for Bath, the outcome would be enlightening, encouraging and cruelly misleading.

Hall and his fellow selectors again made wholesale changes before the game, which was already a sell-out, but Hall stressed that he was merely making use of his full squad and not fielding a second string line-up. The Wigan pair had both been given a brief opportunity to acclimatise themselves to Bath's tactical routines in training and when the team was announced, Robinson was named on the right wing in place of Jon Sleightholme and Paul was selected to partner Phil de Glanville in the centre, with Jeremy Guscott rested.

At half-back Mike Catt and Andy Nicol were omitted, Richard Butland returning at fly-half to partner Charlie Harrison, an inexperienced, but promising young scrum-half. There were six changes to the pack that had lost at Leicester, the front row of Dave Hilton, Gareth Adams and Victor Ubogu being replaced by Kevin Yates, Graham Dawe and John Mallett. Brian Cusack was given a first-team debut in place of Redman at lock, while Nathan Thomas also made his senior bow at the Rec, replacing Andy Robinson. Steve Ojomoh took over the number eight berth from Eric Peters.

Swansea had also made a number of changes, but were still expected to provide tough opposition, having already made a tremendous start to their season with victories over Cardiff and Newport, piling up plenty of points in the process, so most people in an expectant crowd that night were anticipating a hard-fought encounter. What they got, to their utter astonishment and delight, was the biggest rout seen at the Rec since that long-forgotten Pilkington Cup landslide against Oxford back in 1989, as Bath swept all Swansea resistance aside from the opening whistle to post an amazing 87-15 victory.

Adedayo Adebayo began the 13-try humiliation with two in the opening five minutes, Henry Paul, slicing imperiously through the midfield, quickly added two more and after that Bath simply overran a bewildered Welsh side to score almost at will, Callard grabbing one himself, and adding 11 immaculate conversions for a 27-point haul. As Bath supporters gorged themselves on the feast laid before them, Richard Webster helped himself to two tries, and in a stunning last ten minutes Jason Robinson claimed centre stage with two electrifying bursts of pace to set his own personal seal on a Bath performance that had a profound effect on everyone who saw it, even Jack Rowell describing what he had seen as sensational.

After such a dazzling exhibition it was difficult for anyone involved to contain a sense of euphoria as a bevy of reporters flocked round Paul and Robinson, who modestly played down their own influence on the result. Meanwhile, a relieved John Hall admitted to feeling exhausted just watching a display that had exceeded his wildest expectations and represented one of the best games of rugby he had ever seen.

Nobody leaving the Rec that night would have argued with that assessment, and in my back page lead in the following morning's *Chronicle* I described Paul and Robinson's arrival as the launch of a dazzling new epoch in rugby union history.

Sadly, despite all that unrestrained admiration, it proved the shortest epoch on record, lasting precisely three days, as Bath went out the following Saturday and threw away their second Courage League game of the campaign, losing 40-36 to Wasps, who could hardly believe their good fortune in securing such a rare victory at the Rec. That extraordinary form reversal set Wasps on the way to only their second ever Courage League title and left a shell-shocked Bath to face another mortifying Monday morning inquest of the kind the club had become famous for on the rare occasions when they lost.

But post-mortems and inquests were to become an increasingly frequent and contentious occurrence from then on, as what had appeared to be the crest of a wave was suddenly transformed into a whirlpool of indecision and recrimination which would slowly engulf the reigning champions as a torrid winter of discontent began to exert its chilling grip.

Looking back, it can be seen that the seeds of disaster had been sown in an all too brief period of pre-season preparation, while the decision to adopt a breathtakingly ambitious playing style only added to the problems that were piling up. But the biggest mistake of that flawed winter campaign plan was the decision, taken at about the time of Paul and Robinson's arrival, to introduce a system of squad rotation into the team-selection process.

The reasons put forward by Hall and Ashton, apparently with the backing of the squad, for such an unusual policy sounded logical. Bath had accumulated a massive squad of around forty-five players and faced what looked certain to be a daunting and physically exhausting fixture list. So, as Hall explained, it was sensible to systematically protect the club's resources by resting players from time to time, to prevent them from going stale and losing their edge.

Even then the policy raised a few querulous eyebrows among the Bath cognoscenti, who perhaps wondered if it had been introduced as a placatory measure to appease a squad that might have been said to contain too many high-profile stars; others questioned its practicality in terms of maintaining individual form and team continuity. But once the policy was established there was no easy way to divert from it without a loss of face. Its consequences were to be calamitous, until it was quietly phased out long after the damage had been done. Bath had in fact tried squad rotation once before in the amateur days and rapidly cast it aside as unworkable.

Professional sportsmen will always complain when they are dropped, left out, rested or ignored despite consistent form. But they generally accept such ups and downs as part and parcel of the selection process. However, the idea of being rotated on a regular basis was hardly likely to go down well with a player in peak form and eager to retain his place. Nevertheless that was the plan that Bath's management team implemented, and were stuck with for the next few months. Its repercussions began with that unexpected defeat by Wasps, before which Hall announced a team containing no fewer than seven changes from the side that had destroyed Swansea so vividly in midweek.

The biggest shock was the omission of skipper Phil de Glanville, despite his effective partnership with Paul against Swansea. Against Wasps he gave way to a returning Jeremy Guscott, who took over the captaincy for the first time in his career at the Rec. Jason Robinson not surprisingly kept his place on the right wing, while Adebayo gave way to Jon Sleightholme on the left and Catt and Nicol returned at half-back in place of Butland and Harrison, neither of whom had put a foot wrong in unselfishly setting up the demolition of Swansea.

In the pack Dave Hilton resumed his place at loosehead prop at the expense of Kevin Yates; Redman was back instead of Haag to partner the inexperienced Cusack at lock; and Eric Peters returned at number eight, Steve Ojomoh switching to blindside flanker at the expense of Richard Webster, who must have been mystified to be rested after his display against Swansea.

The result of all this selectorial mayhem was a disaster, which saw Bath ruthlessly punished for a litany of forced and unforced errors which cost them the game, although once again they should have won, after recovering from some not surprising early hesitancy to establish a 24-14 lead early in the second half. To their credit, Wasps took full advantage of Bath's lack of cohesion and composure, in defence and attack, to produce some inspired finishing, and with Gareth Rees in lethal kicking form they resisted a desperate late siege and a penalty try to emerge triumphant by a four-point margin.

If ever two League points were carelessly thrown away in the selection process, that was the perfect example as far as Bath were concerned. But, strangely enough, only the players were willing to hold their hands up in acceptance of responsibility afterwards. They shouldered the blame without offering excuses, none more than acting captain Jeremy Guscott, who endured an afternoon to forget as his side turned over far too much possession in the tackle and at the breakdown, which Wasps exploited to full advantage, three of their tries emanating from basic errors by Bath. Apart from that rich purple patch either side of the interval, when Wasps conceded eighteen points and the lead, Bath looked a pale shadow of the team that had routed Swansea in their previous game. But, having regained the ascendancy, they abjectly surrendered it again, raising a spectre that was to dog them for the rest of the winter.

In whatever team sport you care to name, the single attribute above all others that wins championships over an extended season is consistency, which largely stems from belief and confidence in your combined ability. Bath had proved that time and again in their pursuit of silverware and it had always inspired them when the going got tough. But, at Leicester they had surrendered a winning position through careless errors, and against Wasps they were also undone by uncharacteristic mistakes and the fact that they were only at their best for 20 minutes or so either side of the interval. The old ruthless streak appeared to be missing and in its place grew uncertainty even when they were apparently in the driving seat.

At times that season Bath proved beyond question that potentially they were still the finest side in England, as they would amply demonstrate late in the campaign, but occasional and periodic brilliance is not enough to win titles and their inability to attain a high level of consistency was to prove fatal to their trophy ambitions.

Faced with the unpalatable fact that his side had now lost two of their first three league games, unprecedented at the Rec, a disappointed John Hall conceded that Bath were thinking too far ahead, not getting the basics right and committing too many errors. He also surmised that the champions might have to win all their remaining games to retain their crown, a prospect that only inflicted further pressure on a squad who were still coming to terms with the perplexing maelstrom of change going on around them.

Even so, for the rest of September and the early part of October Bath gradually put those two stinging early setbacks behind them, despite constant team changes as the declared policy of squad rotation was adhered to, although Hall conceded that for European and Pilkington Cup games he would select what he felt was his best side.

Phil de Glanville, already tipped as a contender for the England captaincy vacated by Will Carling earlier in the year, was reinstated for the next league clash at Kingsholm, in the absence of Henry Paul, who had sprained an ankle against Wasps. And although Gloucester as usual offered sterling resistance, Bath's extra class eventually saw them through to a hard-earned 45-29 victory. Once again they showed flashes of brilliance to score seven tries, but Hall was still unhappy that the side was still making basic errors and conceding too many points.

In a typically physical contest there were signs of a growing injury problem as well, de Glanville coming off with a broken nose from an alleged punch. But that was tame compared to what lay in store in their next outing at home to West Hartlepool, who along with Orrell would be relegated to Division 2 at the end of the season.

West's coach, the former Welsh international centre Mark Ring, had promised to give Bath a scrap at the Rec and he and his side lived up to that promise in a bad-tempered display that saw their prop, Wayne de Jong, sent off and three of his team-mates shown yellow cards, one of them being Ring, who was lucky not to be sent off after swapping punches with both de Glanville and Jon Callard. Bath won the game comfortably 46-10, Jon Sleightholme scoring twice on his return to the right wing for Jason Robinson and de Glanville racing 90 metres for a conclusive interception try. Afterwards coach Brian Ashton was clearly incensed by the visitors' cynical tactics, while an unrepentant Ring expressed the view that Bath were on their way down from the triumphant pinnacle they had occupied for so long.

Meanwhile, with just two games left before they had to turn their attention to the club's first foray into European Cup competition, Bath were still ringing the changes in adherence to their squad-rotation policy, and it was a barely recognisable team that travelled to Llanelli for a friendly clash the following Tuesday.

With Callard rested after scoring 107 points in his last six games, Bath experimented by switching Paul to full-back and Jason Robinson to the left wing for Adebayo, while youngsters Matt Perry and Joe Ewnes teamed up at centre and Butland and Harrison stepped in at half-back. It was a makeshift back line that struggled to make any impact in a poor game that ended with Bath lucky to snatch a 10-10 draw thanks to late tries from Harrison and Eric Peters. The game itself meant little, but it was revealing for two minor incidents which showed just how much Bath's two rugby league stars still had to learn about the union game. In one Henry Paul actually threw the ball into touch when put under pressure by a Llanelli counter and in the other Jason Robinson tried to run out from behind his own line and was penalised for colliding with a team-mate.

Both men had proved themselves brilliant players, with undeniable try-scoring flair, as they showed in the first half dozen games they played, but it was asking a lot for them to become attuned to a totally strange way of playing in such a short space of time. Paul was undoubtedly a superb centre who could have made a real impact in the union game given time. But sadly for him, a troublesome shoulder injury was to cut short his spell at Bath and he played only a handful of games.

Robinson's impact, so electric in his early appearances, gradually faded as opponents exploited his tactical and kicking deficiencies and he failed to score in his last dozen or so matches, before returning to more familiar pastures at Wigan. Much later, shortly before his four-month contract ended, Robinson explained to me, with obvious frustration, that although he knew he was supposed to turn and make the ball available at the ruck when he was tackled, it still did not come naturally and led to inevitable loss of possession as a result.

I was impressed by both players who were model professionals in approach and were easy to work with from a journalistic viewpoint. Given more time to adapt to a strange environment they would have graced the union game. But although they scored some spectacular tries, mainly in matches that didn't count or were already comfortably won, their arrival on the scene was more disruptive than productive – and expensive at that. The total cost to Bath for four months' work came to £200,000 which, apart from the entertainment value, was money down the drain.

One of Robinson's most impressive tries came in Bath's next Courage League outing at London Irish on the first Saturday in October, when he caught a wayward clearance and spreadeagled the Irish cover in a blistering side-stepping run to the line. However, the game, which Bath won comfortably 56-31, was marred by injuries to de Glanville, who suffered knee-ligament damage, and scrum-half Andy Nicol, whose hamstring snapped after just ten minutes' play. It was a sad blow in a blighted season for Nicol, who missed all of Bath's forthcoming Heineken European Cup qualifying group games and then aggravated the injury when recalled to the side for a fateful quarter-final clash in Cardiff.

Charlie Harrison came on to enjoy a sparkling league debut, and generally did well as Nicol's stand-in. But there was no doubt that Bath missed the combative Scot, whose solid all-round game was vital to the smooth operation of backs and forwards at the Rec. Nicol would be in and out of action for the rest of the season, before making a spirited comeback as captain the following year, when his injury problems abated.

De Glanville also missed Bath's first three European games, but there was to be a surprise consolation in store for Bath's battered skipper, whose finely chiselled features had already suffered a few knocks and would incur more before the season was out. Phil's nickname of 'Hollywood' is apt enough for a player who at first sight gives the impression of being a suave public schoolboy, but his contribution on the field belies the image, no one going into the tackle more resolutely or using the ball less selfishly than this exemplary team performer. He had sat patiently on the England bench in the shadow of Guscott and Carling for the past three seasons since making his international debut against South Africa. But this season was to soon earn him dramatic exposure to the national spotlight.

The RFU had been stricken by constant controversy since the summer, the prolonged row over England's unilateral signing of a television deal with Sky to show their home international games at Twickenham being followed by further conflict with the leading clubs, who at one stage ordered their players to boycott England training sessions.

With Will Carling no longer captain but still keen to play on at international level, there was increasing speculation over who would replace him as skipper and also about the composition of England's back line, notably at centre and at fly-half, where Northampton's Paul Grayson, Wasps' Alex King and Bath's Mike Catt were vying for the role.

Jack Rowell, true to form, was keeping tight-lipped about his plans, and in his initial 45-man squad had included Catt, who had been in excellent form at fly-half for Bath, as a full-back, but had hinted he might take a look at him in the number ten shirt. Also selected in the initial squad were Guscott, de Glanville, Adebayo, Sleightholme, Mallett, McCarthy and Ojomoh, while disappointed to be left out were Jon Callard, Victor Ubogu, and Graham Dawe, who had all been on the bench the previous season.

However, Bath had more pressing concerns, after making a shaky start to their defence of the league title. They now faced four tricky qualfying games in pursuit of their prime objective, the Heineken European Cup, held by the French side Toulouse, who had beaten Cardiff in extra time in the previous year's final, English clubs not having participated in the competition. Bath had now been drawn in a group of five teams that included the French club Dax, Welsh contenders Pontypridd, Italian outsiders Treviso, and Edinburgh, a combined district side of Scottish clubs, who were to be Bath's first opponents at the Rec in what was expected to be a fairly routine opener.

Before the game John Hall tipped Bath and Dax to qualify for the quarter-finals the following month, but admitted that the game at Pontypridd would pose a difficult test for his side, which he confidently expected to get the better of Edinburgh. That prediction proved correct as Bath disposed of Edinburgh 55-26, with Callard again kicking superbly for a 25-point return, although the manner of the victory was less impressive than the result. Leading 38-9 at the interval, Bath slackened off disappointingly in the second half and also suffered another injury setback when Henry Paul damaged his shoulder and was taken to hospital. He would make only two more appearances for Bath – and the last of those would prove to be a fateful curtain call.

The week leading up to the second qualifying game against Pontypool at their Sardis Road fortress proved problematic for Hall, who ridiculed suggestions that his two rugby league stars were struggling to acclimatise to the union code.

It also proved a devastating week for me personally, because on the Wednesday before the game at Pontypridd I received a phone call to say my father had died. I had half expected it, because he had been in and out of hospital for the past two years and had seemed very poorly when he was admitted on this occasion, but it was still a dreadful blow. We had always been close and he was the best friend I ever had, a true and loyal father and incomparably the finest human being I have ever encountered. With my sister and the rest of the family as distressed as I was, and with all the funeral arrangements to contend with, I didn't feel like making the trip to Sardis Road that Saturday. But someone had to cover the game and eventually I persuaded myself that it might take my mind off a sad loss if I got back to my normal match-day routine. So, with a heavy heart, I drove over the Severn Bridge and into the valleys where a depleted Bath were to take on a Welsh side scenting blood. And to dampen our spirits further it was raining (nothing unusual in Wales).

Bath, as well as lacking de Glanville and Paul, were also

without Jeremy Guscott and the in-form Steve Ojomoh, a late flu victim, so it was a much rearranged side that took the field that afternoon, led out by Andy Robinson, who in the absence of de Glanville had assumed the captaincy the previous week against Edinburgh. With Ade Adebayo moving inside to team up in the centre with teenage prospect Matt Perry, the midfield never got going and Bath made the elementary mistake of trying to play expansive rugby in atrocious conditions, which led to a constant flow of mistakes and turnovers.

The contest was one long nightmare for Bath as their forwards were overpowered by a Pontypridd pack inspired by giant New Zealand number eight Dale McIntosh, who produced two shuddering hits on Andy Robinson and Eric Peters, which had the Sardis Road faithful chanting his sublimely apt nickname of 'Chief' (after the character in the film *One Flew Over the Cuckoo's Nest*).

Experienced Welsh international fly-half Neil Jenkins continually drove Bath back with raking kicks for his forwards to chase and, as usual, his place-kicking was unerring. In contrast, behind the Bath scrum, Harrison struggled to grip the ball cleanly, providing a poor service for Catt, which meant wingers Sleightholme and Jason Robinson hardly saw the ball, the latter looking thoroughly miserable and intimidated by the experience. Pontypridd never looked like faltering and eventually were left celebrating a deserved 19-6 victory, which cast Bath's chances of reaching the quarter-finals into the melting pot and left John Hall and Andy Robinson with nowhere to hide in terms of excuses for a demoralising display.

I can't ever remember anyone look so embarrassed as Robinson when he was interviewed by a bevy of press men after that setback. No one suffers the agonies of defeat more than Andy, whose commitment to winning is almost pathological. He has often admitted that he simply can't take losing at anything. And being forced to talk about it afterwards makes it even worse.

Robinson elected to take much of the blame for Bath's demise on his own shoulders, quite unnecessarily, because it was simply a poor team performance arising from a game plan totally unsuited to the conditions. Hall was in no mood to spare his side's blushes, describing the display as clueless. And for the first time he admitted that he was concerned about the contribution from Bath's front five forwards, pointedly refusing to rule out the possibility of dipping into the transfer market in order to boost the squad's forward strength.

The criticism was strong in terms of a manager talking about his players, because normally they are reluctant to voice such candid opinions about their teams. But Hall was clearly devastated by the result, which left Bath needing to beat Dax at the Rec the following week to retain any chance of reaching the last eight. And within 48 hours there was evidence that he was intent on taking action to avert a mounting crisis when it was revealed that he was set to have talks with the Argentine international hooker Federico Mendez, who had been playing in South Africa for Natal.

Bath's crestfallen players were taking collective blame for the setback at Sardis Road, and Jeremy Guscott, fit again after a thigh strain, was optimistic that the team would bounce back to form against a powerful Dax outfit, who had annihilated Edinburgh in their second successive group win. De Glanville, battling to shake of his knee injury, was selected to partner Guscott in the centre, but eventually had to give way to a fit-again Henry Paul, and there were three changes in the pack, with Dave Hilton replacing Kevin Yates at prop, Nathan Thomas coming in for Robinson and Steve Ojomoh edging out Eric Peters at number eight.

In the absence of de Glanville and Robinson, Jon Callard was given the responsibility of captaincy for the first time and fulfilled the role with panache, kicking 17 points and setting up Bath's only try, a superb effort from Paul, before limping out of the fray with a hip injury. But the real heroes of a hard-fought 26-16 victory were the forwards. Ojomoh, back to his powerful, rampaging best, proved an inspirational force and Bath's much maligned front five fully redeemed themselves as they overpowered a daunting Dax side, who led 10-6 at one stage, but whose constant indiscipline was crucially punished by Callard's unerring boot.

It was a triumph which persuaded Hall to retract his bitter criticism of the previous week, singling out Ojomoh and Callard for special praise. And it set up an intriguing battle for the qualifying places the following week, Bath needing a decisive victory in Treviso to go through with either Dax or Pontypridd, who were due to cross swords in France, although the issue looked certain to be settled on points difference.

The trip to Treviso, a small but attractive Italian city with a population of just 19,000 some 30 kilometres north of Venice, was to be my first journalistic assignment on the continent and it would be a memorable one. As it was partly a holiday, I took a flight from Heathrow on the Tuesday before the game and booked into the Hotel Saturnia, a short stroll from St Mark's Square, before sampling the attractions of Venice by night, a rewarding if expensive experience.

I was expected to provide the *Chronicle* with a couple of preview pieces, so the next morning I travelled along the Grand Canal on one of the city's crowded water buses and then by train to Treviso where, after enjoying a meal in the city centre, I took a taxi to the club's expansive training headquarters. Benetton Treviso, as the club's full title suggests, are owned and heavily sponsored by the Italian conglomerate, who had spared no expense in providing facilities for the team, which were superior to any in England.

I was made welcome by the club's general manager, Fabrizio Gaetaniello, a former captain of the Italian national side, and team manager Franco Pavan, and managed to overcome the language barrier sufficiently to learn that Treviso, while unable to qualify for the quarter-finals, were desperate to put up a good show against Bath to further their own and Italy's credentials in European rugby circles.

I watched the Treviso squad train under a balmy autumn sun and gained interviews with home captain and Italian international scrum-half Alessandro Troncon and back-row star Julian Gardner, a veteran, but still extremely effective Australian import, who both relished the prospect of giving Bath a hard time, if not actually beating them. From those interviews I gathered that Treviso were a team who preferred to play open, fast, attacking rugby in the French style and possessed an excellent set of backs. But they were concerned whether their forwards would be able to hold Bath's powerful pack, especially the likes of Steve Ojomoh, whose play had obviously impressed them.

On the Thursday, after phoning through my second preview piece, I indulged in some sightseeing around Venice's staggeringly beautiful harbour and canal network while on Friday I rang the office to be told that Bath had signed Federico Mendez, described by Hall as a world-class player, who would strengthen the squad. The other significant news was that Jason Robinson had been sensational when tried out at full-back in a comprehensive 76-7 demolition of luckless Bristol at the Rec and with Callard not fully recovered from injury he had been selected to fill that role against Treviso, Jon Sleightholme returning to the right wing.

Bath, by this time, were already camped in their hotel just outside Treviso, which, as the BBC 2 series 'The Rugby Club' was later to reveal, proved less than satisfactory as far as the team were concerned, especially with regard to the standard of food.

Saturday dawned to cloudless sunny skies and I again took the waterbus and train route to the gaunt-looking, 9,000 capacity Stadio Communale Di Monego where a thrilling and nail-biting encounter ensued. Despite trailing early on and then flagging badly in the the closing stages of a stamina-sapping contest, Bath produced enough forward power and flair in the backs to clinch a comfortable 50-27 victory and qualifiy in second place behind Dax, who foiled Pontypridd, although the points difference was uncomfortably close. But it took a magnificent virtuoso performance by Mike Catt to see off a talented and determined Treviso and ensure a quarter-final place. Catt scored four superb solo tries and landed five conversions and a penalty to complete a personal haul of 33 points, earning a maximum ten in my ratings list, after a display that also clinched his selection at fly-half for the friendly international against Italy at Twickenham later that month.

But for Catt's brilliance, which included an amazing five-minute hat-trick of tries early in the second half, I doubt whether Bath would have qualified. It demonstrated what he is capable of in broken play and when his confidence is sky high. He has an army of critics who will always prefer a more orthodox fly-half, but on that afternoon in Treviso there was no one to touch him.

After the team had come through what had been a demanding ordeal, it was a happy and relieved Bath contingent who celebrated well into the night, not least the players, who all looked a little bleary-eyed on the flight home the next day. The departure was delayed a couple of hours because of a scare involving an incoming aircraft which had lost one of its doors as it came in to land, but Victor Ubogu, for one, was unperturbed. I sat next to him on the plane and he slept like a log right through a routine flight back to Heathrow.

The good news for Bath was increased a couple of days later when Jack Rowell named Phil de Glanville as England captain. Phil had been a rank outsider for the honour in recent weeks, most pundits tipping Lawrence Dallaglio of Wasps or Jason Leonard of Harlequins to get the nod. But with Rowell intent on adopting a more expansive approach, it was to Bath and de Glanville that he eventually turned. Phil got the call confirming his appointment in the middle of a round of golf the day after returning from Venice. And it was rumoured that at least one of his Bath team-mates had tried to get a long-odds bet on before the official announcement, only to be recognised at the bookmakers who took the hint and hastily suspended all betting on the outcome.

Some people even suggested that Rowell might select an entire Bath back line when he announced his team to face Italy. Brian Ashton firmly supported that idea, but it was perhaps too much to expect, given the likely political ramifications of such action. In the event Rowell compromised, selecting Catt at fly-half, handing Adebayo a first cap on the left wing and picking Sleightholme on the other flank. But the major shock in the line-up was the omission of Jeremy Guscott, which caused a considerable furore, and, in my view at least, cost England the Five Nations Championship and Grand Slam later that season.

There was no doubt that having plumped for de Glanville as his captain, Rowell was faced with a difficult dilemma in choosing between Guscott and Will Carling to partner him in the England centre and many critics suggested that de Glanville was lucky to gain his place by virtue of leading the side. In my opinion Rowell was wrong to prefer Carling to Guscott, who had been in prime form all season, was a natural outside centre of genuine world class and had shown himself far superior in attacking ability and flair than his more orthodox rival. Carling had always been a strong and direct inside centre for England, but had not shown any noteworthy form that season, his last in an England shirt. But, taking into account his record as England captain, it would have taken a brave man to drop him.

So Guscott it was who became the fall guy and spent an international season on the bench, although he came off it with spectacular success against Ireland at Lansdowne Road, and also in a brilliant second half display on the wing against Wales, in the last international to be played at Cardiff Arms Park. But when the Five Nations Championship campaign reached its climax against France at Twickenham, Guscott was still on the bench as Christophe Lamaison danced past a static Carling to score the try that inspired a thrilling comeback and snatched the grand slam from England's grasp.

It must have been a frustrating moment for Guscott, who I felt would have prevented the try. But it must have been even more shattering for de Glanville, who had done all that could have been asked of him as a player or captain all season. Fortunately, an opportunity to gain consolation for that disappointment was readily to hand because, after securing a place in the last eight of the European Cup by the skin of their teeth, Bath were back on a high.

With their quarter-final tie against Cardiff just a fortnight away, Bath's immediate focus switched back to the league and a trip to Northampton, who were in the top half of the table but were not expected to prove strong enough to upset the champions. After their exertions in Italy, however, I had a feeling that Bath might struggle to win at Franklin's Gardens, and it proved justified as they produced a lacklustre performance against a galvanised Saints side who had been well prepared and organised by their astute rugby director and former British Lions coach Ian McGeechan.

It was another wet afternoon, which didn't suit Bath's adventurous running and passing game and, faced by a blanket home defence whenever they gained possession from the breakdown, Bath found penetration almost impossible from the outset. To make matters worse, they lost Graham Dawe with a painful dislocated elbow in the first five minutes and found themselves 9-0 down in the opening quarter as Paul Grayson slotted three accurate penalties. Richard Webster went off with a hand injury early in the second half, and although Callard responded with two penalties it was not enough to prevent Northampton from celebrating a hard-earned but deserved triumph.

That setback was Bath's third league defeat in eight games and, although they were still in second place behind leaders Harlequins, who had lost just once, the pressure was intensifying, as Leicester and Wasps were both level on points with games in hand. It was then, in a tense run-up to their most important game of the season thus far – the European Cup quarter-final in Cardiff – that the cracks and divisions in

Bath's squad morale and management strategy suddenly began to surface, turning an unfortunate situation into a critical one.

It has to be said that Bath suffered misfortune in terms of injuries and late withdrawals from the selected team in those nightmare hours before the kick-off, when players were dropping out like flies. With Graham Dawe out and Mendez not yet arrived, Gareth Adams was the original choice at hooker, but he was diagnosed as having a neck injury, which sadly was to signal the end of his playing career. Neil McCarthy, who had replaced Dawe the previous week, was also ruled out with a bout of flu, and eventually Gary French, Bath's fourth-choice hooker, was drafted into the front row between Dave Hilton and Victor Ubogu. Amazingly, a further mishap befell the team on the morning of the game when Jon Sleightholme was forced to withdraw with a stomach upset. And it was then that a fateful decision was made that would remain a controversial talking point long after the result was consigned to history.

Once again it centred on Jon Callard, who had missed a couple of crucial kicks at Northampton on his return to the side and now suddenly found himself dropped for the quarter-final. Many ardent Bath fans were mystified as to why the country's leading points scorer should be so unceremoniously discarded, when it was generally felt that place-kicking could prove decisive in what was expected to be a close and fiercely contested encounter. On the other hand, Mike Catt had kicked superbly on a dry pitch in Treviso and was considered capable of fulfilling the kicking duties, while Jason Robinson had produced two impressive displays at full-back against Bristol and Treviso and was a proven match-winner in his own right.

So Callard grasped the short straw once again when the team was announced. But then, when Sleightholme dropped out, Bath made a decision that would prove fatal to their chances: instead of recalling Callard and switching Robinson to the right wing, they drafted in Henry Paul on the flank.

Paul, whose shoulder problems had kept him out of action for some time, was short of match-fitness and undoubtedly a risky selection for such a crucial game, but Hall and Ashton took the gamble of including him and Bath took the field with their plans in complete disarray.

To make matters worse, the conditions were once again wet and heavy underfoot, which favoured a powerful Cardiff pack, and then, to cap it all, Andy Nicol, making his comeback from that serious hamstring injury at London Irish ten weeks earlier, was forced to limp off with a recurrence of the injury just three minutes into the game. Ian Sanders, who had himself been out injured for a lengthy spell and had not played a competitive first-team game all season, came off the bench to take over at scrum-half. But for most of the first half, Bath looked the more effective side without showing much penetration against some tigerish Cardiff tackling.

With nerves affecting both sides, the scoring was restricted to penalties by Mike Catt and his opposite number, Jonathan Davies, but Catt's kicking proved erratic as he missed three reasonable chances to put points on the board for Bath, who nevertheless were still well in contention at the interval, when they trailed 9-6.

Although two more Catt penalties put Bath briefly in front for a third time, the rest of the game prove a nightmare for the two Wigan imports. Cardiff had done their homework on Jason Robinson, testing him out with high kicks and chasing through to put pressure on him when, inevitably, he tried to run the ball back. On a couple of occasions Robinson was brought down and turned the ball over with Bath shorn of defensive cover, but the really conclusive moment came midway through the second half, when from a rare Cardiff back move the ball was whipped out to pacy Welsh international winger Nigel Walker, some 35 metres out from Bath's line. Stepping inside from the left touchline, Walker swept past a feeble attempt at a tackle from a flat-footed Henry Paul, accelerated away on a scything diagonal run, and then raced over for a superb converted try, which left Bath chasing the game.

Cardiff replacement Lee Jarvis came on to land two magnificent long-range penalties to extend the home lead to 22-12, and only then did Bath begin to mount the kind of storming rally for which they had long been famous. With a couple of minutes left, Nathan Thomas rounded off one tremendous forward drive by diving over for a try and Catt's conversion left Bath just three points adrift in the dying minutes. Time and again they tried to penetrate Cardiff's defensive screen without success, until in the last seconds they were awarded a penalty some forty-five metres out, but nearly in line with the posts. It was probably too far out for Catt, but, had Bath brought Callard off the bench, it would have been just within his range to tie the scores and send the tie into extra-time.

Whether he would have landed it or not will always be debatable. But instead, Phil de Glanville opted to run the penalty in a last-ditch attempt to snatch a try. It was all in vain. Cardiff held out, and seconds later the final whistle signalled an ecstatic explosion of Welsh joy, and despair for Bath supporters who had crossed the Severn Bridge that morning full of hope and expectancy.

Bath's dream of European Cup glory had blown up in their faces, albeit by a narrow margin of 22-19 – which in retrospect only made it worse. The episode had been a catalogue of disaster from start to finish. And this time the resulting inquest would not be confined to a Monday morning squad discussion, heated but soon forgotten. The fallout from that Cardiff Arms Park débâcle would last for weeks and prove the catalyst for a detonation of even greater magnitude in the not too distant future.

Already struggling to achieve any consistency in the league and with their prime target of European domination denied them, things could hardly get worse for John Hall and his embattled squad. But they did, and savagely so for Bath, as winter tightened its frosty grip to unleash an avalanche of upheaval and aggravation that would engulf the club over the festive season, when tidings of comfort and joy at the Rec were to be in exceedingly short supply.

PART FOUR

Festive Eruption and a New Resolution

(*above*) Master of all he surveyed: John Hall overlooks the Rec. shortly before guiding Bath to a fourth cup and league double in the spring of 1996. (*Bath Chronicle*)

(*below*) Phil de Glanville leads the Bath charge in a sensational 87-15 victory over Swansea in September 1996. (*Bath Chronicle*)

(*above*) John Hall welcomes Argentine giant lock German Llanes to the Rec. shortly before his sacking as Bath's director of rugby. (*Bath Chronicle*)

(*below*) Argentine international hooker Federico Mendez gets a pass away against Orrell, with prop Kevin Yates in close attendance. (*Bath Chronicle*)

(*left*) Watching brief: Clive Woodward runs his eye over a Bath training session shortly after his appointment to the coaching staff at the Rec. Woodward later succeeded Jack Rowell as England coach. (*Bath Chronicle*)

(*below*) The tension mounts: a sombre Jeremy Guscott takes in some last minute advice from coach Andy Robinson before Bath's Heineken European Cup final encounter against reigning champions Brive in Bordeaux. (*Bath Chronicle*)

(*left*) Heat of the battle: Bath lock Martin Haag claims lineout possession against Brive supported by powerful prop forward Victor Ubogu. (*Bath Chronicle*)

(*above*) The Holy Grail: Jon Callard flourishes the Heineken European Cup in front of Bath fans, flanked by Adebayo Adebayo (*left*) and skipper Andy Nicol. (*Bristol Post and Press*)

(*above*) Family celebration: Coach Andy Robinson and his team share their European Cup joy with jubilant Bath supporters. (*Bristol Post and Press*)

(*below*) Champagne moment: (*from left*) Andy Nicol, Nigel Redman, Jon Callard, Richard Webster and Ieuan Evans keep a close eye on the Heineken European Cup at the post-match reception. (*Bristol Post and Press*)

Comrades in arms: Bath owner Andrew Brownsword (*left*) and chief executive Tony Swift toast their Heineken European Cup final success with a drop of the sponsor's brew on their return from Bordeaux. (*Bristol Post and Press*)

Party time: Bath's victorious team share a dressing room celebration after their momentous triumph over holders Brive. (*Bristol Post and Press*)

CHAPTER ONE

Unrest and an Untimely Incident

After that stunning European Cup reverse Bath were without a competitive game for three weeks, but although, ostensibly, a lull descended on the Rec for the rest of November – internationals against Italy and the New Zealand Barbarians taking precedence – behind the scenes a full-scale bout of soul-searching was taking place.

As Phil de Glanville and Bath's England contingent set off to join Jack Rowell's squad preparations for the Italy clash, the club's board and key coaching staff were engaged in a wide-ranging reappraisal of a campaign strategy that was falling into disarray. A secluded Andrew Brownsword-owned country house at Lyme Regis was the secret venue for this crisis summit, which, for once, was kept a well-guarded secret, although the BBC 2 cameras were there to record fragments of the deliberations and would reveal a great deal from the facial expressions of the men who featured in a what was understandably a somewhat muted debate.

Meanwhile, Jon Callard captained a depleted Bath side to a 45-17 friendly victory at Coventry, a Friday night game I missed as I was due to cover the international against Italy the next day, when Phil de Glanville was to lead his country for the first time. It was an awkward baptism for the Bath skipper, because although England were expected to overcome the Italians easily, he was in charge of a new-look side and at the same time his own right to a place in the team was under fierce scrutiny.

The atmosphere in the Twickenham press centre that day was tense with anticipation as a full gathering of national rugby correspondents prepared to pronounce their verdict, not just on de Glanville's merits as successor to Will Carling, but on Rowell's future as the England coach. You could sense knives being honed for a dismissive strike if England failed to impress against such unrated opposition as Italy and detect an unspoken desire for it to happen, since failure would naturally provide much more sensational copy and headlines than a facile England victory.

It is often claimed that the British media take a cynical delight in prematurely idolising our sporting heroes before cutting them down to size when they fail to match the hype the press have generated. But in Phil's case the reaction to his appointment as captain, in place of a cult figure like Carling, was so unenthusiastic that it scarcely registered before his head was being placed in the pillory by sports writers who questioned his right to play, let alone lead the side.

As it turned out England, thanks largely to their dominant pack, ground out a routine, if flattering, 54-21 victory over Italy, who fought back bravely to score three second half tries. De Glanville had a quiet captaincy debut, playing well enough to ward off any untoward criticism, while Sleightholme scored a try and Adebayo did little wrong, only lacking service after twice going close to scoring early on.

England had, however, shown few signs of implementing Rowell's avowed policy of playing adventurous rugby and, denied any other obvious target for their ire, the critics singled out new fly-half Mike Catt for condemnation. Catt, teaming up for the first time with debutant scrum-half Andy Gomersall of Wasps, didn't have a great game, displaying barely a glimpse of the elusive running which had marked his performances for

Bath all season, while he managed to miss three simple chances at goal. But he did land eight far more difficult kicks for a total contribution of 19 points and generally utilised his backs effectively. To be seen at his best Catt requires quick ball from the forwards and a reliable service, and this he failed to get from a pack intent on keeping the ball to itself or from a scrum-half with an eye on his own chance to shine – which Gomersall in fact did, scoring two cheeky solo tries.

Nevertheless, as would often be the case over the next two seasons, Catt took the brunt of the flak for failing to meet the standards expected of an orthodox fly-half, which he is not and has never claimed to be. He is an innovator, an unpredictable but brilliant broken-field runner, who has to have quick ball to show his paces and who thrives on confidence. But he rarely got that service when playing for England and he was unlucky with injury just as he seemed to be making an impact. As a result he lacked the confidence to fulfil his potential at international level. Catt is my kind of flair fly-half, but it's hard to argue with the view expounded by his detractors, who don't rate him in the number ten shirt because, apart from brief glimpses, he has not been seen at his best in that position for England.

The scenario was much the same the following week, Bath winning a routine friendly 40-20 against the Combined Services, while England had the daunting prospect of taking on the New Zealand Barbarians, who fielded virtually a full All Black team. This time the papers were full of praise for an underdog England side who actually led 19-13 early in the second half, but wilted under a relentless New Zealand rally and a brilliant cameo performance by replacement fly-half Carlos Spencer, who scored thirteen points in the final quarter to turn the tables 34-19.

England's forwards again took the major credit for a game first-half performance and Catt took the blame for some errant kicking out of hand and a tepid performance from the midfield, although Sleightholme collected another try and Adebayo's defensive work was impressive.

With those two England games out of the way, Bath found themselves facing two difficult home games in a week before a third international against Argentina. On the Monday night Federico Mendez made his long-awaited debut in a 36-17 win over touring Western Samoa at the Rec. And on Saturday, 7 December, they prepared to face league leaders Harlequins in a contest crucial to their hopes of salvaging some silverware from the season.

For Bath, and John Hall in particular, it turned out to be a day and a performance that will remain etched in the memory, for contrasting and conflicting reasons, although for Hall at least, it ended in a confrontation he will probably regret for the rest of his life.

To preface the momentous happenings of that torrid few hours and the fraught weeks that followed, it has to be stated that Bath had reached a point where the club was fast becoming a pressure cooker of frustrated ambitions, policy disputes and strained loyalties. Ever since that traumatic reverse at Cardiff I had noticed that Hall and Ashton no longer attended post-match press conferences together, as they had frequently done earlier in the season. Yet they still shared the same office, which meant they could hardly avoid regular daily contact. The situation at the club's Queen Square offices had apparently deteriorated to such an extent that the two men were said to be at loggerheads and there were suggestions that the general atmosphere within the camp had become almost unbearably difficult.

I got wind of this from an impeccable source, and around that time I also experienced it at first hand in a strange telephone call from Hall, although it took me a while to understand the implications of what followed. It was highly unusual for Hall to call me at Westgate Street to give me the team for a forthcoming game and to discuss selection. Usually I had to chase him for such information and reaching him was never that easy. But this time the message was that he wanted to speak to me. I don't usually have problems with my hearing, but on this occasion his voice was so subdued and indistinct that I could barely make out what he was saying, and although I asked him several times to speak up he continued to talk very quietly. This situation went on for a while, with me straining to catch what he said, and then the penny dropped: he was whispering because he had no desire to be overheard. Which seemed an odd state of affairs considering his status at the club. I wondered exactly what was going on at the other end of the line. But it was only in hindsight that I understood the significance of that phone call, reflecting, as it did, the mood of intrigue and suspicion that had descended on Queen Square.

A number of factors were combining to increase the pressure on Hall at that time in addition to the inherent problem of achieving acceptable results in a much more competitive professional world.

It was becoming evident, throughout the game, that initial estimates concerning the financial viability of professional rugby union had been wildly optimistic. Spending on salaries and transfer fees had escalated way beyond sensible levels, and operating costs had been underestimated, while revenue at the gate had failed to increase sufficiently to meet those extra costs. Even at the Rec, where Bath had regularly played to full houses in the latter years of the old amateur era, spectators, faced by significant price increases, were becoming more selective and less inclined to turn out for mundane matches on the fixture list. For example, although Bath were guaranteed a full house for the Harlequins game that Saturday, the Rec was less than half full for the evening clash five days earlier against Western Samoa, who as an exciting international touring team would have filled the ground a year or two earlier.

As a result every professional club was ruefully aware of the fact that it was operating at a considerable loss which, for many of the accountants involved at boardroom level, was a situation that required urgent remedial action.

When the new club's first annual accounts were published early in 1998, Bath reported a deficit of around £1.5 million arising from the first year of trading as a public limited company – not as big a loss as those of some rival clubs, but substantial enough to cause concern.

On the playing side, one major problem that had surfaced in recent weeks, despite the rotation system that had been introduced, was the realisation that many players outside the first-team pool were finding they were hardly getting any match experience at all. The main factor in this situation was that Bath, like many of their rivals, had disbanded their third team, the Spartans, principally through the need to economise. But many other clubs had also elected to disband their second team, which meant that Bath United had suffered several cancellations already.

Some of the younger players in the squad were taking part in regular training sessions but were rarely getting the chance to display their skills in a match, which was bound to be frustrating for any aspiring player. That lack of opportunity led to the departure of several promising youngsters, who were not getting regular competitive matches at the Rec and eventually came to the conclusion that they would stand a better chance elsewhere.

Meanwhile, a situation was arising where players selected for midweek friendly games designated by the club as first-team fixtures were not being paid first-team appearance money, which they felt they were due. That led to simmering dissatisfaction in the squad, which some time later had to be sorted out in delicate negotiations between John Hall and squad representatives, led by the players' shop steward John Mallett, and provided yet another irritating diversion for Bath's harassed rugby director, who would have preferred to concentrate on improving the team's performances on the field.

All these contentious issues were beginning to distract Hall by this stage and the situation was not helped by a dearth of competitive matches and the fact that training continuity was again being affected by various international squad requirements which took away many of the club's leading players.

So for everyone at Bath, not least Hall, it was imperative that the team produced the kind of winning performance against Harlequins which would clearly demonstrate it was back on a successful curve and once again challenging for honours.

And when it came to selecting the side to face the leaders Hall showed he had learned at least one lesson from Cardiff and was also prepared to take a gamble by giving league debuts to two forwards who were still relatively new faces at the Rec.

Jon Callard had gritted his teeth over his disappointment at being dropped for the Cardiff game and had fought his way back into contention by leading the side to victory in three subsequent friendlies, and he was restored at full-back, with Jason Robinson reverting to the right wing and Jon Sleightholme relegated to the bench. Federico Mendez, after one friendly outing against Western Samoa, was thrust straight into the fray at hooker, while, in an intriguing ploy, Dan Lyle, who had joined the club as a back row forward, was picked to partner Martin Haag at lock, having recovered from his knee injury and impressed in that position against the Combined Services and the Samoans. Both represented a calculated risk because neither had really been given suffi-cient time to acclimatize to the team's way of playing. However, on the day they proved inspired changes, the powerful Mendez making an instant impression on Rec fans, while Lyle's performance was a revelation, despite his unac-customed new role, which he would reluctantly fulfil on later occasions, before reverting to his preferred position at number eight.

As John Hall predicted in that Saturday's *Chronicle* back page lead, the encounter against Harlequins was destined to be a turning point in Bath's progress. And it was certainly that, although ultimately it had more impact on his predica-ment than that of his team. What he was looking for, he claimed, was a complete all-round performance and a resounding victory. But what he, and a stunned Rec crowd witnessed in wide-eyed disbelief, was another Jekyll-and-

Hyde Bath display that encapsulated the fluctuating highs and lows of the team's erratic form that year.

In a first half of unrelenting Harlequins pressure Callard's second minute penalty gave Bath a brief lead, but the champions then found themselves besieged by a ceaseless onslaught and seemingly powerless to mount an effective counter. Quin's fly-half Paul Challinor levelled the score with a penalty, and then converted a try by scrum-half Huw Harries, after Bath had been driven back by a bull-like charge from Irish international hooker Keith Wood. And then, when Jason Robinson spilled a pass, Harlequins stormed back to set up Challinor for their second try, which he converted to put them 17-3 ahead.

Bath had to defend desperately just to maintain that deficit before the interval, when it seemed their title hopes were in tatters. But after a tongue-lashing from Hall and de Glanville, they were a team transformed in the second half. With their pride on the line, Bath's pack switched into overdrive, pounding forward in a furious display of power and precision that forced Quins back on their heels. Lyle and Mendez, who had struggled in the first half, played like men possessed, Lyle soaring at the lineout to gain a regular supply of possession and also leading the charge in the loose, while the squat Argentine's pace and aggression inspired a Bath stampede that Quins could not withstand.

All it needed was the coup-de-grâce, and Guscott, cool and deadly as ever, provided that, gliding gracefully through the gaps created by the big men to wreak havoc in a retreating defence and score a sensational try, which Callard converted. Callard and Challinor then exchanged penalties, before Bath's forwards drove through for the next try, Lyle leaping salmon-like at the lineout to set up Nathan Thomas for the touchdown. In the final quarter Quins reeled under a ceaseless stream of attacks. Bath's third try came when Callard set up Adebayo for a jubilant scoring gallop, and fittingly it was left to Guscott to wrap up a tremendous 35-20 triumph as he sauntered over unchallenged to send the 8,500 crowd home overjoyed at an amazing comeback.

The sheer quality of rugby Bath produced in that euphoric 40 minutes of near flawless interplay between forwards and backs had been dazzling to behold and, not surprisingly, obtaining quotes was an easy and enjoyable task afterwards. A dejected Will Carling and delighted John Hall paid tribute to the quality of Guscott's performance, both querying Jack Rowell's decision to leave him on the England bench. Guscott himself was typically laid-back, claiming all he aimed to do was enjoy the game and leave the decisions to others.

It was obvious as I left a Rec still buzzing with excitement that it had been a contest to savour and celebrate, which almost everyone who remained was intent on doing. But with a long drive home ahead of me I wasn't able to join in. Instead, I walked back to the office, still incredulous at what I had just seen and sat down to write a report that I hoped would reflect the scale and drama of Bath's extraordinary revival.

I stayed at my desk for an hour or so before deciding to finish the report at home the following day. This was my normal routine, except when I was required to be in the office on a Sunday. However, I felt inclined to enjoy a drink before the journey home and decided on a whim to sample the Saturday night scene at a wine bar called PJ Peppers, a rather grandiose and trendy establishment in George Street, close to the city centre, and a popular meeting place for Bath's younger weekend revellers. I had been there a couple of weeks previously at lunchtime to interview Dan Lyle who was just about to return to action after his lengthy injury absence, but at that stage of the evening, around 8pm, it was rather quiet and having taken my time over one drink, I decided it was not quite my scene and left.

As it turned out, if I had stayed there an hour or two longer, my presence might have prevented an incident that was to have a profound effect on Bath Rugby Club and trigger a shattering saga that would eventually lead to court proceedings nine months later and become a contributory factor in John

Hall's bitter departure from the Rec. I only suggest that possibility for the simple reason that, had Hall and several of Bath's celebrating players spotted me there when they walked in some time later, they might have elected to go elsewhere. Not because they wanted to avoid me personally, but because, if they were in the mood to enjoy themselves, they would have preferred to do so without 'the press' being around.

As it was, I was not there when a group including John Hall, Jeremy Guscott, Adedayo Adebayo, Steve Ojomoh and Ben Clarke (who was in Bath to see some of his former team-mates that day) walked in after attending a post-match social evening at the Rec. Some time later, the police arrived and within days all the local and national newspapers would be breaking the news that Bath's director of rugby had been interviewed in connection with an alleged incident involving a 23-year-old woman who was also in the wine bar.

The sensational revelation finally hit the headlines on Wednesday, 11 December, four days after the Harlequins game, when it was reported that police were investigating an allegation of indecent assault at PJ Peppers wine bar the previous Saturday, when John Hall and several members of the Bath squad were said to be present. The *Chronicle's* lead story quoted a witness who claimed that there had been a lot of swearing and shouting and that a member of a party of about eight people had jumped on a table and started to sing dirty songs, which caused embarrassment.

After that a woman, said to be very upset, had made a complaint of indecent assault and the police were called, arriving at about 10.30pm, just as the party was leaving. According to witnesses, abuse was directed at the police and one Bath player, Jeremy Guscott, had leapt onto the bonnet of the police car and run over the top of it, but no damage had been done and no one had been arrested.

According to the report a spokesman for the wine bar had initially confirmed that an incident had taken place, but had later attempted to withdraw that confirmation and referred any further enquiries to the police. Not surprisingly, no comment was forthcoming from Bath or John Hall that week and for some time, while police investigations continued. And it was widely expected that the matter would be resolved and allowed to drop without charges being filed, but that was not to be the case.

I had nothing to do with reporting the alleged incident or the resulting proceedings, as it was rightly deemed to be a news story. So despite the furore, and the veil of silence that descended in connection with it, I attempted to carry on reporting the rugby side of Bath's affairs, although that was difficult in the circumstances.

On the same day that the PJ Peppers story broke, I reported that Bath were unlikely to extend their interest in rugby league stars Henry Paul and Jason Robinson, whose loan period was due to end a month later. Bath were not too keen to comment on that subject either, but Wigan's chairman, Jack Robinson, confirmed that no approach had been made by Bath to extend the loan or sign either player, who were both expected to return to the league code on 12 January.

I interviewed Jon Sleightholme in a preview of England's clash against Argentina that coming Saturday and talked to Brian Ashton about Bath's prospects. Ashton singled out Leicester, who that week had signed South Africa's World Cup-winning fly-half Joel Stransky, as the main danger to Bath's title hopes.

And as I prepared for the trip to Twickenham on the Saturday, I contemplated the fact that Phil de Glanville had dropped out of England's team with a thigh strain, allowing Guscott to resume his centre partnership with Will Carling.

Argentina were not expected to cause England too much trouble. But it did not turn out that way. England's pack had a combined off day, failing to dominate the Argentine forwards who held their own at the scrummage, foraged gainfully in the loose, and completely disrupted England's lineout, where Martin Johnson and Simon Shaw were given a torrid time by the impressive Argentine locks Pedro Sporleder and German Llanes.

As a result, clean ball to the backs was sporadic and quick ball a rarity. This did nothing to help Mike Catt advance his claims as an expansive playmaker, in a totally lacklustre England display which encouraged even more speculation as to his suitability for the fly-half role. He did, at least, kick five penalties as England, trailing 18-12 with just seventeen minutes left, scraped through to a fortunate 20-18 victory, thanks to a late Jason Leonard try. But a chorus of boos from the stands pronounced the crowd's verdict. Of England's backs, Guscott did well enough, showing the few touches of class on view and having an opportunist try disallowed after Johnson was spotted throwing a punch earlier in the move.

All in all, it was a desultory display by England and an inspired one by Argentina, who took any plaudits going. The outcome would have repercussions for Bath, because one man who must have been impressed by the Argentine second row was John Hall, who had been searching for a formidable new lock forward for some time. I made Sporleder the pick of the Argentine pack, but Hall, aided no doubt by advice from his recent signing Mendez, would soon raid Andrew Brownsword's treasure chest again to bring his partner Llanes to the Rec. It would turn out to be an ill-judged investment that rarely produced much of a dividend.

So, within seven days of that resounding victory over Harlequins it was glum faces all round at the Rec, and at Twickenham, as the festive season drew near. Coming up was a home Pilkington Cup tie against London Irish, which, on form, did not appear to present too great a challenge for the cup-holders.

Bath's somewhat bemused supporters were no doubt consoling themselves with the thought that surely no further disaster could afflict the club after an errant autumn campaign, European Cup woe and that disturbing wine-bar incident. After all, the old year would soon give way to the new, which still held promise of another league and cup double. But, even as Bath's international brigade were making their way back to the Rec in readiness for another cup assault, an even bigger storm was brewing at Queen Square. It was only a minor storm at first, but it was one that would slowly build into a maelstrom of discontent and disharmony, hurling the club into an even deeper crisis that would end in a parting of the ways for two men who had done so much to chart Bath's gloriously successful course over the previous decade.

CHAPTER TWO

A Club in Crisis

Strangely enough, as indecision and turmoil mounted in Queen Square, Bath showed little sign of disruption on the field over the festive period, partly perhaps, because the players themselves were being kept as much in the dark as were the press and public. A measure of just how little information was filtering through to the squad would later be seen in the BBC 2 documentary series 'The Rugby Club', in which concern would be voiced about the fact that the first inkling most players had of situations arising within the club was gained through newspapers, not from internal sources. And although rumours of trouble must have been circulating, true to the Bath family tradition, the players got on with the every-day routine of training, preparing for games and playing, without offering the slightest hint that anything was amiss. While England were struggling to beat Argentina, a largely second-string Bath side trounced Wakefield 71-20 at the Rec, Dan Lyle extending the favourable impression he had made against Harlequins with a rousing display, this time at number eight.

Then on Tuesday, 17 December, ten days after that emphatic Harlequins triumph and its alarming aftermath, Bath were struck by a second earthquake, and one that would have a far

138

greater destructive impact within the club than anything arising from that unfortunate night at PJ Peppers. The information, such as it was, came via a statement issued by the club in response to speculation that morning in the *Western Daily Press*, that the head coach, Brian Ashton, was on the brink of resigning. Bath's brief statement declared that Ashton was taking a week's holiday but was still employed by the club, and this line was confirmed by the team secretary John Allen, who said it had been a difficult week but insisted that Ashton had definitely not resigned.

It was revealed that Bath's players had been called together the previous day to be told by the club chairman Tony Swift that Ashton was taking a week's leave and that training would be taken by Andy Robinson and his fellow coach John Palmer, who would prepare the side for the Pilkington Cup encounter against London Irish that Saturday.

That was about all we had to go on, but it was immediately evident that this was not merely a case of Ashton taking a mid-season break, but something much more serious. I could only speculate as to the reasons for his absence at such a vital stage of the season. All the indications suggested that Ashton was unhappy with the perception of his role within the coaching set-up at the club and was at loggerheads with the rugby director John Hall over matters involving selection and tactics.

Meanwhile, it was revealed that Mike Catt would miss the London Irish game, after aggravating a chest injury which had nearly kept him out of the Argentina game, and that Phil de Glanville was still struggling to recover from the thigh injury that had prevented him from playing against the Pumas. De Glanville was eventually named in the team, but forced to pull out on the eve of the game, again handing the captaincy to Jon Callard, while Dan Lyle, originally selected at lock, was eventually switched to blindside flanker, Nigel Redman resuming his second-row partnership with Martin Haag.

I managed to upset John Hall that Friday when, as a result

of a tip-off, I revealed that James Cockle, a promising 20-year-old back-row forward who had represented England at various youth levels, had quit Bath to sign a three-year contract with second division Moseley. When I had phoned Cockle he confirmed that he was leaving and said he had no quarrel with Bath, but felt there was very little chance for younger players to challenge for first-team places at the Rec and criticised the management for failing to give them enough encouragement. Having gone through the Bath youth system he was ambitious for senior rugby and further representative honours, but felt he wasn't being pushed enough and had missed selection for the England Under-21 side as a result. So, reluctantly, he had decided to accept an improved contract with Moseley who had promised him first-team rugby.

I don't know where the tip-off originated. It was passed on to me and I was asked to follow it up. But the story was guaranteed to bring an irate response from John Hall, especially as it only added to an already inflammatory situation. Later that morning, having read the story, he called me to give vent to his feelings on the subject and ask why I had not contacted him for his reaction. In fact, after talking to Cockle, I had tried several times to reach Hall on the phone, but he was unavailable, and under pressure of a tight deadline the story went in without an official response from the club.

I understood Hall's reaction, but the truth is that Cockle was unhappy at Bath, had decided to leave and was prepared to explain why. So there was no way the story could be described as inaccurate, even if its appearance in the paper at that precise moment was badly timed from the club's viewpoint.

Worse publicity was to follow on the morning of the London Irish game when *The Sun*'s rugby writer, Tony Roche, claimed that Bath were fast disappearing down the plughole in terms of disintegrating morale. The story accused the Brownsword regime of replacing the club's renowned family atmosphere with a puritanical attitude which had damaged relations between players and supporters. And it highlighted the rift between Hall and Ashton over a number of team issues, as well as stating that police were investigating two after-match incidents involving players and management, including an allegation of indecent assault. It concluded that Bath's players were fed up with the situation and urged the team and the club to get their act together, which must have raised more than a few hackles in Queen Square that morning.

Nevertheless, it failed to undermine the team's confidence that afternoon, because Bath easily despatched London Irish 33-0 and although it was not a fluent display, the result was rarely in doubt. Once again it was a stop-start performance as Bath began brightly, establishing a 12-0 lead in the opening quarter with tries from Sleightholme and teenager Matt Perry, ably deputising for de Glanville. However, Bath lost direction midway through the contest before signing off with a flourish, Jeremy Guscott putting his own unique seal on the outcome with a lethal hat-trick of tries in the last thirteen minutes.

What was noticeable that afternoon was the disappointing size of the Rec crowd, estimated at fewer than 6,000, and the subdued reception afforded to John Hall as he made his way to the West Stand dugout. Both factors indicated that Bath fans were none too impressed by the events of the previous fortnight. The attendance may have been affected by the fact that it was the last shopping Saturday before Christmas. But it was still well down on what could normally be expected for such a game. More pertinently, the apparent mood within the crowd was one of anxiety and concern about what was happening at the club and where it was heading.

In his post-match press conference Hall tried hard to play down the significance of Brian Ashton's absence, claiming that Ashton was on holiday and still part of the club, while expressing optimism that the situation would be resolved, with his head coach likely to return the following week. His words failed to convince and only fuelled the impression that Bath were facing a serious crisis, without any real prospect of finding a solution.

All things considered, it was a sombre prospect and not even the news that Bath had been given a plum home tie against Leicester in the sixth round of the Pilkington Cup could lift the gloom, although Hall expressed his delight at the draw when I called him the following Monday. He was only too eager to discuss the prospect of a guaranteed full house for the tie, scheduled for 25 January. (The game eventually took place on 8 February owing to Leicester's European Cup-final commitments.)

As Hall was aware, if Bath emerged victorious from that crucial showdown the second half of the season still held out the hope of some silverware, thus salvaging not only the club's tottering fortunes but his own as well. But while he was happy enough to discuss that scenario, there was still no news on the Brian Ashton controversy, or on the investigation into that sorry episode at PJ Peppers which appeared to have gone very quiet indeed.

Everyone was waiting to see just what would happen next in Bath's troubled yuletide saga, but the immediate answer was very little, as the nation settled down to enjoy the annual bout of festive indulgence. Bath's players enjoyed just a brief Christmas Day break from training before getting back to work in preparation for a Courage League trip to Sale the following Sunday, which turned out to be a wasted journey for all concerned. Despite assurances from Sale on the Friday before the game that their Heywood Road pitch was adequately covered to beat a seasonal bout of frost, the game was eventually called off, a couple of hours before kick-off, just when I and most of Bath's travelling support were arriving, which left us grimly contemplating a wasted 350-mile round trip.

It was a frustrating end to what had been an amazing roller-coaster year for everyone connected with Bath Rugby Club. But the nightmare period was by no means over for the double champions, as within days of a new year dawning the embers of controversy would flare up once more in a spectacular conflagration.

And when the drama unfolded I found myself drawn into it to some degree, thanks to an article I had written reviewing the troubled situation at the Rec.

It was a week that began with news that Bath and Brian Ashton were to have make or break talks on New Year's Eve in a final attempt to settle their differences and avert his intended resignation. That meeting took place, but when I returned to work, having completed my lengthy analysis, there was still no news of an announcement concerning Ashton's future at the club. My full-page article, headlined: 'Bath awake to realities of rugby's new regime', was published in the *Bath Chronicle* on Friday, 3 January, on the eve of Bath's home league game against a Saracens side in which François Pienaar, South Africa's world cup-winning captain, would make his debut, and it was to cause quite a stir.

I was off duty on the Friday when it was published and, when I read it through on the morning of the game, I was annoyed because it had been poorly sub-edited, with spelling mistakes introduced into the text that had not been there in the original. To cap it all, above my byline had been added the words, 'a personal view', which presumably had been inserted in a timid attempt to absolve the *Chronicle* from any responsibility for the views it contained.

Despite those disappointments, I felt that the article was an honest piece of work, although I would concede that it may have shown Brian Ashton in a more favourable light than John Hall. There were reasons for this at the time. Ashton was well liked and respected by everyone at Bath and had always been responsive and helpful whenever I had reason to contact him, whereas Hall, with whom I had to communicate on a regular basis, could be a difficult proposition at times. Considering the lack of reliable information emanating from the club at the time, it was perhaps understandable that the press and public conception of the rift was slanted in Ashton's favour and that he was widely considered to be the wronged party.

Meanwhile, on the same day my New Year article appeared

I was also reporting that Richard Webster had been recalled to Bath's back row against Saracens, after being sidelined since early November, when he had broken a knuckle in the shock defeat at Northampton. Also recalled was hooker Federico Mendez, who had returned to his native Argentina over the festive period for what Bath described as business reasons. It was perhaps too much of a coincidence that during his absence Hall had denied that the club were interested in signing his Argentine international colleague, the giant second-row forward German Llanes. Whatever the truth of the matter, Mendez was back and set to return at the Rec. And Llanes was also reported to be in Bath that weekend for talks with Hall, who was said to be keen to persuade the 6ft 6in, 19-stone lock to sign for the club.

As far as Brian Ashton's position was concerned, it was hinted that a decision might be made that day. But there was no announcement before the game, which had been saved from postponement only by a concerted effort to beat the frost, including extensive pitch covering and the employment of hot air blowers beneath them. Those efforts proved successful. But it was still a bitterly cold day for rugby, and as I made my way to the Rec that Saturday I wondered what kind of reception I was going to get in response to the article that had been published the previous day.

I didn't have to wait long to find out, because, as I walked into the cricket pavilion that served as a press room at the Rec, Ken Johnstone rushed to meet me, shook my hand and offered his congratulations for what he described as a brilliant article, which he felt had hit the nail right on the head – a greeting which startled me at first. Stephen Hands, Bath's commercial and marketing director, duly followed Ken's lead, if less vigorously. And there were other appreciative comments from representatives of the local and national press, including Dave Barton, rugby writer for the *Western Daily Press*, who also shook my hand and expressed the view that what I had written had needed to be said.

With an audible buzz of speculation already pervading the

ground before the kick-off, I climbed up to a West Stand press box that was equally consumed by animated debate over the likely outcome of Brian Ashton's resignation ultimatum. But when they took the field, Bath's players showed few signs of being affected by the controversy.

With their forwards in abrasive mood, Bath rattled Saracens with an early barrage to establish an 18-6 lead in the opening quarter, Mendez and Webster forcing their way over for tries and Callard slotting two penalties and a conversion. But for the rest of the first half Saracens held sway, Michael Lynagh's third penalty and a try by winger Courtney Smith reducing the interval deficit to 18-14.

The second half followed a similar pattern, Bath rampaging forward to stretch their lead to 35-14 through a Callard penalty, a penalty try and a converted touchdown by Guscott, who pounced on a clever chip ahead by Richard Butland, once again proving a more than capable deputy for the injured Mike Catt. But in the last 20 minutes it was all Saracens, as, with Pienaar suddenly beginning to get his bearings, they mounted a tremendous rally to score three fine tries, two Lynagh conversions slashing the lead to 35-33, before a final blast of referee Brian Campsall's whistle ended Bath's increasing fears of suffering another shock upset.

Afterwards Pienaar admitted to being impressed by Bath's forward display, which had certainly earned them the points, a recalled Nigel Redman enjoying an outstanding game, as did the back row of Webster, Nathan Thomas and Steve Ojomoh. But it was Ashton's situation that, not unnaturally, dominated Bath's press conference agenda.

When John Hall arrived, flanked by an equally serious-faced Andy Robinson in his capacity as assistant coach, he imparted very little other than to say that the situation had not changed. Hall intimated that a proposal had been put to Ashton and he expected the situation to be resolved by the following Monday, when it was anticipated a statement would be issued. Thereafter, Robinson did most of the talking and, from the steely grimaces on both men's faces, it was apparent that a torrid saga of dissent and disruption was unlikely to be resolved amicably.

Ashton, who had been engaged in prolonged negotiations with non-executive chairman Tony Swift, declined to comment when I phoned him the following evening, saying he preferred to wait for an official statement from Bath's board. But it was obvious there was to be no last-minute compromise and on Monday, 6 January the die was cast, as Bath and Ashton issued a joint statement confirming that his resignation had been accepted.

In the statement Ashton said he was leaving with some wonderful memories and it had been a privilege working alongside so many talented players. He wished Bath every success for the future and believed that the club would remain a major force. And when I spoke to him later he revealed his sadness that the situation had turned out as it had and claimed that he could not have worked with better players or people.

As expected, Andy Robinson was confirmed as Ashton's successor, although it was interesting to note that he was not allocated the title of head coach but was described as first-team coach by John Hall, who expressed his sadness at Ashton's departure and his appreciation for the contribution he had made to Bath's success in the past, while wishing him well for the future. Hall affirmed that he had every confidence in Andy Robinson, who he felt had done a superb job that season both before and during Ashton's absence. As for the players, who must have been nonplussed by the events of the past month, skipper Phil de Glanville voiced their regret that negotiations with Ashton had proved unsuccessful, but he also thanked him for all his hard work and wished him every success.

Interestingly, especially in the light of developments that would soon arise concerning Ashton's future plans, he was to firmly deny that he had even thought about his future and that, contrary to some reports, no one had been in touch with him with regard to alternative employment. But with his coaching qualifications, unrivalled record of success, and acknowledged reputation as a tactical innovator it was unlikely he would remain idle for long. And it was soon widely rumoured that he was in contention for several high-profile coaching appointments.

At one stage he was strongly tipped to take the coaching helm at Cardiff, while Jack Rowell cagily intimated that he might be contacting Ashton concerning a possible link with the England squad. And it was also being suggested that Ireland might soon be interested in appointing a new head coach – which, in fact would be the case within a few short weeks.

Ashton was named as Ireland's new coaching messiah just before the start of the Five Nations Championship, in a welter of publicity which acclaimed his arrival in terms equivalent to those afforded the revered Jack Charlton, who had inspired Eire's recent soccer revival. Ashton would help inspire Ireland to a surprise win over Wales in Cardiff the following month. But after that initial success a sequence of heavy defeats and his dislike of the intensely political nature of the Irish international set-up would persuade him to resign before he had had time to get to grips with a daunting task.

Some had suggested that when Ashton left Bath he must have been aware of alternative opportunities in the pipeline and had stood his ground in the knowledge that he would be in demand. But I felt he would have stayed at the Rec if the club had seen fit to give him the authority he considered was his prerogative as head coach. For some time it was unclear what his reasons were for first threatening to resign and then carrying out that threat, and he himself has shed little light on the subject. But it was obvious he was unhappy with his terms of employment in the role which allowed him only a limited influence over selection and player recruitment.

Right from the start of that doomed campaign, when he had been the instigating force behind Bath's bold, expansive new playing style, it had appeared that the demarcation lines in the working relationship between Ashton, as head coach, and John Hall, as director of rugby, were not clearly defined. Hall had always looked far more at ease joining in with his players on the training pitch and taking a leading role in tactical deliberations than he ever did wearing a suit in his Queen Square office.

It might have been entirely different if Bath had not suffered those demoralising early setbacks, especially the Cardiff disaster. But when things went wrong on the field and policy disagreements began to emerge, it was always likely that the relationship would come under strain. I don't suggest that Ashton, John Hall, Andy Robinson or any of Bath's coaching team were not wholeheartedly committed to a Southern Hemisphere playing style when they set out that season. But as plans went astray and policies were analysed and reviewed, it was almost inevitable that collective loyalty and unity would come under pressure. Perhaps the strongest criticism of Ashton's actions from Bath's and Hall's point of view was the timing of his decision to threaten resignation, just days after a memorable pre-Christmas triumph over the league leaders and that unfortunate wine-bar incident.

As far as John Hall was concerned, the furore that erupted over Ashton's stance and eventual departure was a critical second blow which further undermined his standing and authority within the club, and would contribute significantly towards his own departure barely a month later. For the time being he appeared to have won the power struggle. But the damage to his credibility was to prove irreparable, particularly in relation to the playing squad, most of whom held Ashton in high regard as a coach and were sorry to see him leave in such regrettable circumstances, whether they supported his argument or not.

On the same day that Ashton's departure was confirmed, I had my own showdown to endure. It was a confrontation I was not exactly looking forward to as I walked down to the Rec that Tuesday, but Bath were training, it had become part of my routine to attend, and I knew it had to be faced.

Although the general response to my analysis published in the *Chronicle* four days earlier had been one of approval, I was certain it would not have been welcomed by John Hall, for whom the timing of it could not have been worse. And I was resigned to some strongly worded condemnation as I mounted the steps up to the members' bar in the Rec club-house, where I saw that just about the entire playing squad and Hall were sitting down to an early lunch.

As I entered the bar it suddenly went extremely quiet. There were a few surreptitious glances from the players, but from Hall, who was sitting facing me at the nearest table, there was not a trace of acknowledgement of my presence.

I stood silently for a while and waited for what seemed like several minutes for some sign of a change in the stand-off situation. But none was forthcoming and finally as one or two players began to drift away I decided to carry on as normal and went over to Phil de Glanville to ask if he would talk to me about the England squad which was due to be announced later that week. Somewhat to my surprise, he readily obliged and we went outside to do the interview, during which he was his usual friendly self, although it was often difficult for Phil to talk freely about his opinions on controversial issues because he held positions of responsibility for both Bath and England.

When that interview was completed, I realised that the air still had to be cleared with Hall, so I returned to the bar and awaited my fate. I knew it would have to come to a frank exchange of views before we could settle our differences. He was nowhere to be seen just then, and I was just about to talk to one or two other players when suddenly he came marching into the bar, headed towards the lounge at the far end of the building and, motioning to attract my attention, announced loudly that it was time we sorted things out.

I followed him through into the next room and sat down, whereupon he immediately began to complain, not just about the article I had written, but also about the personal coverage he had been given in the *Chronicle* since the incident at PJ

Peppers wine bar. The main crux of his argument was that every story that appeared about Bath rugby involving his name seemed to carry a footnote referring to the allegations that had been made with regard to the incident. He claimed that his name was mud in the city because of all the adverse publicity he had received in the past few weeks.

I explained that it was routine policy for newspapers to repeat the fact that allegations had been made, especially in the circumstances of that particular incident, which was of undeniable public interest. And I also gently reminded him that whatever had occurred that night could not be blamed on the newspaper.

After that brief exchange, his tone and demeanour altered appreciably and he became far more conciliatory. We agreed to put our differences aside and within minutes we were conversing about rugby again, which was undoubtedly a relief to both of us.

In many ways I had a great deal of sympathy for Hall, because he had carried a heavy responsibilty for a considerable time. And my intention in writing that article had not been to attack him personally or undermine his position as director of rugby. What I had attempted was to urge the club to act positively to alleviate a deteriorating situation that had dragged on far too long and was having a serious effect not just on morale within the club itself, but, more crucially, on the relationship Bath had always enjoyed with the loyal bedrock of its support.

No one at Bath, and certainly not John Hall, had wanted Brian Ashton to leave, because his coaching ability was valued. But there was a clear reluctance to allow him the influence and authority which he felt was his prerogative as head coach, but was not considered to be his forte. However, once he decided to press his claims to the point of threatening to resign, the club found itself in an extremely delicate situation. And despite efforts to work out a compromise solution, none was forthcoming, and with Ashton not prepared to back down, there could only be one outcome. It was a sad day for

Bath when he left. And the parting should not have been necessary because the deteriorating situation between Hall and Ashton should have been dealt with long before it became a resignation issue. But nothing was done and the rift was allowed to fester until it was beyond healing.

Without doubt Ashton's untimely departure and the way the dispute was handled had a significant impact on the attitude of players and supporters in their assessment of the club's administration at the time. And it was inevitable that the disquiet and unrest that ensued would make life much more difficult for Hall, who was to find himself under increasing pressure. Surprisingly, when the BBC 2 series 'The Rugby Club' was screened later that year, Hall was to claim that his eventual sacking had come as a shock. No doubt he felt he had been stabbed in the back, but deep down he must have known that his own position was in some jeopardy.

It was perhaps symptomatic of the unrest that had gradually infiltrated his squad that in that very same week John Hall announced that two promising Bath players were to be offered on loan to second division Bedford. Hooker Neil McCarthy, who had been in Jack Rowell's provisional England squad at the start of the season, but had hardly featured in Bath's first-team plans since then, and prop Kevin Yates, another on the fringe of England selection, were the players involved. And, although Yates declined the opportunity, McCarthy and the promising young lock Will James leapt at the chance of first-team rugby.

It was an unusual occurrence just before Bath's next league game, a return clash against Harlequins, that left me in no doubt that Hall was now under severe pressure to produce the kind of results that would be imperative to his continued tenure as Bath's director of rugby. On arrival at the Stoop, I found the press room located in a large temporary building at one end of the clubhouse, where the usual throng of rugby journalists were already enjoying some generous Quins' hospitality. The room contained a television set which enabled us to watch Leicester's important local derby clash at Northampton, due to kick off forty-five minutes before Bath's game. Then at around 2.15pm we were joined by Hall.

He had very little to say as we watched the early stages of the Leicester game, an epic scrap which saw Northampton eventually triumph 22-19. But he appeared tense, so much so that he came over and asked me for a cigarette. The request surprised me: I had not seen him smoke before.

He eventually left a few minutes before kick-off, but his presence in the press room at a time when he would normally have been in the dressing room made me wonder what was going on behind the scenes in the Bath camp and why he had made that unusual decision to join the press, whose company he did not usually find congenial.

It was a minor occurrence but indicative of the turmoil the club was going through in the wake of a traumatic Christmas and New Year period. And there was more to come as the inevitable consequences of that upheaval began to unfold.

Meanwhile, whatever Hall's state of mind that afternoon at the Stoop, the tension he had shown appeared to have permeated into the minds of the Bath team on taking the field, because they combined to produce a display that was a far cry from the one which had destroyed Harlequins just a month earlier. Facing a Quins side understandably keen to avenge their recent humiliation at the Rec, Bath enjoyed enough possession and scoring chances to have sealed another decisive victory. But this time the passion that usually inspired them in times of adversity, and the killer instinct that often marked their performances, were noticeably missing.

Jon Callard twice landed penalties to put them ahead in a scrappy first half, but the veteran French international fly-half Thierry Lacroix cancelled those out to keep Quins level at 6-6 by the interval. And, in the second half, Bath looked a shadow of the team that had eclipsed their rivals so decisively in the closing 40 minutes of that epic clash at the Rec. Time after time promising attacks broke down, wrong options were taken, passes went astray and possession was conceded to a

Quins side who scented a first league victory over the champions and were determined to pull it off. Lacroix coolly added two more penalties and a dropped goal to put them 15-9 in front, and then he completed a 17-point haul by converting a 77th minute try by Jim Staples. Bath's fourth Division 1 defeat was confirmed.

It was Jason Robinson's last game for Bath and his performance reflected the lack of confidence in the side, as he wasted one clear chance, and then a second went begging as Mike Catt's errant pass sailed harmlessly behind him with the line at his mercy. Bath had persevered with the Wigan flier, but a run of a dozen or so games without a try told its own story and his return to the league code must have come as something of a relief by the end of his stay, especially in the gloomy circumstances that prevailed at the time of his departure.

The misery on the faces of everyone emerging from Bath's changing room that afternoon was a depressing sight. Although Harlequins' delighted rugby director Dick Best refused to write off their title hopes, it was evident that, in reality, the reigning champions had reluctantly accepted that they now faced an impossible task.

CHAPTER THREE

Fall of a Titan

Throughout what was gradually turning into a winter of bitter discontent at the Rec, Andrew Brownsword had stuck to his avowed intention of staying well clear of the everyday running of the club he had acquired the previous summer. But Bath's apparent inability to shake off the setbacks of the first half of the season and regain an even keel, both on the field and in the boardroom, after the dramas that had enveloped the club over the festive season, must have caused him increasing concern. He had already indicated his strong disapproval of events surrounding the incident at PJ Peppers wine bar, following which Tony Swift had warned Bath's squad that such behaviour was not acceptable and would not be tolerated in future. And, with the reverberations of the Brian Ashton affair still rumbling through the club and the team's form at a low ebb, Brownsword found himself forced to step directly into the fray in a determined attempt to stop the rot.

Direct intervention was not a course of action he had wanted to take. But, reluctant as he was to interfere in the club's affairs, it was a measure he felt was clearly necessary and, once persuaded that action was required, his response was uncompromising. In the aftermath of that Harlequins defeat, Brownsword emerged from the shadows to address the club management and squad, with the BBC 2 cameras in attendance, and announce that he himself would be taking over forthwith as board chairman. Tony Swift was to become chief executive in place of Ed Goodall, who would still be involved but would concentrate more on the core Brownsword operation – a sideways move he perhaps welcomed after the chaos of the previous six months.

That was the extent of the immediate administration changes, but Brownsword made it clear that Bath's pre-season objectives had not been met and he expected a significant improvement over the second half of the season. He reminded everyone that Bath's management had stated that winning all three major trophies was a realistic goal, but that the European Cup had now gone and the Courage League title was unlikely. That left only the Pilkington Cup as a target and he stressed that winning it was something he expected the club to treat as an urgent priority.

Brownsword added that he had recently attended a meeting of club owners and executives and had been impressed by the quality of management personnel that was being attracted into the game. He left no one in doubt that he fully expected Bath to achieve similar levels of excellence. Those words of warning and the realisation that the club's activities were to be much more closely monitored by its financial backer, who confirmed that his commitment to the club was long-term, must have had a salutary effect on players and management, especially on a hard-pressed John Hall. And Hall was quick to respond, exhorting his side to show more consistency and cast off the pressure that had mounted in recent weeks after a campaign that he conceded had not gone perfectly. He highlighted poor finishing as a major reason for Bath losing more matches than expected, but claimed the side could turn things round, were still among the best and had every chance of salvaging some silverware from the season.

As for the squad, still reeling from that Harlequins defeat

and saddened by the news that hooker Gareth Adams had been forced to retire owing to a serious neck injury, it was a time to regroup and face a demanding schedule at club and international level. With the Five Nations Championship in the offing, Bath's next game was a tricky home clash against an in-form Northampton fresh from victory over league leaders Leicester. It would give the club's England hopefuls a final chance to impress Jack Rowell before he named his team for the first international against Scotland on 1 February.

One of Bath's six members of Rowell's provisional squad would take that chance in style against the club he would later join. Jon Sleightholme, who had spent too long in the shadow of Jason Robinson for his liking over the past four months, stepped back into the limelight with a display that sealed his international place in the coming weeks.

To widespread relief, Bath put their troubles aside to produce one of their best displays of the season in destroying the Saints 52-14 as the Rec resounded in appreciation of a supercharged display from the entire team. Bath's forwards took charge from the start, Mike Catt made England rival Paul Grayson look pedestrian with an intuitive playmaking performance and an opportunist try, Guscott and de Glanville dovetailed perfectly in the centre, and Sleightholme was inspired on the flank, running in a hat-trick of brilliant tries, one taking him virtually the length of the pitch. Sleightholme's direct running, blistering acceleration and finishing flair was a revelation after a fairly disappointing season and he rated his hat-trick as the best he had ever scored, while Jon Callard, pleased with his own 22-point haul, felt that Bath had set the record straight following the setback at Harlequins.

John Hall was also delighted, with good reason, describing the performance as outstanding. That it certainly was, but although he didn't know it then, it was to be his last victory as Bath's first professional rugby director.

With the Pilkington Cup showdown against Leicester postponed because the Tigers' European Cup final clash against Brive in Cardiff took precedence, Bath had no game the following weekend and then were forced to cancel a Friday night friendly against Richmond because they had twenty-one players on international duty that weekend. That meant the team would not get together on the field for three weeks prior to the Leicester tie, a factor which did them no favours on the day, while international squad sessions kept many of Bath's leading stars away from the club's training ground.

In an attempt the give the bulk of the squad a break from their usual training routine a three-day trip was organised to the headquarters of 29 Commando Unit of the Royal Marines at Plymouth, with the BBC 2 film cameras in dutiful attendance. It was intended as a toughening-up and bonding excercise and appeared to be enjoyed by the players, who tried the commando assault course, attempted a few intricate army initiative tests, played a friendly game against their hosts and were even subjected to a freezing dip into Plymouth Sound, much to non-swimmer Steve Ojomoh's dismay.

Meanwhile, Jack Rowell had decided to leave out Guscott, Catt and Adebayo from his team for England's opening game against Scotland, decisions which mystified John Hall, who described the omission of Guscott as ridiculous.

Back in Bath the restructured board was busy trying to sort out the complicated issue of appearance money for non-competitive friendly matches and to set a new agenda to revamp the club's tarnished image after two months of controversy and conflict. Newly installed chief executive Tony Swift wasted little time in proclaiming his vision of a new customer-conscious business concern by contacting me to help publicise his plans to improve the club's links with local schools and supporters and make Bath an integral part of the local community.

One of the first initiatives he outlined was an offer of free admission for a thousand schoolchildren to Bath's friendly against the New Zealand provincial side Otago, who were scheduled to play at the Rec four days before the Leicester game. It was the first real sign that Bath had shaken off the bunker mentality that had descended on the club since Christmas and were intent on adopting a more positive, open and welcoming approach. And, as an additional bonus, to improve communication between the club and its local news-paper, Swift extended a lunch invitation to myself and Neville Smith, which was arranged for the Monday following the cup tie against Leicester.

Meanwhile, John Hall's mind was engaged in bringing fresh impetus into the squad by tackling what had long been identified as a weak link in the side's armoury: the lineout. Negotiations with Argentine jumper German Llanes had taken time to complete, but now Hall had got his man, sign-ing Llanes on an extended two-year contract, and soon after stepping off a plane from Buenos Aires, Bath's latest interna-tional recruit was taking a first tentative look at the Rec.

The first problem the new arrival faced was communica-tion, because his English was limited to a few words. But with his compatriot Mendez in attendance to translate, his introductory press conference was less of an ordeal than it might have been. Hall had been impressed with the Argentine's display against England and Leicester's Martin Johnson in the friendly international before Christmas, recalled playing against the 26-year old lock himself back in 1990, and was hoping for big things from his new and expen-sive acquisition.

But although he was to make a sizeable impact on his debut the following week against Otago and performed well enough when selected for the rest of that campaign, Llanes was never able to established himself in Bath's first-team line-up. His lineout work was less productive than anticipated, while his lack of mobility in the loose was not really suited to Bath's preference for a fluid running game. He would serve only 15 months of his contract before being released, along with the marginally more effective Mendez, at the end of the following season. At the time his capture must have felt like a real coup to John Hall, but, in hindsight, it would merely be added to a mounting catalogue of Bath's unwise investments and policy failures that season.

However, as Llanes settled into his strange new surroundings, the week leading up to that vital cup encounter, which had been a sell-out for weeks, was hectic, for Bath and for me, with the prospect of producing another rugby supplement previewing a contest being billed as the turning point in Bath's troubled season. I was at Twickenham on the first Saturday in February to see England slam Scotland 41-13, Phil de Glanville crowning his Five Nations captaincy debut and silencing his critics with a splendid try. Will Carling also scored and Grayson did more than enough at fly-half to justify his selection at the expense of Mike Catt, although it was a much improved display by the pack which routed Scotland.

The following Tuesday a below-strength Bath side went down 31-18 to Otago, Llanes making a favourable impression to encourage speculation that he might force his way into contention for the Leicester game. In the event he was confined to the bench and replaced Martin Haag only in the final 20 minutes.

There was controversy before the Leicester game when Bath's operations director David Jenkins revealed that the Tigers had returned nearly 2,000 tickets out of their 3,000 allocation as they planned to show the game live on a giant screen at their own Welford Road ground, leaving Bath to try and resell the remainder at the last minute. And there was some consternation when both clubs announced their line-ups the day before the game, most of it surrounding the composition of the opposing back rows.

Leicester had decided to leave out their England folk hero Dean Richards in favour of the younger, faster Eric Miller, while Bath appeared to have opted for power rather than pace by electing to play without a recognised openside flanker. Dan Lyle, who had filled every position in the pack bar the front row in his relatively brief first-team career thus far, was selected at openside alongside Eric Peters and Steve Ojomoh and opposite Neil Back, the mobile Leicester and England flanker. It appeared an unlikely reversal of traditional tactics, with Leicester, under the astute guidance of Bob Dwyer seeking to improve their all-round mobility, while Bath, aware of their vulnerability at the set piece against a powerful Leicester eight, had seemingly plumped for the biggest back row they could muster.

Bath's chosen formation would almost certainly improve their lineout options, as John Hall observed on naming his team after what he described as a 'really tough' selection meeting. But there were plenty of Bath supporters who queried the decision because it reduced the side's capacity to gain possession at the breakdown, where the speed of an orthodox openside flanker was crucial.

Bath had two specialist opensides in the squad in Andy Robinson, who had played well in the emphatic win over Northampton, and Nathan Thomas, who had just earned his first senior cap for Wales, while at a push Richard Webster could play on either flank. Arguably those three could have done just as efficient a job as the selected trio, but to ignore a recognised openside and pick Lyle in a position of which he had little or no experience, seemed a strange gamble to be taking in such a vital game. It was a decision that surprised many at the time, and it would be more than six months before many viewers of that BBC 2 series on the club discovered just how contentious that selection debate had been. But it culminated in a calculated gamble John Hall and Bath would rue when the two teams joined combat the next day.

Phil de Glanville was only too aware of the dangers inherent in Bath's proposed back row strategy and argued vehemently that Andy Robinson was the man to fill the crucial openside berth against Leicester, but his plea fell on deaf ears. De Glanville recognised that speed to the breakdown would be essential and felt that Robinson, with his vast experience and expertise in securing ruck ball, was the player who fitted the bill.

The England captain pointed out that, if Robinson played,

he and Bath's other backs would not have to go in and rip ball out of rucks as often as they had recently been forced to do, freeing them to concentrate on exposing Leicester's weaknesses outside the pack. Bath's backs had usually had the edge over their Leicester counterparts in the past and de Glanville was confident they could demonstrate that superiority again, provided they were supplied with sufficient clean possession. He pleaded for Robinson to play, even insisting that it was his duty to the club to do so. But Robinson was adamant in his contention that it was more important for him to concentrate on his coaching role. Hall asked his coach about the state of his fitness and Robinson conceded that he was fit enough for a good fifty minutes, whereupon de Glanville suggested that he start the game and if necessary Nathan Thomas could replace him in the second half.

The dispute ended there, Hall postponing a final decision until the Thursday. But when the team was announced, neither Robinson nor Thomas had been selected and Bath opted to rely on the power and height of Lyle, Peters and Ojomoh and take the risk of letting the loose exchanges sort themselves out. Explaining that decision the next morning, Hall claimed that Bath had wanted lots of lineout options and playing Lyle at openside would give the side those. He would be given free range, because he was a difficult player to stop with the ball in his hands, and although Thomas and Robinson had both been playing well it was felt that the blend in the back row was right for that particular game.

Bath had also completely rearranged the front row that had played in the impressive win over Northampton. Graham Dawe, recalled for that game, was discarded, John Mallett replaced Victor Ubogu at tighthead and Mendez reverted to hooker, allowing Dave Hilton to return at loosehead prop. Hall conceded that the front row deliberations had been just as difficult as the back row, but he felt that it would be an extremely strong pack, despite the numerous changes to an eight that had performed impressively the previous week.

'Hopefully we have got the calculations right, but it's by no means an exact science,' he said. In the event, all those calculations were to come to no avail. With such an array of talent to choose from, a problem in itself all season, Bath got it horribly and fatefully wrong, and for Hall it would be a last throw of the dice.

Coincidentally, and ironically, when the *Chronicle*'s four-page supplement came out on the morning of the game, the main feature was an interview I managed to extract from Andy Robinson. In it he discussed his self-confessed obsession with winning, conceded that Bath had under-performed in certain areas that season and reaffirmed his personal determination never to contemplate defeat. 'Robinson: no time for losers at Bath' was the headline on the piece. And rounding it off was the quote: 'I am confident we will win, there is no doubt in my mind. But, as I have always said, there is *never* any doubt in my mind.'

Andy Robinson was to watch and endure one more example of Bath under-performing that afternoon in a defeat that would culminate in John Hall's departure and his own succession to the hot seat of responsibility for the club's results on the field.

No one among a partisan crowd could have failed to feel the tension in the air as the two sides lined up for the opening whistle that unseasonably bright and sunny February afternoon. From the start it was Leicester who stole the initiative. Joel Stransky put the Tigers ahead with a tenth-minute penalty, and eight minutes later he converted a simple try by Will Greenwood, after Bath had surrendered possession when Ian Sanders committed the first of two basic errors by knocking on as he tried to take a quick penalty.

Momentarily, Bath looked to have regained their composure as a Callard penalty and a typically forceful try by Adebayo cut the deficit to 10-8, but as the first half wore on it became clear that Leicester were gaining the edge in almost every phase of the game. Bath's lineout play, not helped by some atrocious throwing by Mendez, was a shambles from start to finish as they went on to lose fifty per cent of their own ball. The valuable extra options promised by their back row experiment dramatically failed to materialise as Eric Miller cleaned up at the tail and Martin Johnson and Matt Poole once again held sway at the front and middle. Even worse, without a specialist openside, Bath were overrun in the loose where Neil Back had a field day capped by a cheeky opportunist try that was to settle the issue after the break.

A measure of Bath's inadequacy in getting to the crucial breakdown situations could be ascertained from the scrummage facts which told the dismal story that Leicester were awarded the put-in sixteen times to Bath's five, and their front five made the most of it, giving their hosts a torrid time. In consequence, behind the scrum Bath's backs, under constant pressure, lost their rhythm and composure, especially in defence, where centres Will Greenwood and Stuart Potter for once left Guscott and de Glanville toiling in their wake.

Flimsy tackling allowed Potter to grab Leicester's second converted try, and at half time they led 17-11. During the interval John Hall and de Glanville tried desperately to rouse the team from its torpor. But instead of lifting morale their words seemed to have the opposite effect, as Bath deteriorated into an indisciplined rabble for the next half-hour.

In that time Leicester ran in three more tries by Back, Greenwood and Steve Hackney to lead 36-14 with ten minutes left, by which time it was a rout. And although Guscott and de Glanville grabbed a try apiece to make the losing margin more respectable, a Stransky dropped goal assured Leicester of victory, their eventual 39-28 triumph flattering a demoralised Bath side.

Without question, it was the worst all-round display I had seen from a Bath side that for most of the time seemed in utter disarray, bereft of teamwork and organisation and lacking the mental strength and spirit to make anything more than a token fight of it. It was the kind of woeful performance that had not been seen at the Rec for years, and it was inevitable there would be repercussions. Bath had lost games before, occasionally been complacent or below form, but few could recall a Bath side suffer the indignity of being eclipsed in that fashion or look so resigned to defeat. The intense will to win that had fortified the side for so long had simply not been there, a mortifying revelation for a stunned Rec crowd, who could hardly believe their eyes as Bath all but capitulated, against Leicester of all opponents.

A desolate John Hall pulled no punches in his assessment afterwards, accusing his side of lacking the passion normally associated with the club and promising a frank and open discussion at the club's Monday morning team meeting. He pinpointed the team's inability to win sufficient ball, poor defence and unforced errors for the defeat, while praising Leicester for an exceptional performance. Standing alongside him, a grim-looking Andy Robinson claimed Bath's poor defensive work, the key to winning rugby in his view, had been a problem all season and needed a dramatic improvement, as did standards of fitness and communication, which he was confident were areas where adjustments would be made.

'It's not the end of the world, but it feels like it,' said Hall. 'We are going to learn from this and show we can come back.'

Those words were among his last public utterances as the man in charge of Bath's playing destiny. For Hall, the bitter scenario that was soon to unfold might not be the end of the world, but it would cut short his long and distinguished connection with the Rec and this time there would be no way back. He may or may not have realised it, but that Monday's 'frank and open' post-mortem was to be the prelude to his own departure. The thumbs had been turned downwards in rejection as far as his managerial record was concerned, especially the thumb that really mattered, Andrew Brownsword's.

I gathered as much later that day when Neville Smith and I joined Tony Swift for our lunch appointment at the Bath Spa Hotel, where Bath's chief executive dropped a tiny hint that another bombshell was about to explode at the Rec. All Swift divulged was that he faced having to make the hardest decision of his life – but that was all he needed to say. My instincts told me what that decision was and who it involved.

John Hall and Bath were about to part company. And for both him and Tony Swift, the moment of imparting the dread news would be distressing, considering that they had shared such a long friendship and so many outstanding triumphs on the field.

I was off duty the next day when news that an announcement was about to be made gradually filtered through to the media, who began arriving at Queen Square to await a statement that underwent a series of changes before it was released late that afternoon. It began as a detailed release and included a resumé of Hall's illustrious career with the club. But, by the time it had been approved by legal advisers on both sides it was to emerge as a two-line epitaph for the proud career of a man who had guided Bath into the professional light and whose managerial aspirations had perished in the glare of expectation thrust upon him.

And by the time I arrived in Westgate Steet the following morning, another new era was unfolding at Queen Square, although Hall's all-powerful role as director of rugby had been discreetly dropped. Andy Robinson had been put in charge of the playing side, but only as coach, working in tandem with Clive Woodward, the former Leicester and England centre and until recently director of coaching at London Irish. The pair, who had shared responsibility for coaching the England Under-21 side that season, were also joined by Nigel Redman, who was appointed assistant coach.

It was while I was busy confirming and writing up the story announcing Bath's new coaching regime that I suddenly found myself in the glare of the television spotlight. A BBC 2 crew arrived at the *Chronicle* office that morning and asked to film me writing the back-page lead story, a request which proved rather daunting, as I was faced with producing around 600 words of copy to a tight deadline, with a camera and sound boom hovering over me as I tapped away on the Crossfield computer. There was a lot of coming and going around the sports desk, but I had to get the story out, and somehow, despite the intrusion and an understandably nerve-racking hour or so, I managed to complete it and then went down to the paste-up area, again followed by the camera crew, to supervise its insertion into that day's back page.

Until then I had said very little, but when the page was signed off and it appeared that the filming was over I was suddenly confronted with a question, in which I was asked how well I had got on with John Hall and what I thought about his sacking. I responded by saying that we had got on well enough most of the time, although there had been one or two moments when the relationship had come under strain. But that was perhaps inevitable since we had been in regular contact over a difficult period. As for his dismissal, I suggested that such decisions were bound to occur now that the game had turned professional. Bath were expected to win things and now that the club was a professional enterprise that expectation would be greater than ever and those in charge would increasingly be judged by results, as had long been the case in soccer.

In my view John Hall's dismissal was a business decision made because he had lost the confidence and support of Andrew Brownsword, fellow board members, players and fans. After a season of inconsistent results and performance, flawed policy and continual off-the-field controversy, the widespread feeling was that the buck stopped with him and that he should accept the consequences.

Not a single sequence of that morning's filming was included when 'The Rugby Club' series was screened the following autumn, which surprised me. But it was also a relief because I had never harboured any desire to become involved in the politics of Bath Rugby Club. I had a job to do as a journalist for the *Bath Chronicle* and I was also expected to comment on the club's actions and activities from time to time, duties which I tried to carry out as accurately and honestly as I could. But in a rugby hotbed like Bath, where gossip and intrigue are an integral part of the fabric of communal living, it was virtually impossible not to become embroiled to some degree, especially considering the spectacular upheavals that afflicted the club over its first nine months of professional existence.

Hall's removal from centre stage at Bath was doubly sad because it severed a proud family link that stretched back three generations. His contribution to the club's tremendous success on the field, and the efforts he made to keep the squad intact in that crucial first summer of transition from amateur to professional status, were immense.

As a player he was a colossus, a titan, whose reputation and influence overshadowed even the greatest among his many famous team-mates at the Rec, while as a coach he had obvious credentials, and could have handled that role with distinction. But as a manager, which is what his job description entailed, he possibly lacked the experience, organisation, communication and delegation skills that are an absolute requisite of what, in professional sport at least, has long been a precarious existence.

Hall was obsessed with Bath rugby. His overwhelming ambition was not just to keep the club at the top of the domestic pile, but to make it one of the best clubs in the world. It was an obsession that eventually brought about his own downfall, and Brian Ashton's as well. They were among the first high-profile victims of rugby union's professional revolution, but the trickle would soon become a stream as the ramifications of play for pay began to be manifested.

Jack Rowell, Dick Best and Bob Dwyer, who guided Leicester to the European Cup final and Pilkington Cup victory at Twickenham that season, headed a growing list of renowned rugby coaches who would jump or be pushed from office over the next year of uncertainty, strife and political intrigue that showed no sign of abating. They were all, in one way or another, casualties of the conflict that overtook the game once it was thrown open to professionalism. It is a trend already established in rugby union, just as it has been for decades in professional soccer.

While Bath was still preoccupied with Hall's departure, I was bound for Lansdowne Road, Dublin, where Ireland under the newly confirmed coaching guidance of Brian Ashton were to suffer a humiliating 46-6 defeat at the hands of Jack Rowell's revitalised England side. Phil de Glanville enjoyed the second win of his brief captaincy reign, Jon Sleightholme scored twice and Jeremy Guscott came on for the last five minutes to cause mayhem in the Irish defence.

Change was taking place all around me, it seemed, but at least some of the faces would remain the same. The *Bath Chronicle* was under new ownership, having been sold by Westminster Press to Newsquest Ltd. And its staff would soon be looking forward to a move from the outdated confines of Westgate Street to a much more modern, open-plan building at Windsor Bridge, a mile or so from the city centre.

On Wednesday, 19 February, the day I returned to work after an enjoyable five-day stay in Dublin, John Hall was finally charged with indecent assault, just eight days after his sacking as Bath's director of rugby. It was a charge that culminated in a two-day trial at Bristol Crown Court nearly seven months later, when the jury would acquit him of a charge he had firmly denied ever since that fateful episode at PJ Peppers wine bar on 7 December 1996.

Whether foreknowledge of that impending charge had any effect on the club's decision to dispense with Hall's services as rugby director remains unclear, but by then any such speculation was irrelevant. Now Hall, who six months earlier had been the master of all he surveyed at his beloved Rec, was gone. After 14 brilliantly successful years as a player, in a career that featured 276 appearances, 87 tries and 21 England caps, and after a managerial stint that lasted barely 18 months, but was capped by a fourth cup and league double, a titan had fallen.

And I had to contend and communicate with another revered Bath rugby legend, who, as I soon discovered, would waste no time at all in laying down the boundaries and the law governing his new territory.

CHAPTER FOUR

Back to Basics

Andy Robinson, above all else, is unreservedly proud of his reputation as a winner. In that respect he is totally unapologetic. He has an almost pathological hatred of losing, will never contemplate the prospect of defeat, and if he has to accept being beaten, he openly admits that he does so with bad grace. When he took control of Bath's coaching set-up, 'Robbo' (as he has always been known at the Rec), was determined to expunge the word defeat from the club's psyche for the rest of that season, and, more importantly, from the minds of Bath's playing squad.

By the time he and Clive Woodward teamed up to direct playing matters at the Rec, Bath had already lost eight of their 26 games, had crashed out of the European and Pilkington Cups, and were faced by the prospect of surrendering the Courage League title as well, which in Robbo's book was not much of a record to shout about.

Bath had not lost that many games in any season he could remember. And this, given that the club still boasted an unrivalled galaxy of international stars, meant that there must have been something drastically wrong with the tactical approach. He was not slow in putting his finger on the cause and the cure. Brilliant as the side's form had been at times that season, Bath had lost too many games they should have won and had conceded far too many points. So, in his view, the only way to solve those problems was to go back to the drawing board and start from scratch, concentrating on fitness, sound defence and consistency.

He immediately borrowed John Major's ill-fated phrase 'back to basics' and set about revising the way the team played from then on. But his initial concern was to ensure a significant improvement in its collective defensive capability. Although Bath were already being written off as heading for their first barren season for nearly a decade in terms of trophies, they still held an outside chance of retaining their Division 1 title provided further setbacks could be avoided.

Wasps, not among the pre-season favourites for honours, had quietly edged to the top of the table, two points clear of Leicester, with Bath two points further behind in third place. But the champions still had to play both of their rivals, and if they could launch a traditional spring offensive, the league crown was still within their grasp, and this would represent a major consolation prize after all the disappointments they had endured thus far.

They still had ten league games to play, starting with a local derby trip to Bristol. And Robinson immediately targeted that game as the springboard for his vision of a revival in Bath's flagging fortunes. On paper this hardly looked too difficult, as Bristol were floundering at the foot of the table and had been comprehensively hammered 76-7 at the Rec at the end of October. However, much water had passed under the bridge since then, and at home Bristol were no pushovers, so the game posed an awkward test of Bath's resolve and that of their new coach, who was naturally keen to win his first game in charge. Robinson, having missed the Leicester horror show, elected to lead from the front and select himself at openside flanker against a Bristol side that, from the first whistle, looked determined to avenge themselves for a decade of local derby woe and rub his and Bath's noses into the Memorial Ground mud.

They almost achieved that intention, too, producing a gutsy, combative display that saw them lead 13-5 at the interval, Bath's only points coming from Nigel Redman who forced his way over for an unconverted try. But in the second half, despite losing Mike Catt, who had suffered a fearful battering from the Bristol back row, Bath eased their supporters' growing fears with a sterling recovery, capped by a remarkable solo try by Jeremy Guscott, who shot through a gap in midfield, drifted left in search of support, and then dummied the entire Bristol cover to touch down in the corner. Jon Callard, who had already cut the deficit with a penalty, put Bath in front with a precise conversion from wide out and then added a further penalty to seal an 18-13 win. But it was hardly convincing, Bristol launching a relentless assault in the final quarter before being forced to concede a slightly unfortunate defeat.

Robinson, relieved to overcome a side he had never finished on the losing side against, was still wound up by the adrenalin of a pulsating contest in the bar afterwards. He was full of praise for Bath's fighting qualities and resolute defence and described the game and the nine remaining league matches as being solely about winning.

At the same time he also took a verbal swipe at me, over a story I had written that week suggesting Bath might be interested in signing Gloucester's unsettled Scottish international openside flanker Ian Smith, who was rumoured to be seeking a move away from Kingsholm. I had spoken briefly to him on the telephone the previous Thursday, when he had confirmed he was looking for a top class flanker and also a scrum-half as additional cover for the injured Andy Nicol. When I put the question to him, he had intimated that Smith was a possibility, which was all I quoted. But after the Bristol game he took me to task in no uncertain terms for linking Smith with a move to Bath.

As far as I was concerned he had confirmed that Smith was a possible target. But he seemed anxious to let me know, in front of all the other press reporters in attendance, that I was out of order in writing the story and he was not happy about it. We sorted it out the following week in an informal chat at the Rec, when I apologised for the fact that the story had upset him. Although the substance of the complaint was flimsy, because he had confirmed that Smith was a possible target, it was a speculative story that I had been asked to follow up and had done so with some reluctance.

The incident showed me just how careful a course I had to chart in dealing with Bath's hierarchy, who had become extremely sensitive about public relations following the internal ructions of the past three months. Andy Robinson, like many of his peers at the Rec, had always been a fiery, combative player, a scourge of referees and a self-confessed expert at stretching the offside laws to the limit, which often made him unpopular with opposing teams and their fans. Clearly, he would be no less confrontational, when it suited him, in his approach to the press. Like Graham Dawe, although much more aggressively, his attitude towards the media was tinged with suspicion, distrust and often disdain.

It was a stance he never relaxed in all my time at the Rec, which made him an awkward customer to deal with. But that was Robbo. I considered him to be a chip off the old Bath block; but, if anything, he was the core of it: hard, unyielding, relentless in pursuit of his own and Bath's immediate goals. Nevertheless, after clearing up that initial disagreement, we discussed Bath's ambitions for the rest of the season, which not surprisingly centred around winning their last nine league games and salvaging the last major prize available, the Courage League title.

To achieve that goal, Robinson insisted that the playing squad would need to reassess its priorities on the pitch, and that process might involve taking a few steps back before there was much progress. He admitted that Bath had made policy mistakes that season, which he himself had been involved in, and he pledged to put them right. The squad rotation system had not worked; from now on selection would be based on picking the best side available and changes would be kept to a minimum.

He also admitted that, owing to delays in getting the squad together the previous summer, Bath had not been properly prepared at the start of the season, which had caused problems when the campaign began. His 'back to basics' approach would entail a strong emphasis on improved fitness, solid defence and a consistent selection policy. But when that revision process was complete he was confident Bath would rise to new heights of performance, and he targeted April as the month when the team would show the form it was capable of. He predicted it would be an outstanding and historic month for Bath, who always played well at that time of year. And he was almost proved right. But the club's title hopes were to be shattered by one night of tactical disaster when that month was just two days old.

Before that cruel disappointment, Robinson, Woodward and chief executive Tony Swift were to enjoy a brief respite in which to lay their plans for revamping the club's organisation and image. On 25 February, Swift announced that the club was seeking a top class full-time fitness coach to take over from Ged Roddy, who had combined his role as Bath University's director of sports and recreation with the job of supervising fitness training at the Rec. Roddy would continue to oversee Bath's development academy. And in a statement that tacitly acknowledged the somewhat incestuous nature of Bath's previous recruitment policy, Swift stressed that whoever got the job would definitely be from outside the club, although the appointment was unlikely to be made before the end of the season.

A fortnight later, Swift announced that the former coach Dave Robson was rejoining the staff to take responsibility for player recruitment and youth development, a role that would exploit his unquestioned ability for finding future stars. In Robson's case, Bath were turning the clock back, but, although his return was an inside appointment, it was a shrewd move that would pay rich dividends the following season, when an exciting and talented crop of young players would emerge at the Rec.

Meanwhile, with the Five Nations Championship battle approaching its climax and their domestic programme further afflicted by postponements and cancellations, Bath had just two competitive games to look forward to in March: a home clash against London Irish and a midweek visit to West Hartlepool, both of which on form Bath were expected to win.

Before those two games there was to be disappointment for Phil de Glanville as his and England's hopes of a grand slam were capsized by an amazing French recovery at Twickenham. Leading 20-6 going into the final quarter, England looked to be cruising to a deserved victory, but fatally they took their foot off the pedal and the French countered with a stunning fightback that saw them draw level with two opportunist tries.

Winger Laurent Leflamand caught Tony Underwood napping for the first. And then centre Christophe Lamaison, who converted both scores, danced round a flat-footed Carling to score the second, before hammering home the final nail in England's coffin with a match-winning penalty to seal a shock 23-20 win that stole the grand slam and ultimately the championship from England's grasp. It was a devastating blow for Jack Rowell and for de Glanville, who was mortified that the chance of a grand slam in his first season as national captain had been thrown away.

Rowell's eventual replacement as England coach, Clive Woodward, was looking forward to his first home game on Bath's staff the following week against his old club, London Irish, where he had been director of coaching until parting company with the Exiles before Christmas.

I talked to him in the week before the game and found him a calm and lucid character, who was clearly delighted to be involved in rugby again and especially at the prospect of working with Bath's renowned backs. The game itself was hardly memorable. The Irish did well to hold Bath to a narrow 7-3 lead at the interval, before wilting under a seven-try second half barrage and eventually going down 46-3. Jon Sleightholme capped a solid display with his second successive league hat-trick, having scored three tries against Northampton six weeks earlier.

Graham Dawe, restored in place of Mendez, took a couple of strikes against the head in what would be his final competitive appearance at the Rec before yet another cruel injury brought a premature end to his season prior to a final parting in the summer.

And Andy Robinson, who scored one of Bath's eight tries, announced afterwards that he would retire from playing at the end of the season and confirmed he was looking for a young openside flanker to take over the role he had filled with distinction for the past decade at the Rec. He would find and eventually sign one as a consequence of Bath's next encounter at West Hartlepool, when he would come up against a powerful flaxen-haired Cambridge University student named Russell Earnshaw, who had already impressed him when the teams had met at the Rec. But before then Bath's England squad representatives were preparing to end the international season in resounding style.

Cardiff Arms Park, scene of so many epic Welsh victories over the years was staging its last Five Nations Championship match before being replaced by a new national stadium in preparation for the 1999 World Cup. And Wales were hoping to say farewell to its hallowed turf by beating the old enemy, England. But it was never on the cards as Bath's backs, and Jeremy Guscott in particular, laid on a spectacular England performance that sent a passionate full-house crowd home with a tarnished memory of their revered rugby fortress.

With Paul Grayson injured, Jack Rowell gave Mike Catt another chance to establish himself at fly-half and this time Catt grasped it, turning in a skilful display to set up a decisive 34-13 England win. However, it was Guscott, a second half replacement for Jon Sleightholme, who stole the limelight, despite playing out of position on the wing. Left to idle on the bench all season, the Bath legend destroyed the Welsh defence with a dazzling display of pace, vision and bewildering footwork that left no one present in any doubt of his world-class ability. But, while Guscott was lighting up the Arms Park, France were celebrating the title and a grand slam after a facile 47-20 victory over a Scotland side minus the injured Bath trio of Andy Nicol, Eric Peters and Dave Hilton.

As the spotlight reverted to the domestic scene it was apparent that Bath were finally emerging from the paralysis brought on by the club's prolonged internal crisis and coming up with ideas to solve some of the problems that had caused it. And there was evidence that communication was to be much more important under the new regime led by Tony Swift, who set the ball rolling by explaining the club's revised blueprint for securing its future as a major force in professional rugby. Top of his priority list was the need to find a solution to the problem of providing Bath with a viable stadium, which meant either improving the Rec to increase capacity or the club moving to a new stadium elsewhere, within the city boundary or outside it.

On the playing side, Swift said that the board had looked at the essential qualities that had made Bath successful in the past and defined them as good team management, good players and good attitudes. And he stated that Bath would soon make three or four more appointments, including a youth development officer, a post he felt was essential because the club wanted to develop its own players and not rely only on the cheque book, although top class players who really wanted to play for Bath would still be acquired when necessary.

One positive step which had already been taken was the setting up of an official Bath Supporters Club which would expand considerably over the next few months and foster an improved relationship between the club and its following, many of whom had become concerned about what was perceived to a be a widening gulf between the new professional company and the club's members and fans.

All these initiatives helped Bath win back public esteem that had wavered over the past few months, although it would be the team's ensuing performances on the pitch that finally got Rec fans singing their praises again. That return to vintage form was delayed for a couple of games and finally sparked only by yet another traumatic defeat that wrecked their title hopes, but when it came the transformation was well worth it. Meanwhile, after confidence-boosting victories over Bristol and London Irish, Bath faced two awkward trips north in their bid to stay in touch with leaders Wasps, and coach Andy Robinson's back to basics philosophy was still very much top of the tactical agenda.

I missed the return clash with West Hartlepool, Bath eventually winning a dour contest 24-16. But I was back for the rescheduled Tuesday night trip to Sale on 2 April, which always promised to pose a tricky test of Bath's renewed championship challenge and turned out to be a night when the irresistible force was denied by an immovable object. Bath monopolised possession and territorial advantage in a scoreless second half, to an extent that it seemed impossible for Sale to survive. But thanks to some incredible defensive heroics they did just that, eventually winning a titanic forward battle 11-5 to crush Bath's title hopes in the Heywood Road mud.

It was undoubtedly one of the most frustrating matches I saw Bath play, but Sale, who went into the game on a high, having beaten Harlequins to reach the Pilkington Cup final the previous Saturday, deserved full credit for a marvellous rearguard action.

With wind advantage they dictated the early pace, Simon Mannix putting them ahead with a penalty before a well worked try by winger Tom Beim made it 8-0 after an opening quarter of virtual one-way traffic.

Richard Webster then forced his way over for a try after Bath drove through from a lineout, and although Mannix added a further penalty, the Sale lead looked fragile as Bath came out for the second period with a strong wind at their backs.

As the pressure on Sale began to mount, Bath pounded the

home line, their pack driving all before them, and looked certain to score on several occasions, only to be denied by some desperate last-ditch tackling. But still the champions refused to vary their tactics, wingers Sleightholme and Adebayo hardly seeing a pass all night.

Midway through the second half Graham Dawe went off with a broken thumb which ruled him out for the rest of the season, and the longer the game went on the greater Bath's frustration became and the more inevitable their defeat. Sale soaked up everything the Bath forwards threw at them and came back for more, while one flash of Jeremy Guscott magic just before the final whistle summed up Bath's misery. Slipping a tackle in his own 22, Guscott exploded into acres of space, but when he looked for support none was available and Bath's last chance melted away.

The match seemed to sum up Bath's ill-starred season and, as the realisation sank in that their last trophy opportunity had all but vanished, it turned into a night of bitter disillusion and some frank and critical analysis from supporters and players alike. Along with the rest of the press corps, I waited for Andy Robinson or Clive Woodward to turn up for the post-match conference, but there was no sign of either for over an hour, and the reaction from the team, as they emerged from the dressing room, spoke volumes for their opinion of what had gone wrong.

Guscott, unusually, was among the first to vent his frustration, praising Sale's defensive display but openly questioning Bath's tactical approach in the second half, claiming that the team should return to playing the way it had done at the start of the season.

'We have got to go out and enjoy ourselves, get some spice back into the way we play the game and show our commitment to playing some decent rugby,' he insisted, in tones that left no doubt about his view of Bath's limited forward-orientated game plan. Jon Sleightholme was equally scathing about the side's failure to capitalise on a wealth of possession and chances, and try-scorer Richard Webster encapsulated the team's frustration in one sentence: 'The league is a distant dream now, and we don't deserve it on that performance,' he said. And few disgruntled Bath fans were inclined to argue with that verdict as they trudged away contemplating a long and mournful journey home.

I made one last attempt to get the reaction of Bath's coaching team, venturing into a deserted changing area to knock on Bath's dressing room door. But on opening it I quickly changed my mind. Andy Robinson, Clive Woodward and Nigel Redman looked up from their deliberations and one glance was enough for me to apologise for the intrusion and beat a retreat. Sometimes discretion is undeniably the better part of valour, and this was one such occasion. It was a bleak 180-mile drive home that night to write the obituary on Bath's quest for honours that season. Fortunately, there was compensation to come for the rest of April when they relinquished their crown in a style befitting reigning champions.

That night at Sale was a turning point for the rest of the season. It was perfectly clear that the players had no desire to play the restricted style of rugby they had embraced in recent weeks and doubtless their views were forcibly expressed on the subject. Bath had heard quite enough of 'back to basics'. It was time to throw off the shackles and show everyone what might have been. Sadly, it would be too little and just too late.

At least Jeremy Guscott had something to celebrate that night. Despite being left out of England's Five Nations plans, he was the only Bath player selected for the forthcoming British Lions tour to South Africa when the squad was announced earlier that day. It would be his third Lions tour, climaxed by the greatest moment of his rugby career – but that was still to come. For now, having voiced his views about Bath's regression in playing style, he and his shattered team-mates were faced with the challenge of restoring their dented pride in a Sunday confrontation against leaders Wasps, at the latter's new playing headquarters at Loftus Road, soccer home of Queens Park Rangers.

If one thing was predictable about the aftermath of a torrid Bath defeat, it was that the often outspoken Jon Callard would surely carry the can. And when the team was announced for the Wasps game, Callard had lost his place at full-back to Matt Perry, a 19-year-old utility back who was destined to make such an impact that, by the end of the year, he had not only established himself in Bath's first team, but had also made an astonishing international breakthrough.

It was a sign that Callard's career at the Rec was reaching a crossroads and he was not slow to appreciate the fact, as would be evidenced over the next few weeks, when he was to find himself at loggerheads with the club over his future prospects. Being dropped was nothing new for the 30-year-old full-back, who had experienced such setbacks often enough in the past and had invariably fought back to regain his place. But on this occasion the threat to his position looked serious because the talented Perry, eleven years his junior, was clearly being groomed to take over on a permanent basis. And to Callard, who had ambitions of taking up a coaching role when his playing days were over, it was not just his place in the team that mattered but his future. Like many of the Rec's seasoned veterans, he was concerned about what he would do when the time came to retire. And with opportunities at Bath looking extremely limited, he was beginning to feel insecure.

When Brian Ashton had abruptly resigned, Callard had stepped in as temporary backs coach in training. But with the arrival of Clive Woodward that opening was filled, so it was only natural that alternative opportunities might prove a temptation if they arose, as one would within days of his demotion for the Wasps game.

However, he was to show the extent of his value to Bath not just that weekend, but for a good deal longer and, being nothing if not a fighter, he knuckled down to playing for the United that Saturday, kicking three penalties in a 22-17 win over Wasps Vandals at the Rec. He also took his place on the first team bench the following day for a game which was to have a decisive bearing on the destination of that season's Courage League championship.

With the Sale disaster still rankling, Bath took the field at Loftus Road determined to throw off the shackles and play positive, fluid rugby, and that was exactly what they achieved, although in the end, as so often that season, they were left to rue a result that failed to match the performance.

In a scrappy first half Wasps edged 9-6 clear just before the interval, thanks to two Gareth Rees penalties and an Alex King dropped goal. Mike Catt, assuming Callard's kicking duties, responded with two penalties. But then a neat piece of quick thinking by Catt, who opted to run a penalty from in front of the posts, saw Guscott saunter over for an opportunist try to put Bath 11-9 ahead.

A concerted forward surge set up the move from which Guscott put Adebayo over in the corner for Bath's second try soon after the break, and with Catt receiving treatment for a cut, Callard came on to make it 18-9 with a precise touchline conversion, before resuming his seat on the bench again. Rees, whose immaculate kicking played a crucial part in Wasps' success that season, pulled them level with three penalties, but with six minutes left Guscott pounced again to score his second try and Catt's simple conversion left Bath with a 25-18 lead and victory seemingly in their grasp.

Had they clung on to it, their chances of pipping Wasps in the title race might have been revived, but in injury time fate was to decree otherwise. Callard, who had just replaced Perry, missed touch with a clearance, and as Wasps surged forward Bath were penalised for collapsing a scrum near their own line. Suddenly King found room to touch down wide out, leaving everything resting on the conversion attempt by Rees.

It was a difficult kick only a few yards in from touch and the pressure on Rees at that moment must have been immense. But the cool Canadian had not missed all afternoon and never looked like spoiling that record, the ball sailing unerringly between the posts to earn Wasps a fortunate 25-25 draw.

That Rees kick effectively spelled the the end of Bath's belated battle to retain their league title and ensured that the Rec trophy cupboard would be bereft of silverware that season. The draw left Wasps six points clear and Bath knew in their hearts that their last chance had gone. However, as Clive Woodward observed, it had been a greatly improved performance after the Sale nightmare, and with morale restored the rest of April produced a memorable finale and a feast of points to console the Rec faithful.

After so nearly beating the eventual champions, Bath faced four home games in a row before their final clash at Saracens and they made the most of them in a breathtaking return to form and confidence that vividly demonstrated their true pedigree. In the space of those four matches against Leicester, Orrell, Sale and Gloucester they amassed an astonishing 242 points while conceding just 51; more importantly, they made sure of finishing in the top four, thus guaranteeing a place in the Heineken European Cup the following season.

The return clash against an admittedly weary and injury-afflicted Leicester side saw Bath exact emphatic and ruthless revenge for the catastrophic Pilkington Cup defeat that had led to John Hall's abrupt departure only two months earlier. The Tigers, feeling the effects of a debilitating 32-30 defeat at Gloucester in midweek, held the lead for the first 37 minutes, before an Adedayo Adebayo try put Bath 13-9 in front at the interval and opened the floodgates for a remorseless second half slaughter as Bath ran riot in a display of near-flawless running rugby. Six more scintillating tries by Guscott, Mendez, Adebayo, Dan Lyle and Matt Perry, who twice sauntered over for unchallenged touchdowns, sealed a relentless 47-9 rout, and the margin could have been greater had Bath taken all their chances.

It was a champagne consolation for a Rec crowd that had hardly dared anticipate such an outcome and there was more to come as luckless Orrell were despatched 40-14 and a week later a second string Sale side suffered an 84-7 demolition, conceding a dozen tries as Bath ensured European qualification. Guscott signed off his domestic season with a two tries in that game, and with nothing left at stake, other than the runners-up placing, he was allowed to miss Bath's last two matches to rest in preparation for the Lions tour. But his absence made little difference to a rejuvenated Bath side when they hosted Gloucester in an evening encounter on the last day of April.

Richard Hill's side fought hard for most of the first half, but after that it was one-way traffic as Bath ran in a hatful of tries to seal an overwhelming 71-21 victory that left Gloucester contemplating a record mauling.

All Bath wanted, by the time they reached Saracens' new home headquarters at Enfield for their seasonal finale on the first Saturday in May, was a long rest far away from the rigours of a campaign that had begun so promisingly and had gone so sadly astray.

Under cloudless skies and on a hard bumpy pitch they competed well for half a game, establishing a 22-16 interval lead. But with Saracens inspired to greater efforts by their superstar trio of Michael Lynagh, François Pienaar and Philippe Sella, Bath eventually ran out of gas and wearily succumbed 36-29. That defeat, their sixth in the league and tenth in all matches, counted for little, as they still finished runners-up, six points behind new champions Wasps, who celebrated a tremendous achievement in style with a 42-22 victory over Harlequins. That left the latter club in third place, one point behind Bath, with Leicester a point further away.

Whatever Bath's feelings about their own blighted campaign, there was no denying that Wasps were worthy champions of rugby union's first season of professional combat. They lost only three games and dropped just seven points in 22 matches, a magnificent feat over a gruelling eight-month slog, although it helped that, as unlikely contenders, they came under less pressure than Bath and Leicester. For Leicester it was a disappointing end to a campaign that, at one stage, looked likely to be their most successful ever, but defeat by Brive in the European Cup final sapped their morale at a vital stage, and after that injuries and a demanding run-in saw them fade badly. However, they did manage to gain Pilkington Cup consolation in a dour Twickenham final against Sale which was a deserved return for their seasonal efforts.

For Bath, there was only the minor comfort of a valedictory late season resurgence to alleviate the disappointment of a fractious and traumatic year which had promised so much the previous summer. At most other clubs a seasonal return of 22 wins, two draws and ten defeats might be considered satisfactory. But not at the Rec, where trophies had come to be regarded as part of the furniture and a barren season was a prospect not to be contemplated. Runners-up in the league and two cup quarter-finals added up to unmitigated disaster in Bath eyes, after such a prolonged period of dominance, especially in comparison with that tremendous double celebration 12 months earlier.

It could easily have been so different, because in my view Bath, on their day, were still the best team in the country that season. But they simply failed to prove it consistently, when it mattered in the big games, a characteristic which had once been their forte. Too many mistakes were made from the outset that were not recognised and rectified until far too late. While rival clubs were re-examining and redefining their priorities and their business structures in response to the onset of professionalism, with the sole aim of closing the gap between them and the old amateur champions, Bath naïvely assumed that their supremacy would remain unchallenged.

They already had the best squad, the finest coaching expertise, guaranteed support and that fabled family ethos, or so they imagined. And when the financial power of Andrew Brownsword was put at their disposal, the final element for continued success was in place. After all, who in their right minds would seek to change a winning formula? But change was the key aspect that Bath got entirely wrong that season. On the field there was too much experimentation – in strategy, playing style, recruitment policy and selection procedure.

But, behind the scenes, where in hindsight it was obvious that drastic change was urgently required, there was far too little, in terms of attitude, approach, administrative infrastructure and long-term planning. Add to that the other crucial factor, a lack of sufficient time to prepare and organise an efficient business structure and strategy before that first professional season got under way, and the ingredients for Bath's unexpected downfall were already in the pot waiting to boil over.

I find it hard to apportion too much blame to the playing squad, who, gave everything that could have been asked of them and more. If anything they were more prone to let victory slip from their grasp than they had been in the past, notably in the first two league defeats by Leicester and Wasps, which lit the fuse of uncertainty and unrest that followed. But otherwise they trained and played in accordance with the highest standards of professional discipline and pride, at times in extremely trying circumstances.

The crux of Bath's problems, as Brian Ashton had put it so succinctly in that crisis meeting at Lyme Regis after the European Cup débâcle in Cardiff, was down to unreasonable expectation, poor communication and inadequate organisation. 'We are talking about being a professional club with a semi-pro organisation. We've deluded ourselves if we think we've got a professional organisation because we haven't,' he said then, and his blunt words hit the mark.

Tony Swift, in response to a question posed by Sky TV pundit and former team-mate Stuart Barnes near the end of that doomed first professional crusade, conceded that complacency and arrogance had played a part in Bath's failure to achieve the success that had been so eagerly anticipated. 'I genuinely don't feel that the other other clubs have got it right, I just think we got it more wrong,' he said. As an epitaph for a season of unparalleled upheaval and strife, it was spot on.

Meanwhile, as the rugby spotlight switched to the Southern Hemisphere in anticipation of a challenging test series in South Africa for the British Lions, and in Argentina for Jack

Rowell and his depleted England tour party, Swift and his new managerial team were already laying plans for Bath's second professional crusade. It was destined to be no less daunting, controversial and problematic than the club's initial professional venture. But this time, although much would again go wrong at the Rec, one cherished dream was to be realised in thrilling fashion against overwhelming odds.

Bath had learned some hard, but crucial, lessons from the ordeals of their professional baptism. And the next time around they would be better prepared to confront the huge challenge that lay ahead.

PART FIVE

Bath Against the World

CHAPTER ONE

Survival of the Fittest

One factor rugby union's newly professionalised players may not have fully taken on board, when they eagerly signed those lucrative contracts nearly 12 months earlier, was that now they were no longer free agents and that eventually there would be a price to pay for their new-found prosperity. Initially, not much changed from the old amateur routines. They trained more often and at different times, but for those who had given up jobs there was much more leisure, which, for some at least, posed a problem of filling their spare time. That situation did not last long. By the end of a demanding first season most of Bath's senior players were exhausted, apart from those like Andy Nicol, Graham Dawe and Eric Peters who had been injured for much of the winter.

As the game became more competitive and their club and international commitments intensified, the top players began to get stale with the constant pressure of training and competing at the highest level. And Bath, with their huge squad of quality players, were affected more than most clubs. The first signs of weariness began to show through that spring, with Jon Sleightholme a particular case in point. Having struggled to retain his club place against a formidable challenge from Jason Robinson, and after performing prominently in

England's pre-Christmas friendlies, Sleightholme had been in peak form early in the new year, scoring successive league hat-tricks and also playing well in the Five Nations Championship. But by the time he returned from the Hong Kong World Sevens tournament, in itself a gruelling test of fitness and stamina, Sleightholme was feeling the strain both physically and mentally and admitted as much to me before the season ended. What he needed was a proper rest period when it was over. But what he and half of Bath's squad were faced with was yet more competitive rugby on international tours around the globe.

Jeremy Guscott at least had a couple of games off to recuperate for the Lions tour to South Africa, but with eighteen England men on that trip, Jack Rowell selected eight Bath players in his squad of thirty for England's six-match tour to Argentina. Sleightholme, Phil de Glanville, Adedayo Adebayo and Mike Catt were the Bath backs in the party, along with forwards John Mallett, Kevin Yates, Martin Haag and Steve Ojomoh, while Nigel Redman, miraculously recovered from a knee operation, was soon called up as a replacement and then amazingly drafted into the Lions squad as injuries mounted in South Africa.

Both Federico Mendez and German Llanes were picked to play for Argentina, Mendez suffering a serious shoulder injury in the first game of the two-test series. Mallett damaged his back early on and had to be flown home, and Ojomoh aggravated a finger problem which took a long time to heal.

Meanwhile, Bath supplied three members of the Scotland party for their six-match tour of Zimbabwe and South Africa, with Eric Peters, recovered from a hand injury, and the reliable Dave Hilton joining tour captain Andy Nicol on the trip. The captaincy was a deserved accolade for Nicol after his injury-dogged season, when persistent hamstring problems and then a dislocated shoulder, incurred against England A at the end of January, kept him sidelined most of the winter. His absence had been a critical loss to Bath, who missed his strength, aggression and skill in crucial games. But he endured it all philosophically and firmly admonished me for voicing a fairly common whisper during his third spell on the sidelines that he might be injury-prone.

Nicol did a sound job for Scotland on that tour and was to do even better as Bath's new captain when Andy Robinson asked him to replace Phil de Glanville later that summer – the first time a Bath skipper had been appointed rather than elected by his fellow players, but absolutely the right choice nonetheless.

Of the other Bath players, Dan Lyle flew back to America to lead the US Eagles in a challenge series against Wales and Canada, a tournament that involved travelling huge distances across the American continent, which would affect his form and fitness when he eventually returned to the Rec to prepare for the new season. Nathan Thomas joined the Welsh squad for that series, while Bath also supplied four players for the England A tour of Australia, two of whom, Matt Perry and Andy Long were to make full international debuts against Australia at Twickenham in the autumn, while Chris Horsman and Richard Bryan would break into Bath's team within months.

That meant half of Bath's squad were playing competitive rugby, mostly on bone-hard pitches, for a good part of the close season, and risking serious injury, which in several cases was the inevitable outcome. With so much valuable talent in action thousands of miles away, it must have been a worry for Tony Swift and Andy Robinson. But they had other important matters on their mind as they sat down to review their policy and playing requirements for the 1997/98 campaign.

Among the concerns uppermost in Swift's mind had been the need to revamp Bath's staff and management structure to create a more professional organisation. He had already made a start by snapping up the highly rated Jim Blair as the club's full-time fitness consultant. Blair, a 62-year old Scot, had lived and worked in New Zealand for over three decades, building a reputation for producing superbly fit rugby squads for the powerful Auckland district side and the All Blacks, who he had prepared for two World Cup tournaments in 1987 and 1991.

Curiously for someone who enjoys the occasional cigarette (an apparent weakness that endeared him to me, an habitual smoker), he was an acknowledged all-round fitness specialist, who had devised training programmes for four Kiwi America's Cup yachting challenges and also prepared New Zealand's international hockey teams.

I considered him a real breath of fresh air at the Rec. At Bath's recently refurbished Lambridge training ground, to which the club would return for training purposes after using Bath University for most of their daytime squad sessions the previous winter, he was approachable, articulate and highly professional in outlook and attention to detail, and was welcomed by the squad, although his novel and demanding fitness schedules would test the players' durability and stamina to the limit in the build-up to the season. Blair was uncompromising in ensuring his standards were met. But he soon came to admire the squad's positive attitude and adaptability. And despite being an outsider, he was quickly accepted as a valuable member of the Bath rugby family.

Another popular recruit was Gareth Adams as Bath's director of youth development, with responsibility for liaison with local schools and colleges to find and develop local rugby talent. His career as a hooker with Bath had been ended by a serious neck injury at the age of 26, just when he was making a real impact at first-team level the previous autumn. His appointment demonstrated that the club was still concerned for its loyal servants, and it could not have gone to a nicer or more unassuming sportsman.

Two more new faces were introduced in June, Andrew Brown arriving as marketing and commercial manager and Liz Pritchard as media and communications manager. Liz, a cheerful, attractive public relations consultant and former Gloucester fan (no less), took over much of Ken Johnstone's workload, although Ken continued his press liaison duties on match days while helping her settle into her new role.

Both these recruits came under the wing of commercial director Stephen Hands, whose sponsorship and marketing brief was becoming increasingly important as the club struggled to establish itself on a sound financial footing. But it was apparent that the crucial factor in achieving that aim was Bath's ability to maximise its income on home match days. That meant something drastic was needed to improve revenue from home attendances, but prolonged negotiations with Bath and North East Somerset District Council over increasing the capacity of the Rec were making scant progress, largely owing to strong resistance from local residents.

The club was still reluctant to take the major decision to leave the Rec and move to a new stadium. Apart from the problems of finding a potential site and gaining planning approval, it would involve massive financial investment at a time when the viability of the professional club game was still in doubt and virtually every EPRUC club was running at a sizeable loss.

The dilemma presented Swift and the Bath board with a puzzle to which there appeared no logical solution. The product was exciting, finance was available to improve the squad and the potential crowd support was sufficient to make the business viable if, as they hoped, the game began to take off as a major attraction. But they were faced by the reality that the Rec was council-owned, and its tenure governed by a set of covenants restricting its use and development. And opposition to their plans to turn it into a top-class stadium from local residents was intense and organised.

Improving the Rec to a profitable capacity was undoubtedly Bath's preferred option at that time because a new stadium represented a massive long-term gamble. But Swift was aware of the need to retain the club's loyal supporters, who for years had put up with inadequate facilities and poor viewing, which had been a constant source of complaint, especially when the ground was full to capacity for big games.

Bath had felt no pressure to solve such problems in the amateur days, when admission prices had been stable, big crowds were guaranteed because of the quality of rugby on offer, and overheads were controllable. But professionalism was a different kettle of fish. And faced with a daunting salary bill, escalating costs and a customer base that was becoming more selective and value conscious, the club had to find some way of improving the situation for all concerned.

So, in a summer close season that was all too brief, Bath initiated a short-term compromise plan to carry out limited redevelopment that would increase revenue, not upset residents unduly and placate their fans by drastically improving viewing facilities all around the ground. The plan actually reduced the Rec's capacity by about 300, but it involved increasing seated accommodation to around 5000 seats, and an appropriate price increase meant that revenue would rise appreciably, if not yet sufficiently to make a dramatic impact on the club's financial viability.

In the circumstances it was the best option available. Work around the ground began in July, under the scrutiny of operations director David Jenkins, and continued apace, right up to the start of the season. By that time the Rec, while not exactly transformed, at least resembled a reasonable first-class rugby venue.

And for the fans the improvement in viewing facilities would be appreciated, despite the extra cost. It also demonstrated that their concerns were being considered and acted upon, which was another plus factor in Bath's favour as the club sought to secure its future in a city that had tradition, but not size, on its side in the harsh commercial world that rugby had embraced.

With limited ground improvements under way and new staffing arrangements almost complete, Swift and his coaches turned their attention to player recruitment, where the club's requirements were easier to define but no less difficult to fulfil in a highly competitive market place. Top of the priority list was the need to assemble a squad capable of winning trophies in the season ahead and, above all else, the Holy Grail - the Heineken European Cup.

The French sides Toulouse and Brive had captured the honours in the first two years of competition and Bath's long-held desire to prove themselves the best club in Europe and become the first British side to win the trophy still burned fiercely. That target had been Bath's key ambition twelve months earlier when John Hall and Brian Ashton had assembled what was to be regarded as an oversized squad, and the desire to conquer Europe had, if anything, intensified – although this time around the club had wisely learned not to proclaim it so publicly.

To achieve it would require meticulous planning, judicious transfer investment and astute management of resources as well as a large slice of luck. And, in deciding their recruitment priorities, Bath chose to concentrate on quality rather than quantity, while an increasing need for financial restraint forced the club to cut the size of the squad from 36 contracted professionals to between 25 and 28, hopefully without reducing its effectiveness. This time there would be no expensive loan signings from rugby league or gambling on unknown quantities. The potentially weak areas within the squad were identified and a short list of targets drawn up, although this was subject to change through the summer.

The initial shopping list included a hooker, a lock forward and a scrum-half. And the three players originally targeted were England stars Mark Regan, Simon Shaw and Kyran Bracken, all from neighbours Bristol, who had avoided relegation but were struggling financially and inevitably faced problems in retaining their top performers.

Theoretically Bath still had four hookers on their books, but Federico Mendez was expected to be out of action for weeks, if not months, with his shoulder problems and Graham Dawe, enjoying a deserved benefit year, had announced his retirement after twelve successful seasons at the Rec. At nearly 38, the Cornishman was still a fearsome competitor, but he had been dogged by injury throughout the previous season. When

Mendez was injured there was a brief period when it seemed Dawe would be recalled by Bath, who had retained his registration, but the signing of Regan eased that situation and it seemed he had played his last game at the Rec.

Happily for Dawe's many admirers, he eventually surprised everyone by extending his career for another swansong season with Sale (where he had broken his thumb in his last game for Bath), the Manchester-based club snapping him up just a day before the 15 August registration deadline. Typically, 'Dawesy' was concerned that the move might be deemed disloyal by some of his fervent fans at the Rec, thousands of whom turned out for his farewell testimonial match at Bristol City's Ashton Gate stadium early in August. But few begrudged him the chance of a further share of the professional pot. He had earned it, having put up with that marathon travelling routine over the years in Bath's cause. And he certainly gave Sale good value as back up to his old adversary, Steve Dymond, as he would prove with a rousing display against his old club late the following season.

In the event Regan, whose ambition to join Bath was not exactly secret, was the only one of the Bristol trio to arrive at the Rec. Bristol were reluctant to let him join their arch-rivals and unhappy about the transfer, but his contract had only a year to run. Rather than keep an unhappy player and then see him depart for nothing, Bristol realised the weakness of their position and allowed Regan to move.

Shaw, a 6ft 9in giant who had made an impressive start to his international career with England the previous season, showed little interest in Bath and signed instead for the new champions Wasps, while Bracken moved to Saracens, briefly recapturing the England scrum-half berth before a persistent shoulder injury deprived him of it again.

Bath were linked with Cardiff's Welsh international scrum-half Rob Howley, but that interest never got off the ground and, with Regan's arrival delayed, it was an openside flanker, Russell Earnshaw, who became Andy Robinson's first major signing, the former West Hartlepool player arriving just before training recommenced in earnest under Jim Blair on 10 June.

Earnshaw found his first training session at the Rec an eye-opening and lung-bursting experience, as did many of his new team-mates, or at least those who were not still on international duty abroad. I shall never forget watching Martin Haag go through the pain barrier that morning, his face contorted with effort and his shirt dripping with sweat just hours after flying home from England's tour of Argentina, on which he had performed with distinction, playing in both tests to earn his first England caps at the age of 28. After almost giving up hope of getting the call, Haag had earned the right to have his photograph hung among a long line of famous predecessors in the Rec's international hall of fame. He was overjoyed about that accolade, especially as, having played in two tests, he could never be described as a one-cap wonder.

Many of Bath's touring stars missed that initial introduction to the Blair fitness regime. But their turn would soon come in an intense pre-season build-up that would herald Bath's first major crisis, waiting to unfold with potentially disastrous consequences for a season that was still more than two months away. Those ten weeks of the so-called close season were to be as eventful and momentous as any equivalent period in the previous eighteen months and would change the lives of many of the household names associated with Bath, England and the British Lions, as rugby's explosion continued to erupt with dramatic consequences.

The first murmurings of discord in what had until then been a relatively productive and harmonious summer had been sounded on England's Argentina tour, which after one early setback had looked to be flourishing. After trouncing Argentina A 58-17, Phil de Glanville led an England side containing seven Bath players into the first test and emerged triumphant after a scintillating 46-20 victory, highlighted by two tries from Adedayo Adebayo and a brilliant fly-half display by Mike Catt, who contributed a try, five conversions and two penalties.

Within hours of that success Jack Rowell's plans were seriously disrupted, as first Catt was called up by the Lions to replace Paul Grayson, and then Nigel Redman, who had enjoyed a superb test return, found himself on a plane to South Africa after the Scotland lock Doddie Weir fell victim to a vicious stamping by Mpumalanga's Marius Bosman and suffered serious knee-ligament damage.

Jon Callard flew out to Argentina at short notice to replace Catt, but was not selected for the second test, which saw England slump to a disappointing 33-13 defeat, a result which took the gloss off an otherwise successful trip. But, much to Rowell's chagrin, England's needs were deemed secondary to those of the Lions who, despite mounting injury problems that robbed them of the services of key performers such as Rob Howley and Ieuan Evans, were beginning to warm up impressively for their daunting three-test series against the Springboks.

Back home Dan Lyle was voted supporters' player of the season; Andy Nicol, Eric Peters and Dave Hilton flew out on Scotland's African tour; and John Mallett heard the good news that his back problems did not require surgery. But for the next three weeks the spotlight was firmly on the Lions – and Jeremy Guscott in particular.

The Lions went into the first test at Cape Town's famous Newlands stadium on 21 June as rank underdogs, their chances being dismissed by the local rugby fraternity. But they produced a performance and a victory that would stun their South Africa critics, and many at home as well. Displaying remarkable defensive resilience and aided by the lethal place kicking of Neil Jenkins, they came from behind to produce two tries in the last seven minutes by Matt Dawson and Alan Tait which shattered the tiring Springboks. The outcome was a famous 25-16 victory that laid the foundations for a momentous series triumph.

A week later at Kings Park, Durban, the Lions were forced

to defend with even greater fortitude against a ferocious assault from a much more powerful South African pack that threatened to smash their heroic resistance. But once again, although tries rarely looked on the cards, they took every chance that arose and with just three minutes remaining were on the brink of sealing the series with the score level at 15-15, Jenkins landing five majestic penalties.

What occurred next will remain forever enshrined in the annals of rugby union folklore and will surely stand as Guscott's supreme moment in a long and illustrious career with Bath, England and the British Lions. Breaking out of their own half, the Lions drove downfield only to be thwarted by some desperate Springbok defence, but Irish lock Jeremy Davidson set up clean possession, Dawson rifled an accurate pass and in a trice Guscott steadied himself, took aim with his right boot and let fly a drop-kick that sailed unerringly between the posts.

Those agonising closing seconds must have felt like hours to the exhausted Lions. But there was no response from the shattered Springboks. A miraculous 18-15 victory had clinched an historic series win against all odds, and Guscott was the undisputed hero of the hour, as the ecstatic tour party celebrated their triumph in style.

It was the outstanding sporting highlight of that eventful summer, but the euphoria was to be cruelly short-lived. And for Guscott, and Bath, it would be replaced by pain and adversity that would blight their progress for months.

Seven days later in a meaningless third and final test at Ellis Park, Johannesburg, South Africa exacted some measure of consolatory revenge over a weary and unmotivated Lions side 35-16 to round off a memorable series.

Mike Catt was selected for his Lions debut in place of an injured Gregor Townsend, but he had little chance to shine in a one-sided encounter. And Guscott broke his arm in a freak tackle that put his rugby career in jeopardy and left Bath's plans in turmoil. Guscott did not reappear all year, leaving Bath to cope without him. The problems were already piling up at the Rec and there were still six weeks to go before a ball was kicked in anger in a second professional rugby season that was to be every bit as chaotic as the first.

As Guscott flew home to his family, and a first meeting with new daughter Saskia, his wife Jayne having given birth a week before the first test, Phil de Glanville was urging Jack Rowell's critics to cut out the sniping, and Andy Robinson hinted he was looking for two new players.

The July sun was hotting up and there would be no respite from its rays for Bath's hard-pressed players, nor from the rigours of an international tour circus that traversed the globe that summer. Soon after the Lions jetted out of South Africa, England were in Australia for a one-off test, and on the eve of the game Jack Rowell was coming under fire from a familiar quarter, his predecessor, Dick Best urging the RFU to appoint a full-time coach for the national side.

It was soon revealed that they were already seeking Rowell's successor, reports circulating that Auckland coach Graham Henry had already been approached, while other names openly touted included Northampton and Lions coach Ian McGeechan and Leicester's Australian World Cup-winning coach Bob Dwyer.

Meanwhile, both Jon Sleightholme and Kevin Yates had been called into the squad for the game against the Aussies, which saw a jaded and lacklustre England side beaten 25-6, de Glanville himself turning in a lifeless performance and missing two crucial tackles that led to Australian tries.

Two days later, Rowell, who was unwilling to forsake his extensive business interests to coach England on a full-time basis, announced his desire to guide the side through to the 1999 World Cup. But he was clearly under pressure in a political power game that was beyond his control.

At the same time Matt Perry and Andy Long played for England A in a 27-7 defeat by their Australian counterparts, while prop Chris Horsman missed the game with a leg injury. Who could have predicted then that the first two would share a debut for the full England side four months hence, and the unfortunate Horsman would be facing a terrifying battle against cancer.

Fate can be cruelly fickle at times and it wasn't about to do Bath any favours, although for a few days there were glimmers of encouraging news to briefly raise the gloom of defeat abroad and an increasing injury crisis at home. The first item of news was good from Bath's point of view, but not necessarily for Jon Callard, who had set his mind on leaving the club to take the vacant post of director of rugby at ambitious third division Worcester. Instead, the job went to England's assistant coach and former Leicester stalwart Les Cusworth. Despite a protracted pursuit by Worcester's millionaire chairman Mike Robins, Bath had steadfastly refused all offers for Callard, who still had two years of his contract to run. Callard was bitterly disappointed at the time and complained about the club's intransigent attitude in a rugby magazine. But Tony Swift considered Worcester's offer was insufficient to compensate Bath for his loss and was in no mood to relent, a stance he, and Callard, would be thankful for one day in the not too distant future.

Further proof that Bath meant business in pursuit of the club's ambitions came to light the following day when it was revealed that London-based stars Victor Ubogu, Steve Ojomoh and Adedayo Adebayo would be required to move to Bath to make it easier for them to fulfil their training and playing requirements.

The propitious omens remained constant for a while longer, with encouraging news that Bath's other London-based player, Simon Geoghegan, had again been given the go-ahead to commence full-time training. But the Ireland winger was soon destined to be disappointed for the umpteenth time as his troublesome toe joints failed to take the strain and three weeks later he was contemplating yet another complicated operation.

Then on 24 July, it was revealed that Bristol had relented and Mark Regan was set join Bath. And within a week, on the same day that Andy Nicol was confirmed as Bath's new captain, Regan paraded for the cameras at the Rec and pledged his future to his new club.

Two days later the squad got together to bid farewell to Graham Dawe at his Ashton Gate testimonial against a Fran Cotton Home Nations XV, a game that I was sad to miss owing to a prior commitment to Bath Cricket Club's annual tour to Blackpool. That venture ended abruptly when I discovered that my car had been broken into and vandalised. But it was a minor disaster compared to the crisis that was breaking back at the Rec when I returned to Windsor Bridge that August, the *Chronicle*'s staggered transfer from Westgate Street having been completed late in July.

With a lone friendly game at Newbury only days away and their opening Allied Dunbar Premiership One clash against promoted Newcastle due in less than a fortnight, Bath's injury problems had suddenly taken a concerted and drastic turn for the worse. Just about every member of the squad had been afflicted by one problem or another over a hectic summer on tour or in training. Even Tony Swift had managed to pull a muscle on a rare training foray. But now the injury crisis was acute and, frustratingly, the recovery process from this litany of ailments seemed unaccountably slow.

Apart from a long term absentee list that included Guscott, Mendez, Geoghegan, Mallett and Ojomoh, nearly everyone seemed to have muscle damage in some degree, mainly in the groin or hamstring region, which led some sages to wonder whether Jim Blair's new routines might have stretched the squad's fitness beyond breaking point. Andy Nicol, Jon Callard, Dan Lyle, Jon Sleightholme and Andy Long were all trying to ward off leg-muscle injuries. Bath's real crisis was on the wings where Geoghegan was ruled out long-term, Adebayo was likely to be out for some time with a stress fracture of the shin, and Sleightholme was troubled by a niggling groin strain. With those three international fliers crocked and no other winger of first-team standard available, Bath were facing a major problem, with only two league games, against Newcastle and Harlequins, before the European Cup group matches got under way. It was imperative that some way of solving the dilemma was found, and urgently.

Swift and Bath's management team came up with a two-pronged plan that involved scouring the transfer market for a couple of quality players, while at the same time recruiting two short-term replacement wingers who might see the club through the opening months if the efforts to complete major signings fell through.

One possible recruit was already being lined up. Brian Lima, the 25-year-old Auckland winger who had played for Western Samoa in the last two World Cup tournaments, was highly rated by Jim Blair, who knew him from his time with Auckland. Lima was keen to come to Bath, but just when it seemed his signing was cut and dried, the New Zealand RFU ruled it out because the Samoan was under contract to them for another 12 months and they were unwilling to release him.

The other target was Scotland and British Lions fly-half Gregor Townsend, who like Mike Catt could also play in the centre, but was said to be unsettled at Northampton because he wanted to play fly-half and the Saints preferred Paul Grayson in that role. Cardiff were Bath's main rivals for his signature, but although Townsend talked to both clubs, neither managed to lure him away from Franklin's Gardens, a disappointed Andy Robinson claiming that the Scot had not fancied the prospect of competing with Catt for the number ten shirt at the Rec.

The collapse of both deals was revealed the day before the friendly at Newbury. But fortunately Bath had also acted quickly to bring in two relatively unknown wingers as a stop-gap measure if attempts to beat that Friday's transfer deadline proved fruitless.

Brian Roche, a stocky 22-year-old Irishman, whose club rugby had been played for Sunday's Well, an obscure club near Cork, but who had played for Munster and also been part of the Irish Under-21 squad, was given a three-month trial. And Michael Wood, a promising right wing who had scored four tries on the England Under-21 tour of Australia that summer, was hastily signed on a month's loan from West Hartlepool, for whom he had already made around 30 appearances.

Roche made an instant impact by scoring two tries within ten minutes of coming on as a second half replacement in Bath's erratic 57-31 at Newbury that Thursday evening. And he would serve the club well over the next month, earning an extension to his trial period before eventually returning to Ireland, while Wood also made a useful contribution before returning north at the end of his loan period.

While I was at Newbury watching Bath look superb in attack and poor in defence, Tony Swift and Andy Robinson were completing a sensational transfer coup just hours before the deadline elapsed in a last-ditch swoop that gave the club a huge morale boost and provided a real fillip to their trophy ambitions.

Ieuan Cenydd Evans, one of Welsh rugby's greatest wingers for over a decade, had agreed to sign a two-year contract to play at the Rec, after twelve seasons with Llanelli. At 33, he was getting close to the veteran stage, but no one could question his quality or his pedigree. Welsh captain on 28 occasions, Evans had scored a record 33 tries in 71 appearances for his country and only Jeremy Guscott could equal his three British Lions tours, the latest of which had been with Guscott in South Africa.

The only problem was that, like Guscott, he was out of action, having suffered a bad groin injury in the first test victory over the Springboks which had forced him to return home. But although he would miss the first month of the season, just having him in the squad was a huge bonus to Bath. Small and wiry, Evans might not have looked too impressive at first glance. And his injury history was frightening, including a broken leg, five shoulder dislocations and a horrific ankle dislocation. But Tony Swift and Andy Robinson were only too aware of his calibre and had been prepared to back their judgement with hard cash, knowing they had every chance of being repaid in full in the major confrontations to come. As indeed they would be on one particular day in January when the chips were down.

For Evans and cash-strapped Llanelli the move made sound financial sense and the opportunity to compete at the highest level in the Allied Dunbar Premiership and the Heineken European Cup was just the kind of challenge he would relish. His arrival could not have been better timed. It lifted the club out of its injury gloom and sent a buzz of anticipation through the ranks of Bath's regular supporters, who must have wondered when the catalogue of bad news would ever end.

They were also relieved to hear that one of their favourite sons, Jon Callard, had set aside his disappointment at missing out on the Worcester opportunity and pledged his full support for a club he described as one of the best in the world. He was used to setbacks at Bath, but had never let them down and his renewed loyalty was another plus factor in their eyes.

Now it was time for the family to close ranks and meet the challenges that were about to arise. And this time there would be no unguarded talk about winning everything on offer or lame excuses over injury woes, especially from Andy Robinson, who named his rookie recruits Brian Roche and Michael Wood in the side to face Newcastle. A host of familiar faces were still not fit to play, but Newcastle would still come up against a Bath team containing no fewer than twelve internationals in a contest that would serve as a litmus test for their own Premiership One ambitions.

Meanwhile, three days before serious rugby action resumed in earnest, Jack Rowell resigned as England's coach, the timing of his departure leaving the RFU with egg on its face and apparently no one to replace him, their surreptitious attempts to line up a successor having been met with rejection. However, Rowell's departure was to have a significant impact on Bath's already disrupted campaign plans. For Clive Woodward, the Newcastle encounter was to herald his exit from the Rec, six months after coming to the aid of a club in dire crisis. Not that much had changed.

After the game, Woodward confirmed that he had been approached and would meet RFU playing committee officials Don Rutherford and Bill Beaumont the following week to discuss the situation. However, he stressed he had not been offered a job, had promised Bath he would stay until the end of the season, and intended to stick to that promise.

Not surprisingly, Tony Swift was more than disturbed to hear rumours of Woodward's impending departure. According to him, no one at Twickenham had bothered to consult him or the club about it. At one stage it seemed that both Woodward and Andy Robinson might depart. Certainly, in the final episode of 'The Rugby Club', Swift spoke of both men being approached without his knowledge and insisted that the RFU would not get much co-operation from Bath until it was prepared to talk to the club.

In the event, it was another three weeks before an embarrassing bout of musical chairs was finally resolved. Woodward's appointment as England's new full-time coach was confirmed on 16 September, with Roger Uttley installed as team manager and Sale boss John Mitchell appointed to coach the England forwards.

Andy Robinson stayed with Bath, where he was soon to be joined by a familiar face as his new backs coach. And the RFU agreed to pay Bath compensation of £150,000 for the loss of Woodward's services.

For Phil de Glanville, who had publicly criticised the way Jack Rowell had been treated, Woodward's elevation was to signal the end of his reign as England captain, and also cost him his place in the team. And with Andy Nicol assuming his captaincy duties at the Rec, a year that had begun so brightly was about to end despondently. It had been a hugely demanding and fraught period with which de Glanville had coped admirably. But with all that had happened he was probably relieved to get out of the firing line and return to the relative tranquillity of being just a professional player and family man.

Clive Woodward was not the only departure from the Rec

that summer. Ian Sanders and Neil McCarthy had already joined Richard Hill at Gloucester, and two more high-profile players would be leaving before long as Bath sought to reduce the size of the squad and the wage bill.

One recent appointment would prove extremely short-lived. Ian Jones, who was completing a masters degree in sports medicine at Nottingham University, had become Bath's first full-time physiotherapist early in July, replacing the familiar team of ladies who had treated the club's injured players for several years.

I had interviewed him for a feature in the *Chronicle*'s usual pre-season supplement, when he stated that he would strongly resist pressure to speed up the recovery process of injured players or pass them fit before they were ready to return to action. Shortly after that Ian Jones and Bath parted company. Apparently he resigned, but his sudden exit was not a subject on which the club had any wish to expand, then or later. In his place the ladies were quietly restored to duty, and Bath's injury crisis gradually eased, although not before a controversial reverse in the opening game of the 1997/98 campaign had put the club back under intense pressure. Another rugby season was under way, and Bath were back on a second crusade to conquer the world.

CHAPTER TWO

A Road Littered with Casualties

There was little doubt about which game Sky Televison would select for live coverage on the opening day of the Allied Dunbar Premiership One season, the new sponsors having taken over from the brewers, Courage, who had withdrawn after a decade of support for rugby union. Newly promoted Newcastle, launched into the top flight by Sir John Hall's immense wealth, against the once all-conquering overlords of the English domestic game, was a natural and intriguing attraction, and the Rec, still recognisable, but greatly improved from a spectating viewpoint, was guaranteed a full-house for the big kick-off.

Everyone was keen to discover just how competitive the new Premiership season was likely to be, and a contest between the former champions and a rising force in English rugby looked likely to provide an ideal gauge. But when the two teams ran out it was evident that a true comparison was not on the cards. Newcastle, after an uneventful preparation, were virtually at full strength, while Bath's line-up, especially in the backs, revealed the full extent of the ravages of the club's pre-season injury blight.

The Falcons fielded a strong pack, with Irish internationals

Nick Popplewell and Ross Nesdale bolstering the front row, England's Garath Archer and Scotland giant Doddie Weir (happily recovered from his Lions tour injury) at lock, and the aggressive Dean Ryan and the Samoan flanker Pat Lam, who would be voted player of the year that season, in a mobile, combative back row. They also possessed immense experience outside the scrum, with Gary Armstrong and Rob Andrew at half-back, Va'aiga Tuigamala and Lions tourist Alan Tait at centre and Tony Underwood and former Bath player Jim Naylor on the wings, while at full-back Tim Stimpson had only recently made a promising England breakthrough.

In contrast, Bath were without a dozen internationals, although they were still able to field a strong enough pack to leave three more – Dave Hilton, Nathan Thomas and Mark Regan – on the bench. Gary French was preferred at hooker, while, in the injury absence of Dan Lyle and Steve Ojomoh, Richard Webster and newcomer Russell Earnshaw packed down alongside Eric Peters in the back row.

Bath's back line, however, was barely recognisable with novice wingers Roche and Wood on the flanks, youngster Jon Pritchard alongside de Glanville at centre, and Matt Perry a late susbstitute at full-back for Callard, whose thigh strain had again ruled him out. The inexperienced Charlie Harrison had also been drafted in to replace Andy Nicol, who was again hit by hamstring trouble.

Viewed in that context it was bound to be a daunting test of Bath's depleted resources and the fact that they only lost a controversial game to a late try by replacement wing Stuart Legg, having played the final forty-five minutes with fourteen men, said much for the courage and resilience of their patched-up side.

The major flashpoint that signalled Bath's downfall was the 38th minute sending-off of Nathan Thomas, who had been on the pitch for only three minutes, as a replacement while Webster was receiving treatment for a cut. But in a fateful lapse of discipline Thomas aimed a stray boot at Stimpson who was preventing release at a ruck, and referee Steve

Lander sent him off. Webster was all set to return by then, but the dismissal meant that was ruled out and, already 6-0 down to two Stimpson penalties, Bath suddenly found themselves with a mountain to climb, although they fought back to within inches of scaling it.

Mike Catt cut the deficit with an early second half penalty, but then a powerful burst by Tuigamala and Stimpson's simple conversion put Newcastle 13-3 up, before Catt added a second penalty and Bath began to rally. Matt Perry's incisive break and searing pace earned him a superb try, Catt's conversion tied the score at 13-13 with 14 minutes left, and then Bath pounded the Newcastle 22, despite their numerical disadvantage.

But, just as it seemed they might snatch victory or at worst a draw, Newcastle broke away, stole two lineouts, and suddenly Andrew and Tuigamala combined to send Legg over behind the posts, Stimpson's easy conversion sealing a 20-13 win that set them on course for a successful championship challenge.

But for Bath's injury problems and Thomas's dismissal, which earned him a 60-day ban, Newcastle would almost certainly have lost that opening encounter. Instead, they went from strength to strength, while Bath's defeat left them staring down a gun barrel, with only one more league game before the European Cup qualifying pool series.

For Andy Robinson, Thomas's indiscipline could not have been less timely. After the game he was furious at the way the game had been handled by the match officials, particularly the two touch judges, claiming that a Catt penalty had been ruled out when it had in fact gone over, while conversely one of Stimpson's kicks was flagged as good when it appeared to drift wide. Whatever the merits of his argument, the unalterable fact remained that with one match gone Bath, who had never lost their first two league games, were facing the prospect of their worst start to a league season ever and Thomas's rush of blood had merely intensified their chronic manpower crisis.

Losing that opening game was potentially disastrous. But, by this time, adversity and Bath were familiar travelling companions and the steadfast way that beleaguered squad responded to the challenge over the next crucial six-week period was illuminating. In fact, it wasn't a case of just six weeks, because the sheer scale and frequency of the setbacks and challenges that Bath were forced to confront from that moment on would multiply dramatically over the next six months.

On the playing side the situation could hardly have been worse. Bath were resigned to the fact that many of their Premiership rivals had caught up in terms of squad strength and performance. A rapid increase in the influx of top-class foreign stars had seen to that.

In their amateur days Bath could count Leicester, Wasps and Harlequins as probably the only serious obstacles to trophy success. Not any more. The Premiership was now full of ambitious clubs with abundant resources, and, with the onset of European involvement, the French were invariably difficult to beat, the top Welsh sides always had been and the Italians, Scots and Irish were intent on making their mark. Just twelve months earlier Bath fans could still point to fixtures regarded as second rate. And back then the club had not encountered anything like the injury spate it now faced. To cap it all, Clive Woodward's impending departure meant that the coaching set-up was to be disrupted for the third time in nine months.

The overall scenario was not exactly inspiring as Bath prepared for a trip to the Stoop on the last Saturday in August, where they had performed so poorly and lost in January. And the team news was hardly encouraging. Andy Nicol's hopes of a return had been dashed, while Callard was forced to drop out again, and although Lyle and Sleightholme were back in action, the latter was still unhappy about his fitness, and it showed in a strangely ineffective display which would have consequences as the season progressed.

What Bath needed against Harlequins was for someone to

213

produce an outstanding individual performance. And they were given that by fly-half Richard Butland, who was brought in only because Catt's groin strain allowed him to run, but not kick.

Too gifted to leave out, Catt switched to centre alongside Phil de Glanville, with Perry continuing at full-back. But it was Butland who stole the limelight as Bath fought back from the brink of a second league defeat to snatch an amazing victory. Butland kicked five penalties after Quins appeared to be taking control of a fluctuating contest. And then, with Bath trailing 20-15 in injury time, he first converted a penalty try to snatch the lead and then added a further try to seal a match-winning 22-point haul.

It was a spectacular solo contribution that raised the side's morale after that Newcastle mishap, and he played well the following week at Pontypridd. But it wouldn't be long before Catt took over again and the unlucky Butland was forced to resign himself to another long stint on the bench. He would endure a strange and wildly fluctuating winter, encompassing odd periods of inactivity, injury, international prominence for England A (which took him close to a full cap at one stage), and eventually a spell on the transfer list. But by then nothing surprised the 26-year-old Butland who was used to ups and downs at the Rec.

Had they succumbed to Harlequins that afternoon, Bath would not only have been left contemplating their worst league start ever but would have gone into their European Cup Pool C games at a low ebb. Instead, after that incredible injury-time flourish, they went on to savour an unbeaten September, winning all four games, albeit by narrow margins, and virtually ensuring a place in the quarter-finals, where they were to be given the chance to avenge a defeat that still awoke painful memories at the Rec.

It was to be a momentous and eventful month, not just for Bath, but in other quarters as well: a month of new beginnings, new faces and changing circumstances, and by the time it was over nothing would be quite the same for a good many people connected with the club, myself included.

The commencement of a new European adventure was just a week away, and the Heineken Cup was beckoning Bath's convalescing warriors into the breach once again, with a string of six consecutive Pool C matches in what was deemed to be the hardest qualifying group.

Twenty teams from England, France, Italy, Wales, Scotland and Ireland were lined up in five groups of four to meet on a home and away basis (a variation on the previous year when the teams only met once), with the side finishing top qualifying automatically for the last eight, accompanied by the winners of play-offs between the five runners-up and the third-placed side with the best record. Bath, drawn in Pool C with Pontypridd, their conquerors 12 months earlier, the reigning champions Brive, who had beaten Leicester 28-9 in the previous year's final, and Borders, reputed to be the strongest of the Scottish district sides, were only too aware that this time there would be no easy games.

Bath's programme began with two away games at Pontypridd and Borders, followed by Brive and Borders at home, and then Brive away, before a final pool clash against the Welsh champions at the Rec. It was obvious that a winning start was essential and that meant beating Pontypridd at Sardis Road, where Bath had surrendered in a muddy nightmare the season before.

Bath had just been installed as tournament favourites by the bookies, which was ludicrous considering their injury plight. But perhaps they knew something Tony Swift and Andy Robinson were unaware of. Oddly enough, I had a feeling this would be Bath's year. And even when, much later on, it seemed the fates had conspired to wreck their aspirations, it was a faith that never died. Somehow, I just knew it had to be.

Andy Robinson, meanwhile, had more tangible considerations on his mind. Slowly but surely his injured troops were limping back to fitness and he wanted to ensure they were in the right mood to atone for the misery of Bath's last visit to Pontypridd. His selection options, however, were still limited.

And with Phil de Glanville reluctant to continue as acting captain in Nicol's absence, he needed to find a leader capable of inspiring the level of passion required to beat Pontypridd on their own soil. The player he eventually chose was Jon Callard, recovered from his thigh strain, who had led Bath to victory in several European games the previous season, and Robinson clearly felt he could do so again.

There were other surprises in Bath's line-up that Saturday. Jon Sleightholme was dropped after his lifeless performance at the Stoop. Matt Perry moved to the right flank to make way for Callard, while Brian Roche retained his place on the left wing. At scrum half, Robinson took a gamble by leaving out Charlie Harrison, Nicol's recognised deputy, and handing a virtually unknown 19-year-old his first team debut. Ricky Pellow, a former pupil of Robinson's at Bristol's Colston Collegiate School, had only just received his A-level results. But he had already shown promise for the United and was now set to play his first senior game for Bath in a crucial European Cup tie.

Not surprisingly, Pellow was overwhelmed at his selection to partner Richard Butland at half-back, but he was confident and Robinson's gamble was vindicated as Bath set the record straight with a hard-earned 21-15 win, although they had to beat off a fierce late rally from Pontypridd, before victory was assured. Tries from Butland and Victor Ubogu and three penalties and a conversion by Callard, who resumed the kicking duties, saw Bath build up a 21-8 lead after an hour. But then their defensive capacities were stretched to the limit as Pontypridd stormed back in the final quarter, Neil Jenkins converting a Daffyd James try to cut the deficit to six points. Bath were pinned back in their own 22 in a nail-biting finale, but managed to hold out and from that moment on they were up and running. None of their group games would be easy, but the days of huge victories were gone. Consistency, sound defence and the ability to take chances were to be the key elements of their success over the next six weeks and Bath showed they had acquired those vital attributes.

A long trip to Mansfield Park, Hawick, where they would take on Borders, was next on Bath's agenda, but that encounter was preceded by a week of interesting revelations on and off the field.

On 9 September, nearly seven months after he had been charged with indecent assault and nine months after the alleged incident at PJ Peppers wine bar, John Hall stood trial at Bristol Crown Court and pleaded not guilty to the offence. The following day, after the court had heard evidence from Hall and the student teacher who had accused him, and had been told that there were no independent witnesses, he was acquitted by the jury, who took just 40 minutes to reach a verdict. Hall's long torment was over and at last he could begin to put his life together again. Soon after his sacking as Bath's director of rugby, he had joined a sports management agency and later married his long-time girlfriend Kirsty, who had supported him throughout his lengthy ordeal.

On the same day that Hall was acquitted it was announced that Newsquest had sold its Wessex Division, which included the *Bath Chronicle*, to Bristol United Press, the parent company of our rivals, the *Western Daily Press* and the *Bristol Evening Post*, for a total of £35 million. We had been in residence at Windsor Bridge for only a few weeks, but it was clear that a new era had begun for the paper and that major operational changes were on the way.

In the meantime, Bath were getting ready for their second European Cup Pool C clash against Borders. The pre-match bulletins were encouraging, as it was revealed that Ieuan Evans was back in training, having recovered from his groin injury, and was in contention for a place in the side at Hawick on the Sunday, while Jeremy Guscott and Steve Ojomoh were also ready for a return to action.

In the event, Evans was forced to wait a bit longer, while Guscott was selected but obliged to drop out with a back injury incurred in training. Ojomoh played and made an encouraging comeback.

No one realised it then, but Guscott's new injury, described as a back muscle strain, would turn out be be much more serious than that, and far worse even than the broken arm that had already kept him out of action for over two months. The extent of it, however, was not revealed for some time and Bath were again forced to carry on without him.

They accomplished that task comfortably enough in a low-key contest at a windswept Mansfield Park, thanks to a commendable performance by the pack, which always had the edge over a much lighter Scottish eight. Russell Earnshaw set Bath on course with two opportunist tries in the opening quarter, Matt Perry wriggled through for another and two Callard conversions put Bath 19-6 ahead by the interval. But after that they were forced to pull out all the stops against a dogged Borders side, who cut the deficit to five points before further tries by Ojomoh and the giant replacement prop Chris Horsman, in his European Cup debut, clinched an unconvincing 31-17 win.

Two down, four to go – and I picked up a scoop by predicting that Jon Callard was in line to replace Clive Woodward as Bath's new backs coach. After the game Andy Robinson had revealed that a statement was imminent concerning Woodward's future and that his successor had been earmarked, although he refused to disclose his identity. Callard, who was with him at the press conference, brushed aside suggestions that it might be him, but I was certain enough of the outcome to speculate that he was the man and went ahead with the story. Clive Woodward was named as England's new coach two days later, and although it took nearly a fortnight for Bath to confirm the name of his replacement, Callard it was.

Meanwhile, after heartening victories in Wales and Scotland, Bath were now faced with successive home games, the first against holders Brive, a meeting seen as their most crucial Pool C encounter, and then what looked to be their easiest qualifying game, the return clash against Borders at the Rec. And, if their first two games had been close-fought affairs, Bath would soon find these two even more nerve-racking.

Over the next few days the main concern about the Brive game was whether it would go ahead at all, as a sudden and unsavoury explosion of violence left the entire tournament in disarray. The trouble, soon referred to as 'the battle of Brive', erupted in a controversial climax to their home game against Pontypridd, when, with the Welshmen on the brink of winning, Brive were awarded a disputed injury-time try to snatch a fortunate 32-31 victory. Instantly a mass brawl broke out on the pitch, resulting in Brive flanker Lionel Mallier and Pontypridd's Dale McIntosh being sent off.

Even worse shame followed later that night when French players found themselves in the same city centre bar as a Pontypridd side, still seething at their narrow defeat, and violence broke out again in another unseemly brawl, which allegedly left the Brive international trio of Christophe Lamaison, Philippe Carbonneau and David Venditti nursing painful injuries. In the uproar that followed, Pontypridd's McIntosh, Phil John and Andrew Barnard were detained by the French police. The incidents threatened the entire tournament, while Brive tried to get their game at the Rec postponed because of the likely absence of their battered stars.

Bath's Tony Swift gave that suggestion short shrift, claiming that postponement would cost the club a fortune and cause mayhem in European rugby, while pointing out that Bath had already played two games with up to a dozen players on the injured list. Fortunately, common sense prevailed. The tournament organisers, European Rugby Cup Limited (ERC), ruled that the game must go ahead and the furore gradually died away. But it made Bath's first encounter against the European champions even more intriguing the following Saturday.

When the teams eventually took the field at a packed Rec, Venditti was sufficently recovered to play at centre, but Lamaison, his eye heavily protected, and Carbonneau sat it out in the stands, while Bath fans were at last able to give Ieuan Evans a rousing debut reception as he took his place on the right flank for the first time at the Rec.

Bath were soon in for a shock as Brive displayed the outstanding quality of their backs with two superb tries by wingers Pascal Bomati and Jerome Carrat to give them an early lead. Bath were hard pressed to contain the French side in the first half, but gradually their pack began to take control, especially at the lineout, where Nigel Redman enjoyed an outstanding afternoon. And, with Callard in deadly kicking form, they gradually fought their way back to set up a thrilling climax that could have gone either way. Matt Perry and Mike Catt plundered vital tries as Bath, trailing 15-14 at the interval, edged in front early in the second half. But Argentine centre Lisandro Arbizu hit back with Brive's third try and, in a pulsating finish, it was Callard's 17-point contribution that settled the issue 27-25 in Bath's favour to leave them top of the group, after a victory that was on a knife-edge until the final whistle.

That narrow success was a vital psychological factor in Bath's progress in the rest of the qualifying campaign, because, having beaten the holders they now knew there was a realistic chance of winning the tournament. But victory was achieved at a price. Ieuan Evans had played well, but his lack of match fitness resulted in a recurrence of the groin tear which had kept him out for so long. It was the same muscle, fortunately less seriously damaged than before, but it sidelined him for the rest of the pool games.

Adedayo Adebayo, however, was back after recovering from his stress fracture. And there was encouraging news about Simon Geogheghan, who played a full 80 minutes in Bath United's 26-10 midweek win at Ebbw Vale, a game which saw John Mallett taken to hospital with ankle ligament damage. And there was still Jon Sleightholme. The England winger had been cast into the shadows after making a fairly anonymous return from injury at Harlequins three weeks earlier. But with Evans out of action again, he found himself back in the picture as Bath prepared for the return clash against Borders at the Rec on the last Saturday in September. The problem was his confidence, which had been sky-high at the start of the year, but was now at a low ebb. And in the wake of so many injury disruptions and the loss of coach Clive Woodward, Bath's backs in general were barely firing on one cylinder, let alone their full quota. The pack had taken most of the honours in the three European Cup ties so far, but outside the spark was missing.

On paper, having already beaten Borders by 14 points on Scottish soil, Bath should have encountered few problems in the home clash, but the anticipated easy win failed to materialise and in the end they were lucky to scrape home by just four points. The fans seemed complacent too. A crowd of only 5,500 turned up to see the game and they must have wondered what was going on, as Bath floundered for most of the first half, allowing Borders to edge 8-6 in front after an early try by scrum-half Bryan Redpath who pounced on a mistake by Ricky Pellow.

Mike Catt lifted the gloom with a glorious break which saw him driven over by the pack for a try, Callard's conversion and an injury-time penalty giving Bath a 16-8 interval lead. But the second half failed to follow the expected script as Borders hounded every lapse. Dan Lyle and Eric Peters were sent on to bolster a struggling back row and Peters quickly made his mark with a storming 40-metre burst to score in the corner. But Borders scented blood and when Bath's backs committed more glaring errors, they were punished by two more Scottish tries.

First Michael Dods touched down after Sleightholme failed to ground the ball behind his own line and then, when Phil de Glanville failed to release in the tackle, a quick penalty move put Tony Stanger racing clear for Borders' third try. That left Borders just a point behind, with their tails up, but two late slips denied them a shock upset as Callard's fifth penalty sealed a fortunate 27-23 victory for Bath, but only after a spilled pass in the dying seconds prevented Borders from stealing the honours.

Nevertheless, it was Bath's fourth successive Pool C win and with Brive drawing 29-29 in a thrilling encounter at

Pontypridd, where both teams were on their best behaviour, it meant that Bath had only to win one of their last two games to make sure of topping the group and sealing a home quarter-final draw, a huge advantage in the later stages.

First they had to take on the reigning champions on French soil, and that had always looked likely to be a supremely daunting test, particularly as Bath's form had gradually waned in recent weeks. It had been a hard month for a team still awaiting the return of many of its most influential leading lights and winning those four initial cup games had already taken a toll on the entire squad.

There was one piece of encouraging news just before I flew out from Bristol with the team on the first Thursday in October with the game against Brive scheduled for the following Sunday. Skipper Andy Nicol was hopeful that he had finally shaken off the hamstring problem that had forced him to miss the first part of the season and was set to take over from Ricky Pellow, who had suffered a similar injury against Borders. Nicol lacked match fitness, which presented something of a risk, but his mere presence was a boost to the squad selected for the trip, who were in optimistic mood when we touched down in Limoges, before completing the last 100 kilometres or so by road to the picturesque town of Brive.

I managed to do my preview pieces while we waited at the airport, taping interviews with Jon Callard and a new face in the first team picture, Iain Balshaw, an 18-year-old Lancastrian who had joined Bath's rugby academy only five weeks earlier. Balshaw had already represented England up to Under-18 level and had shown such precocious talent at full-back for the United that he suddenly found himself catapulted onto the replacement bench against the reigning European champions, a staggering prospect which didn't seem to overawe him in the slightest. In the event he would get just three three minutes' exposure in the limelight at the Parc Municipale des Sports that Sunday. And by then it would be far too late for him to make any significant impact, but even in that short time he did enough to show that Bath had discovered a player with an exciting future.

On a hot autumn afternoon and backed by a partisan 12,000 crowd, Brive took the initiative right from the first whistle, Lamaison landing the first of four immaculate first-half penalties within 45 seconds. But for the next half hour Bath managed to stay in contention and create a couple of scoring chances which sadly went astray. A mistake by Callard set up Brive's opening try, Arbizu exploiting an overlap to send Bomati over in the corner. But two Callard penalties pulled it back to 10-9, before Lamaison took over, three more penalties for rash infringements stretching the French lead to ten points at the interval.

Sadly, the second half saw Bath gradually fall away after Callard had kicked his fourth penalty, as a strangely restricted tactical game plan failed to pay dividends and the heat began to melt their dwindling reserves of stamina. Obsessed with driving forward from set piece and ruck, Bath got nowhere, Ojomoh and Richard Webster gaining precious little yardage and by the time they began to move the ball wide it was too late.

Brive applied constant pressure and extended their lead with a Laimaison dropped goal and then settled the issue in style with a brilliant try created by Arbizu and finished clinically by full-back Alain Penaud, Lamaison converting easily to take his personal tally to 19 points in a clear-cut 29-12 revenge win for their narrow reverse at the Rec.

It was a somewhat downcast Bath party that boarded the plane back to Bristol that night, a flight which provided me with one moment that will linger long in my memory.

I sat next to the 20-year-old Chris Horsman on the return journey and when we came in to land I noticed he had his head in his hands in silent prayer. He didn't like flying and particularly landing, but we touched down without incident. Less than a month later he was found to have testicular cancer, which threatened to end his promising career, not to mention his life. But in true Bath tradition he fought back, enduring two debilitating spells of chemotherapy, before regaining his fitness and playing again before the end of the season.

The setback in Brive left Bath needing to overcome Pontypridd at the Rec six days later to make sure of finishing top of Pool C. But there was to be a major shock in the run-up to the game, with the announcement that Jon Sleightholme had been placed on the transfer list by mutual consent.

For Sleightholme, it was a move he felt he had no option but to make. In the past 12 months his place had been constantly under threat from Jason Robinson and latterly Ieuan Evans. He had lost confidence, form and his England place, and the only way he could see of regaining it was by moving to a club that could guarantee him regular first-team rugby. Bath, with a promising crop of youngsters coming through, and under growing pressure to make squad economies, were not prepared to stand in the way of an unhappy player who could not be assured of first-team selection.

Cardiff were one of the first clubs to show an interest, but soon thought twice about following it up, accusing Bath of pricing themselves out of the market by demanding a fee that was reported to be in excess of £100,000. Another month elapsed before Sleightholme finally signed a three-year contract with Northampton, who must still have recalled the stunning hat-trick he had scored against them back in January. Sleightholme was selected for that Saturday's final Pool C clash against Pontypridd, but made little impact of note in a game which was dominated by Bath's pack and the return of one sorely missed forward in particular. Dan Lyle, restored to health after his hectic summer exertions with the US Eagles and an early season injury, had impressed in a 20-minute replacement spell against Brive and was drafted into a reshuffled pack in place of Steve Ojomoh at number eight, while hooker Mark Regan was dropped in favour of Andy Long. Within weeks, Long would also be preferred to Regan in Clive Woodward's new-look England side. And Steve

Ojomoh, resigned like Sleightholme to the prospect of limited first-team opportunities, would be contemplating a move to Gloucester, where they were distinctly brighter.

As for Pontypridd, they found a resurgent Lyle and a fiercely committed Bath side too strong for them at the Rec that Saturday. In a scrappy, niggling contest that produced few moments to savour, Bath ground out a decisive 17-3 lead at half-time and never looked like surrendering it, emerging comfortable 23-10 winners. Lyle, back to his inspirational best, scored a try, Mike Catt dropped a goal and Jon Callard kicked five more penalties, taking his total points tally to 78 in six matches, an overall contribution to the team's progress that was beyond price.

Bath seemed to have overcome the worst of their dire injury plague and booked a home quarter-final tie against Cardiff on 8 November, a revenge encounter they had thirsted for since that disaster at the same stage nearly a year before. I wrote and phoned over that Monday's back-page lead from a hotel bar in Fishguard, where I was waiting for a ferry to take me on a golf holiday to Ireland, a crossing that was delayed for five hours by bad weather in the Irish sea.

The news for Bath fans was infinitely worse. Jeremy Guscott's back strain had been diagnosed as a bulging disc requiring major surgery and there was no telling how long it would be before he was back. The injury curse had clearly not yet been lifted.

While I was away, Bath were able to cast aside the pressure of their European Cup exploits and give some players a brief respite as they beat Oxford University 60-15 in a friendly. Then, in the first of three successive league matches, they brushed aside Bristol 44-15, scoring seven tries.

Their next outing was at Welford Road against Leicester, always a difficult place for any visiting side to win. And it was a game that Bath were to throw away in irritating and controversial fashion.

Leading 19-13 thanks to a try by Richard Webster, and a conversion and four penalties from Callard, Bath allowed themselves to be sidetracked by an unedifying second half display by Leicester, who continually disrupted the scrummage, collapsing it time and again. And with the French referee Patrick Thomas doing little to punish the culprits the contest degenerated into near farce. Mark Regan, recalled in place of Long, was hoping to press his England claims with an impressive display against arch-rival Richard Cockerell, but he did himself no favours by overdoing the belligerence and ultimately Bath lost their discipline and the game, 33-22, leaving Andy Robinson to lament that his side had cut their own throats.

Bath had now lost two of their first four league games, and the injury news was hardly reassuring. Nathan Thomas was back after completing his 60-day ban, but now Richard Butland was found to have a stress fracture of the shin and Federico Mendez, who had pulled out of the Leicester game complaining of a back problem, had been given leave to return to Argentina for three weeks. It was not exactly a great week for Phil de Glanville either as Clive Woodward named Wasps flanker Lawrence Dallaglio to succeed him as England captain. But he was still in the 28-man England squad along with Adebayo, Perry, Catt, Regan and Andy Long.

At least Bath's young guns were still firing and one legendary veteran was working his way back to fitness. A youthful and talented Bath United side stormed to a rousing 71-17 rout of Moseley at the Rec in midweek, Kennedy Tsimba scoring a hat-trick at fly-half, while Ieuan Evans came through his comeback game unscathed. The wing wizard and his Welsh compatriot, Nathan Thomas, both returned to first-team action against Richmond the following Saturday, Thomas producing a storming display and Evans celebrating his recall with two marvellous tries, as Ben Clarke and his new club were given the runaround. Bath were 22-0 up at the interval and 42-7 ahead before easing off and eventually winning 47-31, Tsimba coming on late in the game to cap his senior debut with the final try.

It was a satisfactory return to form a week before their

European Cup quarter-final, and Bath's opponents were confirmed the following day when Cardiff narrowly ousted their old rivals Llanelli 24-20 in their play-off encounter. Meanwhile, a depleted Pontypridd side were back in Brive to contest another play-off place. It was the third time the two teams had met in two months and once again it was close. But the holders again came from behind to win 25-20, and there were no violent disturbances.

Cup fever was rife in Bath that week, as the countdown began for an eagerly awaited return clash against the Welsh giants. And this time Bath ensured that their preparation would not be marred by the last-minute mishaps that had undermined their chances the previous year. No one at the Rec doubted it would be another close and fiercely contested battle, but Bath were confident of winning on their own turf and they hardly needed motivating for the task in hand.

The key areas of conflict appeared to be at scrum-half, where Andy Nicol faced the livewire Rob Howley, and in the kicking duel between Lee Jarvis and Jon Callard, who was not to be controversially discarded this time. On the day, both Bath men met the challenge with aplomb. Nicol, in inspirational form, overshadowed his world-class Welsh counterpart and Callard's kicking, as it had been throughout the tournament, was unerring in its accuracy.

Cardiff, encouraged by the first of two tries from their powerful centre Leigh Davies, made a real fight of it in the first half and trailed only 12-11 at half-time. But after the break Bath's more mobile and athletic pack gradually got on top and, urged on by a Rec full house scenting revenge, they were in no mood to let victory slip away. Victor Ubogu, back to his rampaging best, powered over for a try to add to Phil de Glanville's touchdown, and Dan Lyle, a towering influence in all phases, wrapped it up with Bath's third try, Callard slotting a conversion and five penalties to complete a deserved 32-21 triumph and erase the bitter memories of that last meeting in Cardiff. The semi-final was still six weeks away against as yet unknown opponents. Bath were to play, and lose, three games in that time, as the rugby focus switched to England's four-match international series against Australia, South Africa and New Zealand for the rest of November and early December.

Coincidentally, two of Bath's three intervening fixtures were also against opponents from the Southern Hemisphere. Four days after eclipsing Cardiff, a depleted side lost 29-13 against touring Tonga. And at the end of November the Australian outfit, ACT Brumbies, losing finalists in the Super 12 series, gained a hard-earned 20-13 success over a below-strength Bath team.

Otherwise, it was a period of excitement, uncertainty, new horizons and conflicting fortunes, at Twickenham and at the Rec. Two days after the Cardiff win, Matt Perry and Andy Long discovered they had been called up for England debuts at full-back and hooker respectively against Australia the following Saturday, along with Adedayo Adebayo and Mike Catt at fly-half, Phil de Glanville earning a place on the bench. For Long it was perhaps too early, as he lasted only half a game before being replaced. But Perry grasped his opportunity with both hands, playing all four games against the top three teams in the world and looking more assured with each outing. Adebayo did little wrong, showing admirable defensive qualities in the first two games, before being prematurely discarded, while little changed in Catt's eccentric England career. He had few chances to shine in a drab, rain-ruined draw against Australia, but gave a nightmarish kicking display as the All Blacks overcame a game England side in the first union international ever played at Old Trafford. Then he suffered bad luck against South Africa, as he was stretchered off with concussion after his elusive running had inspired England to a first half lead. The Springboks eventually secured a decisive win.

For Clive Woodward it was a daunting introduction to his new coaching role. But he and England eventually emerged with credit, as they nearly upset the All Blacks in their second encounter at Twickenham, leading 20-3 after the opening quarter before being held to a 26-26 draw.

Back at the Rec it was a time of departures, continuing concern over financial losses and fears over the club's long-term future in the light of the continued stalemate that afflicted plans for stadium development. Shortly after the victory over Cardiff, Jon Sleightholme finally signed for Northampton and by the end of the year Steve Ojomoh had left for Gloucester, both for undisclosed fees. It was a torrid time for Bath and the only reassuring news was that they would be at home for their European Cup semi-final on Saturday, 20 December. Their opponents would be Pau, rated the weakest of the three French sides in the last four. Brive, who had knocked out Wasps at Loftus Road in their quarter-final clash, would take on the former winners Toulouse in what promised to be, and was, an epic semi-final.

The scene was set for a tantalising pre-Christmas confrontation. But Bath were to suffer an unprecedented setback and a record league defeat just seven days before what was already being described as the most vital game in the club's history. On Saturday, 13 December, I drove to Vicarage Road, Watford to see Bath take on league leaders Saracens, who had won their opening six matches and sat two points clear of Newcastle, who had also gained maximum points from their first five games.

Saracens had just begun to share Watford FC's ground and the spectacle that awaited a 10,658 crowd that afternoon – a record attendance for a Saracens' home game – was like a surrealistic vision of the future for diehard traditionalists in the stands. An American football-style team of cheerleaders, blaring music whenever there was a score, and even a radio-controlled cart to bring on and remove the tee whenever a place-kick was awarded, were some of the incongruous accompaniments to a riveting contest, at least from a Saracens viewpoint.

For Bath it represented one long nightmare, as their depleted side, with teenage centre Mike Tindall making a first-team debut he will always recall with anguish, were torn to shreds, conceding six superb tries. Trailing 28-9 at the interval, Bath hit back with tries by Richard Butland and Mark Regan to add to Callard's three first half penalties, but they were simply no match for Saracens on the day, and eventually suffered the humiliation of a record league reverse, losing 50-23.

No one wanted to say anything as Bath's entire staff left Vicarage Road in grim-faced silence after the game. When Andy Robinson emerged his barely restrained anger was so evident that rational explanations were out of the question, the Bath coach uttering a few words of praise for Saracens before striding away into the night.

The match report of that débâcle was to be my last as rugby writer for the *Bath Chronicle*. A situation had been developing in my working life which came to a head later that week and would herald the end of my association with the paper. The problem was simple. Since the *Chronicle* had been acquired by Bristol United Press, the company had been formulating plans for new working arrangements within the group, including proposals to extend my duties in reporting Bath rugby. I was unhappy about the proposals, rejected them – and that was it: no one backed down, and on Friday, 19 December (my day off) I was told that I had been suspended pending a disciplinary hearing the following Monday.

Ironically, my last story, a front-page lead involving an exclusive interview with Tony Swift, had revealed his and Bath's grave concern over the club's future in the light of its parlous financial state. The report reflected Swift's fear that Bath could soon decline into third or fourth division oblivion unless its stadium problems were solved over the next few months. He warned that although Andrew Brownsword was continuing to invest a huge amount in the club, it was currently operating at a serious loss and the chairman could not be expected to bankroll Bath for much longer, without any prospect of improving the club's current facilities at the Rec or of moving to a new stadium. Indeed, no one seemed to be happy that week preceding the season of goodwill, particularly thousands of Bath fans who were unable to gain entry to the Rec that Saturday because the demand for tickets far exceeded the ground's paltry 8,200 capacity.

There was one glimmer of hope: Bath were on the brink of reaching the Heineken European Cup final. And as Andy Nicol led them out against Pau that afternoon the elusive possibility of unique conquest was suddenly within their grasp – not to mention the prospect of financial salvation that success would inevitably help to secure.

The tension and pressure on both teams as they fought out a nerve-racking contest was immense. But, although Pau did not lack for commitment, skill or courage, Bath were in no mood to give any quarter or let destiny take its own course. It was no classic. But Bath's overall discipline and sterling defence stood them in good stead as they ground out an 11-9 interval lead, thanks to Victor Ubogu's third try of the tournament and two pinpoint Callard penalties to three successful kicks from Pau's David Aucagne.

Flying winger Philippe Bernat-Salle caused dismay among Rec fans with a smartly-taken try to keep Pau hopes alive in a frenzied second half. But the French side's tendency to yield penalties under pressure brought about their undoing as Callard's unerring boot punished them three more times, his last kick extending a narrow lead to 20-14. The closing moments were agonising for Bath fans, until a final blast of referee Derek Bevan's whistle triggered an eruption of joy and relief that must have been heard across the city. Bath were through to the final in Bordeaux and a tantalising dream was close to fulfilment.

There was more welcome news after the game when Andy Robinson revealed that Jeremy Guscott was recovering well after his operation and hoping to be back in action by mid-January, two weeks before the final, although Robinson was cautious about his chances of being ready in time.

The following day Bath's final opponents were identified. In a dramatic semi-final clash in Toulouse a last gasp penalty by Christophe Lamaison put Brive level at 22-22 at the end of extra time, and the rules decreed that they went through on a

2-1 try count. Bath would have to overcome the reigning champions once again to lift the trophy, in their third meeting of the season. And, with the scores even between the two teams, it was the perfect scenario for the climax of an epic tournament.

Four days later David Gledhill was forced to sack me as the *Bath Chronicle*'s rugby writer. I cleared my desk at lunchtime on Christmas Eve and walked out of the office for the last time, my head swimming in a whirlpool of conflicting emotions, unsure of what the future held.

But of one thing I was in no doubt. If Bath were going to be in Bordeaux on Saturday, 31 January, for their date with European Cup destiny, I would be there to share it with them, come what may.

CHAPTER THREE

Bitter Prelude to a Family Reunion

Strangely enough, I enjoyed that Christmas, perhaps because for the first time in many years I was not committed to a busy working schedule over the holiday period and for once could relax. It was quite a relief not to have to make the long journey to Sale for a Premiership clash the day after Boxing Day, and then spend half the night and most of the next day hammering away on the computer, although I did regret missing the game.

After the adrenalin surge of beating Pau, I half expected Bath to come unstuck at Heywood Road, as they had done so fatefully the previous April. But this time it was Sale, two places above Bath in mid-table, who were destined to be thwarted. John Mallett made a welcome return that afternoon after a prolonged injury absence, caused initially by the back problem that flared up in Argentina with England and then when he damaged ankle ligaments on his comeback at Ebbw Vale. Matt Perry took over from Jon Callard at full-back and Mike Catt reverted to centre allowing Richard Butland to step in again at fly-half as Bath squeezed a narrow 13-11 victory in a dour game. Butland scored their only try and Catt kicked a conversion and two penalties to keep Sale at bay.

Three days later I was back in the Rec press box to watch Jon Sleightholme run out in the green and black of Northampton. But it was a subdued return for Sleights, who saw little of the ball as Bath ground out a decisive 26-3 victory. Russell Earnshaw, out of favour since the Leicester defeat, was recalled, capping an effective display with a try, as did Andy Nicol, while Callard kicked sixteen points.

Thus, as a new year approached, things were looking up at the Rec. And Bath, with a European Cup final awaiting in the offing, turned their sights to the apparent formality of a Tetley's Bitter Cup fourth-round tie against Premiership Two side London Scottish, Tetley's having taken over cup sponsorship from glassmakers Pilkington.

The game, originally scheduled for Richmond's Athletic Ground, which they shared with Scottish, had been switched to Bath because it clashed with Richmond's home tie, and was postponed twice after heavy rain left the Rec waterlogged. But on paper Bath looked sure to overwhelm a side who were challenging for promotion but were not rated in the same class.

Some time previously I had spoken to the Scottish chief executive, Richard Yerbury, a Bath resident and member at the Rec. He had been keen to publicise the fixture in the hope of boosting the attendance, and had outlined his and Bath's plans to make the day a fun occasion with a real Scottish flavour. That was the admirable intention. But it all went horrendously wrong, thanks to a single moment of inexplicable madness which shook the rugby world and ignited a raging controversy that left Bath's European Cup preparations in disarray and the club's reputation under a cloud.

The game was 35 minutes old and a lifeless Bath were struggling to contain a lively Scottish outfit when the two packs locked horns at a scrummage, which promptly collapsed in an unruly heap. But when the players regained their feet, flanker Simon Fenn, an Australian making his debut for Scottish, was staggering around clutching his left ear and eventually had to be taken off, bleeding profusely. He returned, heavily bandaged, but was replaced midway through the second half, by which time Bath were facing a sensational defeat.

When fly-half Iain McAusland kicked a penalty to put the Exiles 23-21 ahead with four minutes remaining, it seemed they would win. But, in the dying moments, they were penalised for a needless obstruction and Callard's penalty snatched a 24-23 victory for Bath, whose performance could only be described as abysmal.

I had no idea then that anything was amiss. The Fenn incident had occurred on the far side of the pitch from the press box, which made it impossible to see what had taken place among such a crowd of bodies. And I doubt whether anyone on the ground had any better view, including most of the players. Some discussion took place between Bath officials and players in the private area next to the bar afterwards. But nothing seemed unduly untoward and I was still unaware of any major controversy, when I encountered Jon Callard and began a conversation about the forthcoming European final.

He made no mention of the Fenn incident. But I was taken aback to hear him express doubts about whether he would be selected for the team to take on Brive, as he felt that Matt Perry, England's full-back, might be preferred as a more attacking option, with Mike Catt undertaking the kicking duties. As assistant coach, Callard was certain to have a say in team selection, but he seemed almost resigned to not playing, which, considering the contribution he had made to get Bath into the final, sounded ridiculous to me. I told him so, even going so far as to suggest it was his destiny to play in the final, which was perhaps a trifle over the top and produced a rueful smile and a shrug of the shoulders. But in a jocular response, he intimated that, if he played, and Bath won the trophy, the champagne would be on him.

I was to remember that promise three weeks hence. But over the next few hours it was forgotten. The Sunday papers bore banner headlines proclaiming Bath's shame and revealing that Simon Fenn and London Scottish were furious that part of his ear had been bitten off by a Bath opponent and had called for the culprit to be named and severely punished.

That was just the opening salvo in a barrage of controversy and condemnation that was to engulf the club over the next fortnight, when the identity of the player who had committed the deed was the subject of nationwide speculation, fuelled by endless debate and comment in the media. The furore was heightened by the fact that no one on the field, not even Fenn himself, seemed able to say with any certainty who had bitten his ear and none of the video evidence available appeared to shed conclusive light on the incident. But on the Monday, London Scottish made a surprise decision to cite the entire Bath front row of Kevin Yates, Federico Mendez and Victor Ubogu, while revealing that Fenn had received 25 stitches in the wound and might require plastic surgery.

Richard Yerbury proclaimed his disgust over the affair and called for the culprit to own up. But Tony Swift countered that it was irresponsible to speculate about the incident before all the evidence was examined, and claimed that evidence the club had gathered so far was inconclusive. However, Mendez and Ubogu both denied any involvement, the latter going so far as to threaten legal action, which left the spotlight to fall firmly on the other member of Bath's front row, Kevin Yates. Bath duly announced that the club had suspended the 26-year-old prop pending further investigation and an internal disciplinary hearing. The newspapers claimed his rugby career was hanging by a thread, although Yates denied being the culprit, a stance he maintained throughout the intense saga that ensued.

Besieged by media attention, Bath still claimed that the club was not convinced that Yates was the offender or that there had even been a bite. But with Mendez and Ubogu officially cleared of involvement, the furore focused Yates, who was forced to withdraw from the next two England training sessions, although Clive Woodward confirmed he would remain in the squad until any guilt was proved.

It was a desperate time for Yates and Bath in the run-up to

the cup final against Brive, which had been almost forgotten in the welter of publicity that surrounded the biting incident. I was relieved not to be part of it. I liked Kevin Yates, who had a warm and friendly disposition and a great sense of humour, earning him the reputation as the joker in Bath's pack. And of the Bath's entire squad, he was one of the last I would have considered as a potential culprit. I couldn't bring myself to believe he could commit such a vicious act on a rugby field. And, despite the fact he was subsequently found guilty and banned for six months, by an RFU disciplinary hearing which took 25 hours to reach a verdict, I still can't credit that he was the offender.

He was a superbly effective forward who had only recently fought his way back into Bath's side and was close to a major England breakthrough at the time. It seemed so incongruous and out of character that, even in a moment of aberration, he would risk the loss of a potentially glittering career by such an ugly assault.

The Kevin Yates affair – 'Bath's week from hell' as one paper described it, although its ramifications were to linger much longer – could not have erupted at a worse time for the club. And it undoubtedly had a detrimental effect on squad morale. The club captain, Andy Nicol, Yates' flatmate, admitted that he and the other players had been affected by the controversy, which was heightened by the fact that Bath were denied an opportunity to vent their frustration on the field the following week. Bath were due to play the unbeaten championship leaders Newcastle at Gateshead in a crucial Sunday game that was expected to see Jeremy Guscott given an opportunity to prove his match-fitness. But after Bath had made the long journey north, the match had to be postponed as the pitch was waterlogged.

It was yet another setback to Bath's preparations for their big day in Bordeaux and meant that, having played only one game in January, they were left with just one chance to restore their sagging morale before taking on Brive.

For Andy Robinson that harrowing three-week period must

have been a nightmare. He had been distraught at his side's performance against London Scottish, the squad was low on morale and short of match practice, and there had been scant opportunity for him to assess current form or begin to finalise his selection plans in readiness for the biggest game in Bath's history.

Nothing seemed to be going right and there was still a serious question mark over the fitness of his trump card, Jeremy Guscott, who had not played since breaking his arm in South Africa six months earlier. Guscott, in company with another injury concern, Adedayo Adebayo, had been to Lanzarote for warm weather training in an attempt to accelerate their recovery. But it was a race against time, and whether either would be fit to perform at their peak in Bordeaux, or even make the team, was still uncertain.

Such was the estimation of Guscott's value that, even after a six-month absence, Clive Woodward had recalled him to the England squad for their game against France a week after the final, along with Perry, de Glanville, Catt, Yates and Regan. He was named in the squad on the same day his former England partner, Will Carling, announced his retirement from the game, following a long-running dispute with the Harlequins coach, Andy Keach, who had accused him of a part-time attitude towards his club commitments.

Rancour and disruption was clearly not confined to Bath. And even before they were due to fight England's cause in that European Cup final, the leading Premiership clubs and the RFU were re-opening hostilities over future control of the tournament, the clubs announcing their intention to boycott the event in 1998/99, after agreeing unified action at a meeting in London.

Meanwhile, back at the Rec, Bath's bemused and apprehensive squad were aware that crunch time had arrived. Places in the team for the final were still up for grabs and the last opportunity to secure one was presented by a fifth-round Tetley's Bitter Cup clash against Richmond, who had been beaten 47-31 on their last visit to the Rec in November but whose form had improved of late. And, with several former Bath players in their line-up, they were eager to avenge that defeat against a side who were way below par, short of match practice, and had other things on their mind.

Making several changes to the team that had played so badly against London Scottish, Bath rested Andy Nicol, Ricky Pellow taking over at scrum-half, while Guscott and Adebayo were given the chance to prove their fitness and Matt Perry was preferred to Jon Callard at full-back. It was a back line that suggested Bath were seeking to rediscover the fluent running game they had so nearly perfected under Clive Woodward the previous spring. But it had ominous implications for Callard, whose reaction to being omitted suggested he felt his place in the final was in doubt. 'I would love to play, but sometimes you have got to say this is the side for the way we are trying to play. It's a bold and brave statement by Robbo and the club,' he said. But his real feelings were probably quite different.

In the pack Mendez switched to prop in place of the suspended Yates, allowing Mark Regan to resume at hooker, while Brian Cusack replaced Llanes as Nigel Redman's lock partner. Neither Yates nor Llanes would appear in the final. Yates' disciplinary hearing had been postponed, to give his legal advisers more time to prepare his case, but the suspension ruled him out. For Llanes it was the end of the road. He had featured regularly over the past two months, but his display against London Scottish had, to put it mildly, not pleased Andy Robinson. It was his last first-team outing for the club, as he was ignored for the rest of the season before being released from his contract.

I missed that Richmond game owing to a funeral, but when I discovered the result it was yet another tale of woe. Bath had been eclipsed 29-17 in extra time and the London side had emphatically deserved their victory over the European Cup finalists, who had struggled to achieve any cohesion or penetration in their play. On the credit side, Jeremy Guscott had emerged unscathed in a lively comeback and Adebayo amply demonstrated his fitness with a first half try. But Perry had made little impression at full-back and Catt's kicking had been erratic although he did land two late penalties to level the scores at 14-14 at the end of normal time.

However Bath had slumped badly in extra time, conceding fifteen points and two tries to a rampant Richmond side, whose hero was a forward Bath had released as surplus to requirements just nine months earlier. Craig Gillies had departed the Rec, frustrated by the lack of first-team opportunity, shortly after Bath had bought Llanes in a bid to solve their lineout problems. He soon made rapid strides at Richmond and proved it that afternoon, outjumping Redman and Cusack at the lineout and enjoying an impressive game. Another Rec old boy, winger Jim Fallon, scored Richmond's opening try, Ben Clarke was a constant menace, while prop Darren Crompton and replacement flanker Adam Vander also figured prominently in an embarrassing defeat of their former club, which left Andy Robinson ruefully conceding that decisions to let players go can return to haunt a club.

'We have some serious talking to do, but I am confident we will have things right for Brive,' he declared. But Bath's perplexed supporters must have wondered how the club were going to turn their fortunes around only days before embarking for France. The Richmond game had been Bath's last chance to shrug off the depressing setbacks that had assailed the club since the turn of the year and produce some convincing form. Instead it heightened the sense of foreboding that preceded their departure for Bordeaux the following Thursday. Even that didn't exactly go according to plan, Phil de Glanville being forced to take a later flight after his wife Yolanda was taken ill. But by then Bath were almost immune to the tribulations that fate seemed to be stacking up against them. It was as if their resolve was being tested to the limit by fickle gods. But the ultimate test was too close at hand for anything else to go amiss and only then would it be seen whether they truly had the character and the discipline to conquer it.

They had no shortage of incentive to upset the odds. The English press had already written off their chances of overcoming the reigning champions on French soil, having taken into account their disastrous recent form and the effects of a month of non-stop controversy. However, there was one body of opinion unwilling to share that view. And even now they were preparing to unfurl their blue, black and white flags, don brightly dyed wigs and paint their faces in readiness to support the club to the bitter end. The Bath family were gathering en masse for a continental pilgrimage in pursuit of their Holy Grail and they were determined to be there at the moment it was raised aloft in triumph. By ferry and plane, car, coach and train they were heading for Bordeaux, intent on relishing every minute of a weekend to cherish for the rest of their days.

They had not been impressed by events of the past month, particularly the team's performances in the Tetley's Bitter Cup. And they knew precisely how hard the task would be against a high-quality Brive side playing in their own country with the fervent support of 30,000 Frenchmen urging them to victory. But they were reassured by two facts that everyone else seemed to have forgotten. Bath, by tradition, were always at their most dangerous when under pressure, with their backs to the wall. And the club had never lost in ten previous cup finals.

I was on my way to join them, along with my family. My wife and two daughters had become afflicted by European Cup fever. My eldest, daughter Lisa, flew out from Gatwick, her sister Anna arrived by train from Marseille, and my wife and I were booked on a private flight from Bristol Airport, chartered by Danny Sacco, who had helped organise those inter-code challenge matches against Wigan nearly two years earlier. It was a convivial but uneventful flight and, on arrival at Bordeaux Airport we were ushered into coaches and, in a short detour on the way to our accommodation, were given a brief glimpse of the imposing Stade Lescure, where Brive and Bath were due to settle their differences the following day.

Bordeaux was teeming with blue, black and white regalia that night. We settled for a quiet meal and a nightcap back at the hotel. But thousands of Bath fans enjoyed a prolonged dress rehearsal for the anticipated celebration just 24 hours hence, and the night was largely spent in animated debate over the rugby feast that lay in store. One or two indulged themselves to the extent of failing to make the game the next day, or so I heard. But otherwise it was a friendly invasion, which the locals welcomed, especially as the tills were kept busy until the small hours. I slept fitfully but awoke to cloudless blue skies and a warm January sun, which felt like a positive omen for Bath, who had a habit of hitting form as winter turned to spring.

After breakfast we headed for the city centre to relax over coffee and croissants in the balmy sunshine and survey the scene as Bordeaux began to fill up with black and white-bedecked hordes of Brive fans, most of whom were clearly convinced they were about to witness a contest with only one possible outcome. I parted company with my family entourage at around eleven and set off to walk to the stadium, which I had been informed would only take fifteen minutes. Half an hour later it was still not in sight, but a growing stream of fans led me to it. And suddenly there before me stood the Stade Lescure, burnished white, like a colossal Spanish bullring.

Only then was I struck by the magnitude of Bath's task that afternoon. With the heat intensifying by the minute, they were facing a relentless ordeal against the champions of Europe, in a gladiatoral amphitheatre where their support would be outnumbered six to one by a French crowd baying for a ritual slaughter of the English invader.

Just about every rugby journalist in Europe appeared to be there and it was pleasing to renew acquaintance with many former colleagues and rivals. I sat with Ken Johnstone, hale and hearty as ever, and as the wine and banter flowed we scanned the team lists and expounded our theories about how the game would unfold. But the consensus of opinion was that Bath had a mountain to climb and precious little chance of scaling it.

The solitary saving grace from Bath's standpoint was that Andy Robinson had at last been given the opportunity to field his strongest side. And he had grasped it with both hands by calling on all the club's most experienced and battle-hardened warriors. Jon Callard's fears had not been confirmed. He was down to play at full-back, with an unlucky Matt Perry confined to the replacements bench, despite his recent success with England. It had often been so at Bath in the glory years, and this day was no exception. Adedayo Adebayo and Ieuan Evans were there to roam the wings, combining power, pace and defensive resilience. And in midfield, Jeremy Guscott's talismanic presence was restored alongside Phil de Glanville, a centre partnership guaranteed to instil doubt into any opposing back line. At half-back Mike Catt and Andy Nicol were Bath's selected combination. They were a proven pair, Nicol's resilience, passing accuracy and all-round competence blending perfectly with Catt's unorthodox, often unpredictable genius, which, on this occasion, he would temper with restraint and a disciplined cutting edge.

But Bath knew it was up front, in the forward exchanges, where the battle would be won and lost. And there Robinson had chosen men he could rely on under extreme pressure, when mental and physical strength would be of paramount importance. Denied the services of Kevin Yates at loosehead prop, Robinson had no need to look further than the consistent Dave Hilton for his replacement, while his preference for Mark Regan instead of Mendez at hooker was tactically shrewd, because with the versatile Mendez on the bench it gave him an extra replacement option. A fit John Mallett must have entered his calculations at tighthead. But Victor Ubogu's inspired form had been one of the major features of Bath's progress to the final and there was no way he could be overlooked.

At lock, where Robinson had tried a variety of combinations in recent months, it was no time for gambling. Neither

Llanes nor Cusack had grabbed the chance to get their names on the teamsheet so Robinson turned to the tried and trusted pairing of Nigel Redman and Martin Haag, men who had served Bath superbly for nearly a decade. For Haag, disregarded since late October and desperate to restate his credentials, it was the perfect motivation, and he would not be found wanting.

The back row confrontation was always going to be a crucial area of conflict against Brive and here there was only one real certainty. Dan Lyle had the power, pace and handling skills to stretch the French side from number eight. And his dynamic jumping was invaluable at the lineout, which meant his inclusion was never in doubt. On the flanks it boiled down to a difficult decision of choosing two from four. Russell Earnshaw and Eric Peters came up with the short straws as the two Welshmen, Nathan Thomas and Richard Webster, narrowly got the nod.

It was a full line-up of fifteen internationals, which I and Bath fans could scarcely question, and with four more on the bench, in Mendez, Mallett, Perry and Peters, there was no shortage of top class experience. Ricky Pellow, Richard Butland and Earnshaw completed the replacement quota.

Ranged against them was an equally formidable array of talent assembled by the Brive coach Laurent Seigne, whose selection dilemma must have been greater than Robinson's, particularly in the backs, where his options were innumerable. Alain Penaud, Christophe Lamaison and the Argentine international Lisandru Arbizu were all well capable of playing fly-half, Lamaison having filled the role effectively in Brive's 29-12 qualifying group win over Bath. But on this occasion Seigne plumped for Arbizu, and selected Penaud and ace kicker Lamaison in their more accustomed roles at full-back and centre respectively. On the wings, again from a wide choice, he had settled for the spectacular pace of the Carrat brothers, Sebastien and Jerome, the latter sharing the honour of being the tournament's leading try-scorer with seven. David Venditti, another elusive runner, was teamed with Lamaison at centre, while in their scrum-half and captain Philippe Carbonneau Brive boasted an experienced French international of the highest class who would do much to wreck England's Five Nations Championship hopes in Paris a week later.

Didier Casadei, Laurent Travers and Richard Crespy were as formidable a front row as could be found anywhere in club rugby, while the locks Eric Alegret and Yvan Manhes were also more than capable of holding their own in any company. In the back row Brive were confident that they had a match-winning trio. Luic van der Linden had been the outstanding player on the field at openside in the last meeting of the two teams, while on the opposite flank Olivier Magne had earned a worldwide reputation for his destructive power. Number eight François Duboisset completed a pack that had cut a swathe through the best teams in Europe for the past two seasons.

In terms of quality, the two teams represented the cream of English and French rugby. But on their native soil, and with 30,000 French rugby fanatics adding a fearsome vocal backing to their cause, Brive had every advantage on their side, except perhaps the choice of referee.

Jim Fleming, a Scot, had been nominated to officiate the final along with the touch judges David McHugh, from Ireland, and the Welshman, Clayton Thomas. The choice of Fleming at least offered Bath hope of a familiar and consistent interpretation of the laws governing crucial areas of the conflict. He had refereed their home pool victory over Brive, when he had been assiduous in punishing French indiscretion at the lineout, and Bath were banking on that strict approach being applied once again. But it was only a minor factor in their favour. Every other advantage seemed to be squarely arranged on Brive's side.

I have no idea what went through the minds of Bath's players as they prepared to take the field. They were all used to the big occasion at international level, but this was a new experience and even more intimidating in many ways. As I took my seat to one side of the press box, at the back of a stand filled with partisan French supporters, I felt surrounded, intimidated and overawed by the frenzied atmosphere in the colosseum-like stadium, while the minutes ticked away to the kick-off in the most important game in Bath's history.

The majority of Bath's support was assembled directly opposite me, surrounding the electronic scoreboard in one tiny corner of the ground, while a smaller segment waved their flags and banners behind the nearest set of posts. But they were merely a splash of blue in a sea of black and white stretching around the rest of the stadium. Bath's fans did their best to make their presence felt as the teams emerged and went through the pre-match formalities. But their efforts were eclipsed by the welcome that greeted Brive, whose entrance was accompanied by an explosion of tickertape, clouds of smoke from an avalanche of brightly coloured flares and a cacophony of music, beating drums and rousing acclaim that hardly abated until the final whistle.

It was more like the frenzied carnival atmosphere of a South American soccer stadium than anything I had ever encountered, the sheer volume of noise from the passionate 36,500 crowd putting any Wembley cup final in the shade. But there was nowhere for Bath to hide as they lined up for the start. And before they had a chance to get into their stride, they fell behind, as Brive took the opening lineout, launched a ferocious driving maul and, when Bath took it down, Lamaison punished them unerringly from the ensuing penalty.

The first blow of a remorseless first half barrage had been struck. And when, in a brief foray into Brive territory, Callard hesitantly miscued a simple penalty chance wide, the howl of derision that greeted the miss, from massed Brive ranks at that end, merely confirmed that Bath were a long way from home and seemingly out of their depth. As the drums pounded out a constant bombardment of encouragement, Brive surged forward time and again, stretching Bath's defensive capabilities to the limit. And as the penalty count rose,

Lamaison extended the lead to six and then nine points with two more immaculate kicks before the siege was momentarily lifted and Callard this time found his range to make it 9-3 after nineteen minutes.

Had Brive managed to snatch a try in that stormy first half-hour the eventual outcome might have been altogether different, but twice they were to be denied certain scores. The first chance arose when a decisive break through the centre was halted by the referee's whistle for an earlier infringement. And the second was prevented by an an unbelievable finger-tip tackle by Ieuan Evans on Sebastien Carrat, who was brought down with Bath's line at his mercy.

That was the first of two defining moments in the game from Bath's viewpoint. It kept them in contention at a crucial time and, more importantly, persuaded Brive that the best way to achieve victory was not to be found by moving the ball wide. Instead, they elected to restrict their tactical horizons and concentrate on forward domination and the reliable boot of Lamaison. It was a limited, negative ploy, but it had already paid dividends and soon yielded more, as Lamaison landed two further penalties in the last ten minutes of the half, while a lone response from Callard left Bath profoundly relieved to be only 15-6 adrift at the break.

They were down, but thanks to a tremendous defensive effort they were not yet out, although the message from the Brive hordes during the interval indicated their certainty that it was only a matter of time and perseverance before Bath were finally put to the sword. It had hardly been a classic first half, but as a spectacle it had been riveting, dramatic, with Bath content to soak up pressure, mount the occasional back-row offensive in which the athletic Lyle was invariably prominent, and wait their chance to counter.

But such opportunities had been rare, and as the taunting notes of 'Mission Impossible' blared out over the tannoy system during the interval, Bath's worried fans must have secretly feared a French landslide in the closing forty minutes. That prospect looked ominously on the cards as Brive drove forward with renewed vigour shortly after the restart, pouring through from two lineouts near the corner flag only to be repulsed by fanatical resistance. But then a series of scrums close to the Bath line seemed certain to be rewarded with a pushover try. Time and again, Carbonneau put the ball in, the Brive pack forced their way forward to within inches of the line and a try looked certain. But every time Bath somehow found the combined strength to hold them at bay, force them back and close the door.

Seven times Brive repeated the pushover tactic, but failed to make sufficient ground. And suddenly, when they were turned over and lost the scrum put-in, Bath controlled it superbly, enabling Catt to clear his lines with a booming touch kick. The pressure was off and, once repulsed, Brive were never to impose the siege so potently again.

That heroic stand was to provide the second and most decisive turning point, because, when it ended Brive were a force on the wane, their dominance broken and confidence undermined. Had they scored then the issue would almost certainly have been settled. But, still only nine points adrift, Bath suddenly grew in stature, took renewed heart and began to thrive. All of a sudden that beleaguered front row went on the offensive, Redman and Haag began claiming their own lineout ball with clinical ease, and in the loose Lyle, Webster and Thomas, relieved of constant defensive duties, began to forage forward, commit the Brive half-backs and gain vital yardage. And then, with nearly an hour gone, Bath secured the try which stunned 30,000 Frenchmen into bemused silence.

Redman inspired the initial assault, soaring to claim lineout possession, Catt hoisted a high ball deep into the Brive 22 and Guscott retrieved it to force his way to within metres of the French line, where Bath were awarded a penalty. Scorning a kick at goal, Bath chose a scrum instead, processed it cleanly, and when Lyle broke infield to find Nicol, his whipped pass was instinctively flipped on by Guscott, who might have scored himself, but Callard was there at his shoulder on the overlap to scurry over unopposed and then slot a straight-forward conversion.

Only 15-13 down, with twenty minutes remaining, Bath were back in contention with a vengeance and their ecstatic followers found renewed vocal strength, which faltered momentarily when, five minutes later, in a sudden Brive counter, Penaud dropped a cultured goal to extend their lead to five points. However, seeds of doubt had been sown in French minds by that galvanising try and a minute later Bath drove straight back down the pitch, Brive were penalised within easy range, and Callard placed the kick between the posts with absolute conviction.

The scoreboard duly registered 18-16 with fourteen minutes remaining. And suddenly I sensed that this was history in the making, that Bath were on the threshold of a triumph unrivalled in their entire 133-year existence.

Nathan Thomas, nearing exhaustion, gave way to Russell Earnshaw, his job superbly done. But as the final minutes ticked away and the two sides became enmeshed in a last nailbiting scramble for supremacy it was obvious that one last score would decide the outcome. However, none seemed forthcoming as the contest edged into injury time.

And then, as Bath roused themselves for one final lung-bursting effort, it happened. Penaud, cornered deep in his own 22, missed touch with his clearance, Adebayo made ground down the line before chipping the ball forward, and as he followed up the kick, he was barged into touch by the covering Manhes. It was a blatant bodycheck, instantly spotted by the touch judge. And when he raised his flag, Fleming responded by awarding a penalty fifteen metres in from where the ball landed just inside the 22 metre line. The kick would have been straightforward enough in any routine encounter, but it was still at an awkward angle. And as Callard stepped up to place the ball, 5000 Bath hearts were in their mouths.

With a sea of blue, black and white banners as his background, Callard paced out his run, glanced up at the posts, steadied himself for what seemed an age and, almost in slow motion took a couple of paces forward. As he swung his right boot in a sweet arc an exultant explosion of joy accompanied the ball on its unerring flight between the uprights. But the celebration was premature.

Even then there was to be a final twist of the knife. A scrupulous Jim Fleming allowed three more agonising minutes of injury time, in which Bath almost contrived to throw away the historic victory they had fought so heroically to achieve. Brive, in desperation, mounted a concerted attack down the left, Bath conceded a lineout and then a flagrant penalty for collapsing a maul, and suddenly Lamaison had only a slightly more difficult kick than Callard's to snatch the trophy back again, as legions of French fans awaited the outcome in silent prayer.

As Lamaison's kick rose skywards a thousand black and white flags were hoisted in joyous anticipation, only to fall back again in dismay as the ball dropped short and wide of the posts where, incredibly, Andy Nicol fumbled it, conceding a scrum five metres out to the right of the posts. It was Brive's last throw of the dice and the whole stadium was transfixed in suspended animation as the ball came back. Carbonneau set up Arbizu for a routine dropped goal and amazingly the ball sliced off his foot, curved slowly wide and fell to earth still in play in Bath's in-goal area.

None of Bath's players seemed aware of the danger of conceding a fluke try even then. Except for Richard Webster, who ran back and touched the ball down as Fleming put his whistle to his mouth and blew a final blast to signal that it was all over, unleashing an outbreak of hysteria that Bath and their fans will never forget.

The celebrations that followed in that small corner of the Stade Lescure were a sight to bring tears to the eyes. And there were plenty of those, as players and fans joined together in unrestrained delight. Bath were champions of Europe and a dream had been realised in miraculous fashion.

All I could do was watch in silence, hemmed in by

hundreds of speechless French fans equally dumbstruck by the dramatic events of that epic finale, and the sheer effrontery of Bath's triumph over the fallen champions, who lingered, distraught and disbelieving, on the pitch, unable to absorb defeat in a battle they had assumed would be won.

When Andy Nicol led his Bath team up the steps and towards the gleaming trophy that awaited them, I found myself rising to my feet. And as he turned and hoisted it aloft, I raised one arm, fist outstretched, clenched in tribute. Bath's European crusade was complete. And, reunited once again in euphoric acclaim of a feat unparalleled in its annals, the family was intent on a celebration party that would more than do it justice.

I made my way to the press conference through a mingling throng of Bath and Brive fans, many still unable to absorb the full impact of what they had just seen. But not for long. Bordeaux was about to host a night of Anglo-French revelry on a scale it had not seen for decades, and few would still be sober by the time it ended.

And once the post-match formalities were over and the media army had filtered away to file their glowing tributes to Bath's European conquest, I set out on the walk back to a city centre already busily preparing for the festivities ahead. I had not seen my own family since mid-morning and had hardly considered how we would spend the evening. But, on my return, plans had already been laid and we were soon heading for a special rendezvous.

We ordered bottles of wine in a crowded side-street bar and shared our recollections of the day's heady events, until an hour or so later some very familiar faces began to troop through the door and congregate in a private room up a flight of stairs. After a few minutes, a beaming Victor Ubogu came down to say hello. And shortly after he went back upstairs we were joined by another member of Bath's victorious elite. In fact, the undisputed hero of the hour. Jon Callard carried a tray bearing a bottle of vintage champagne and five glasses which he filled to the brim, before we shared a toast to a truly remarkable day in all our lives.

I still have the bottle as a memento of that night. It's empty of wine, but full of memories, a constant reminder of two unforgettable years of conflict and comradeship, on a professional crusade in the company of champions.

PART SIX

The Epilogue

The Place Gambetta was gradually returning to a more normal Sunday routine the next morning as we gathered, bleary-eyed in the sunlit square, to bid farewell to Bordeaux and go our separate ways.

It was past lunchtime and we awaited a bus to take us back to the hotel, and thence to Merignac Airport, when a coach pulled up nearby and waited equally patiently for its missing party of revellers. And shortly afterwards they materialised ambling round a corner, unshaven and slightly dishevelled, a dozen or more swarthy celebrants, some with bottles jutting from coat pockets, evidence of a night of unrestrained indulgence.

I didn't recognise them at first as they filed past, stopped, turned and playfully teased my two daughters in French. Only then did the penny drop. It was the remnants of the Brive team returning from a late night wake and the bitter dejection of defeat was still evident in their restless eyes. The vanquished champions were going home to a less than ecstatic reception.

We were on our way home too, on a flight back to Bristol filled with weary, contented travellers, still savouring the afterglow of a weekend well spent, while back in Bath the unlucky ones, those who had stayed at home glued to television screens, were getting ready to afford their returning heroes a triumphant welcome.

A joyful crowd of over 2,000 fans assembled in Victoria

Park to see Andy Nicol and his team brandish the Heineken European Cup from the top of the *Bath Chronicle* bus that Sunday night, in the aftermath of the proudest day in Bath's chequered history.

Andrew Brownsword, replete with his own 'Allez Bath' supporters cap was pictured in a celebratory embrace with an equally delighted Tony Swift, and was moved to sum up his own feelings on seeing his club engrave its name indelibly on the European Cup.

'I am delighted for the club and Bath and am very proud of the guys. This is not about money. It's about achievement,' he said.

And so it was. But money was inevitably an ever-present factor in Bath's minds as the club slowly returned to normal over the next week or so and began to contemplate the tentative prospect of further glorious achievement over the remainder of a season that still had more than three months to run.

The adrenalin inspired by their exertions in Bordeaux would sustain a renewed Allied Dunbar challenge through February and March. And, in the meantime, commercial director Stephen Hands and his marketing team were gearing themselves up to exploit ready opportunities to clinch lucrative sponsorship deals over the next few months.

European conquest had not entirely dispersed the financial crisis that had loomed large before Christmas. And there remained a host of daunting problems to be confronted and resolved, both locally and nationally in a game still riven with chaos and division. But it had bought the club vital time to consolidate and progress in the hazardous minefield of professional rugby union.

Over the next few weeks Bath proudly announced valuable new sponsorship deals with sports equipment firm Adidas and the Cider company, Blackthorn, while continuing discussions with local authorities in its quest for a stadium fit for European champions.

Meanwhile, for the club's playing squad there was a brief

respite to recuperate before the season resumed in earnest, which, for Jeremy Guscott, Mike Catt and replacements Matt Perry and Phil de Glanville, meant an early rematch against several of their Brive opponents for England against France in Paris seven days after their win in Bordeaux.

However, for Clive Woodward, it was to be a vividly disappointing start to England's Five Nations Championship challenge. He elected to leave out Perry and bring Catt back at full-back in a side committed to running the ball. But two devastating tries in the opening 10 minutes gave the French the upper hand and they went on to secure a deserved 24-17 victory over a side that failed to fulfil its potential.

France never looked back after that success, recording victories over Scotland, 51-16 at Murrayfield, Ireland 18-16, in a near-upset in Paris, and then Wales by a derisory 51-0 margin in Cardiff, thus clinching their second successive grand slam.

England contented themselves with another consolatory triple crown, crushing Wales 60-26 in an unreal contest at Twickenham, Scotland 34-20 at Murrayfield, and Ireland 35-17 in their final game, which saw Catt recalled on the right wing to score their third try before limping off with a hamstring injury.

Jeremy Guscott celebrated his 50th cap by leading England out against Wales, and Matt Perry returned to consolidate his position at full-back. But otherwise, it was an unsatisfactory Five Nations campaign from a Bath viewpoint, although their domestic form had begun to encourage burgeoning hopes of a familiar spring revival and even the outside chance of another trophy to swell the Rec silverware cabinet.

Eleven days after capturing the European Cup in Bordeaux, Bath proudly paraded the trophy around the Rec before a midweek Premiership One clash against Gloucester and promptly set about rekindling their receding title pursuit of Newcastle and Harlequins with a decisive 47-3 win. Eric Peters, a second half replacement for Dan Lyle, rounded it off in style, with a late hat-trick burst.

That comprehensive victory was followed by five more in the next six weeks as Bath overcame Wasps (43-27) and Harlequins (39-13) at home, Bristol (22-16) away, Leicester (16-5) in a dour Rec encounter and then a rousing 49-35 victory at London Irish to register their eighth successive league victory.

By the time they reached Easter, and two crucial holiday fixtures against Saracens at home on Good Friday and Richmond away on Easter Monday, Bath had pulled themselves right back into the championship race.

Newcastle now headed the table, after losing just one of their 15 league games, but Saracens had suffered three defeats, the same number as Bath, who trailed them by four points with two games in hand. However a familiar spectre had returned to haunt the European champions in that post-Brive premiership flourish – a rising injury list.

Nathan Thomas had not played since the final and his back row partners in Bordeaux, Richard Webster and Dan Lyle, both succumbed to serious knee ligament injuries in the next two games against Gloucester and Wasps, requiring surgery which put them out for the rest of the season.

It was bad enough losing an entire back row, but then, in a bruising win over Bristol, Mike Catt was badly concussed in a late tackle by Eben Rollett, which angered Andy Robinson, who accused him of deliberately trying to maim his fly-half. Catt was thus resigned to a mandatory 21-day absence, but he too would not reappear again that season. And when regular deputy Richard Butland suffered a similar fate at London Irish, Bath suddenly found themselves facing a fly-half crisis.

That spate of injury setbacks in crucial positions could not have come at a worse time and their impact on a flagging squad was soon evidenced as their title hopes effectively vanished over the four-day Easter period. Saracens beat them 29-13 at the Rec on Good Friday, Matt Perry unsuccessfully taking over the number ten shirt. And then Richmond eclipsed a depleted side 32-14 on Easter Monday, when Jon Callard undertook the fly-half role, but fared little better.

After that double blow, Bath's season was all but over and they knew it. With little left to play for except third place and their pride, it was perhaps inevitable that the team's performance went into decline and Andy Robinson was forced to face what, for him, was an unacceptable prospect – losing on a regular basis.

In fact six of their last eight league games ended in defeat, a frustrating finale that saw them beaten 27-17 at Gloucester and then crash 29-19 at home to a Sale side that included the evergreen Graham Dawe, making a fiery return to the Rec that must have filled him with mixed emotions.

The losing streak was briefly interrupted by a 20-3 home win over relegation-haunted London Irish, but that was followed by a 16-15 reverse at Northampton early in May. And, although Bath put up a terrific fight when they met champions-elect Newcastle at Gateshead in their penultimate game, Rob Andrew's men ground out a 20-15 win that virtually assured them of the title, in their first season in the top flight.

That left Bath facing a final encounter against outgoing champions Wasps at Loftus Road, before their labours were over, and they signed off in positive style, a vintage four-try first half blitz setting up a 28-0 lead, before Wasps reduced the eventual margin of defeat to 31-17.

Overall, that victory concluded a season that had been marginally less successful than the barren season the previous year. In all they had lost nine times in Premiership One, but still finished third with Leicester, well adrift of Newcastle and runners-up Saracens, both of whom enjoyed the rare distinction of a league double over Bath.

Such a disappointing end to the campaign had taken the gloss off that European Cup triumph by the time the squad dispersed for a hard-earned summer break. And when Bath announced a list of non-retained players for the following season, at least one responded by taking a public swipe at the club, and Andy Robinson in particular.

Federico Mendez, later to join Northampton, had made only two starting appearances, since coming on as a late replacement in Bordeaux and, after being released, he vented his spleen, criticising Robinson's coaching methods and his management of the squad. Bath's cursory response indicated that, in their view, the complaints were a case of sour grapes by a player whose contract was not being renewed.

Mendez' Argentine compatriot German Llanes and Irish fellow lock Brian Cusack were also released, as were youngsters Joe Ewens and Ricky Pellow among others, Pellow later joining Premiership Two newcomers Exeter, a club with whom Bath would forge a mutually beneficial links in the close season.

With Llanes and Cusack gone, Bath were obviously in need of second row back-up for the squad as a priority in their recruitment plans over the summer. But they were to find that, despite being European champions, the club did not hold quite the same compulsive attraction to the top names in world rugby as in years gone by.

Frustrated by the Welsh RFU in their efforts to sign Ponytpridd fly-half Neil Jenkins, who had been a target before their European Cup final triumph, Bath made feverish efforts to sign several other top stars to boost squad strength.

London Irish lock Malcolm O'Kelly, who had made a big impression in Ireland's Five Nations Championship campaign was one persistent target, but eventually decided to stay at Sunbury. And Bath also made vain efforts to sign French fly-half star Thomas Castaignede, Sale's England winger David Rees and South African world cup scrum-half Joost van der Westhuizen. But none of these moves came to fruition.

Bath did pull off one major coup, when, in the middle of England's doomed tour of the Southern Hemisphere, Ben Sturnham, a rising young star in Saracens' powerful back row contingent, announced he was joining Bath, efforts to recruit former All Black scrum-half Jon Preston, a versatile back who could also double as fly-half and goalkicker, eventually ended successfully with the revelation that he would arrive in November.

And Jim Fallon, the powerful 31-year-old former Bath winger, who had switched codes to play rugby league for Leeds a few years previously, was tempted back to the Rec from Richmond. But otherwise, it was a relatively quiet summer on the transfer front.

Meanwhile, for almost all the squad, it was a summer of rest and recuperation from the rigours of competitive rugby, with most of Bath's international complement declining to go on tour with their various national squads, who all sent severely depleted parties to the Southern Hemisphere and were humiliated as a result. England suffered the most, enduring a record 76-0 defeat by Australia in their first major test and improving only marginally in further setbacks in New Zealand and South Africa.

Matt Perry was Bath's only representative in a second-string England party and was one of the few outstanding successess on an otherwise profoundly depressing trip, which caused coach Clive Woodward to openly castigate his RFU employers for allowing the national side to venture abroad without so many front rank performers.

Not surprisingly, the home unions also came under fire from their Southern Hemisphere counterparts, who implied that sub-standard touring teams would not be welcomed again and urged the Northern Hemisphere governing bodies to put their house in order and regain control of their domestic situation.

However, the ever-widening chasm between the clubs and the more hawkish elements within the RFU, led by management board chairman Cliff Brittle, left that prospect unlikely, as rugby union's unholy civil war raged on with only tentative signs of a lasting settlement.

As internal divisions surfaced between Brittle and members of his own board, he was deliberately kept out of negotiations in May between the RFU and the clubs, which culminated in approval of the Mayfair agreement, a seven-year deal designed to end the bitter conflict over the future structure of the domestic game.

That agreement was hailed as a victory for common sense by the clubs, but condemned as a sell-out by Brittle and his supporters in the RFU hierarchy, sparking the resignation of his vice-chairman (playing), Fran Cotton, who had been acclaimed for guiding the Lions South African tour triumph less than 12 months earlier.

Cotton's outspoken reaction to the way Brittle had been excluded from the talks led the RFU to accuse him of bringing the game into disrepute. But the ratification of the Mayfair agreement and the prospect of peace between the game's governing body and the clubs was seen to hinge on Brittle's re-election as chairman at the RFU's annual meeting in July.

Brittle, backed by widespread support among the game's grass root clubs, had twice fought off challenges to his leadership in the previous two years. But his power base had been eroded, and when retired policeman Brian Baister was elected to replace him by a clear 520-345 majority, the outcome was greeted with undisguised relief by the clubs and more moderate members of the RFU council, who could now conduct their negotiations without the acrimony that had undermined them for so long.

Brittle's departure was no guarantee of harmonious progress to a compromise treaty that would satisfy all parties in the prolonged power struggle, but at least it was a significant step towards a permanent solution to rugby union's pressing problems.

The dispute had inflicted significant damage to governing bodies and the clubs, many of whom were already fighting to survive in a climate of financial uncertainty and constant change. And Bath had not escaped the consequences.

Barely two months after concluding sponsorship deals with Adidas and Blackthorn the club announced that Stephen Hands had resigned as Bath's commercial and marketing director, Hands claiming that he had achieved everything possible at the club under the current structure and after recent discussions had decided it was right to move on. No replacement was sought for his role, but operations director

David Jenkins was given an extended brief as sales director.

At the end of June, Bath announced a major change in its youth development policy by scrapping the club's University-based academy, in favour of extending links with local clubs whose young players would be invited to play for the Under-19 side.

And early in July there was news of a real breakthrough concerning Bath's ambitions to develop a stadium capable of making the club financially viable, with the setting up of a joint working party with Bath and North East Somerset District Council to try and solve the stadium dilemma.

Welcoming the progress, Tony Swift warned that a solution had to be found within six months, because the club could not continue to run a commercial operation without the stadium capacity problem being resolved, while Paul Simons, the council's head of economic development and tourism, claimed that the club was part of the life of the city and the council wanted it to stay within its boundaries and not be relocated elsewhere.

Three weeks later, another significant announcement revealed that Bath's chairman Andrew Brownsword was retiring as chief executive of Hallmark Cards, Europe, to concentrate on his other business interests.

There was no indication as to whether the tycoon would take a more active role in the club's affairs, but the prospect was not being discounted at Queen Square and on the eve of the new season it was confirmed that Tony Swift was set to revert to his former role of non-executive chairman, and Brownsword would indeed become more involved in the everyday running of the club.

Meanwhile, Bath's playing squad reported for pre-season training in July, not knowing who they would be playing on 5 September, the opening Saturday of the 1998/99 season, or whether they would yet be defending their European Cup crown. With the clubs maintaining their boycott in the forth-coming season, in protest at the way the tournament's governing body, European Rugby Cup, had run it, publication of a fixture list had been delayed, just one indication of the chaos that still engulfed the game.

At one stage several French clubs, including Brive and Toulouse, threatened to join the boycott and support a break-away European tournament, while the idea of forming a British League of 20 clubs, to include the fourteen Premiership One clubs, four Welsh teams and two Scottish sides, received wide support. But with the new season less than a month away it was rejected by the Welsh Rugby Union and was reluctantly shelved.

Meanwhile, the clubs themselves were counting the cost of a bitter civil war. Bristol, once giants of the English domestic scene, went into receivership, sparking a bitter wrangle and hasty rescue bids from rival consortiums seeking to gain control of the ailing club and ostensibly save it from oblivion.

And Bristol were not the only club under threat of bank-ruptcy as the harsh realities of rugby union's professional revolution hit home. What had started out as a bold crusade was rapidly becoming an undisciplined, inglorious retreat for many aspiring clubs, who had flocked to join the professional ranks with such fervour just two years earlier.

Bristol's sorry demise yielded fringe benefits elsewhere. With the club's entire playing staff made redundant, several leading players were quickly snapped up by rivals, one of them, Ireland centre Kevin Maggs, signing a two-year contract with Bath, who had recently appointed Richard Webster as club captain in place of Andy Nicol.

And when the takeover battle for Bristol's future was resolved, the successful bidder had a strong Bath connection. Malcolm Pearce, a Bath-based millionaire, who had been an influential benefactor behind the scenes at the Rec for years before Andrew Brownsword's arrival, was revealed as Bristol's new owner.

Pearce had provided employment for a host of Bath's inter-national recruits in the heady days of amateur triumph, when Jack Rowell reigned supreme as coach. And now they were teaming up again, with Rowell installed as non-executive director alongside Bob Dwyer as Bristol's new director of rugby. The *eminence grise* was back in harness, ironically, just ten miles down the road from his former stamping ground. But he will find it a different game.

Rugby union has changed beyond recognition since Rowell left the Rec four years ago. That unique family ethos he founded has been consigned to history by the professional revolution. I fancy Bristol's fortunes may soon be on the rise. But they have a long way to go to rival the glory that was Bath.